# TOWARDS A
# CRITICAL THEORY
# OF SOCIETY

COLLECTED PAPERS OF HERBERT MARCUSE
EDITED BY DOUGLAS KELLNER

Volume One
TECHNOLOGY, WAR AND FASCISM

Volume Two
TOWARDS A CRITICAL THEORY OF SOCIETY

Volume Three
FOUNDATIONS OF THE NEW LEFT

Volume Four
ART AND LIBERATION

Volume Five
PHILOSOPHY, PSYCHOANALYSIS AND EMANCIPATION

Volume Six
MARXISM, REVOLUTION AND UTOPIA

# TOWARDS A CRITICAL THEORY OF SOCIETY

## HERBERT MARCUSE

### COLLECTED PAPERS OF HERBERT MARCUSE

Volume Two

*Edited by*
*Douglas Kellner*

London and New York

First published 2001
by Routledge
11 New Fetter Lane, London EC4P 4EE

Simultaneously published in the USA and Canada
by Routledge
29 West 35th Street, New York, NY 10001

*Routledge is an imprint of the Taylor & Francis Group*

Typeset in Sabon by Keystroke, Jacaranda Lodge, Wolverhampton
Printed and bound in Great Britain by University Press,
Cambridge

*British Library Cataloguing in Publication Data*
A catalogue record for this book is available from the British Library

*Library of Congress Cataloging in Publication Data*
Marcuse, Herbert, 1898–
Towards a critical theory of society / Herbert Marcuse; edited by Douglas Kellner.
p. cm. – (Collected papers of Herbert Marcuse; v. 2)
Includes bibliographical references and index.
1. Sociology–Philosophy. I. Kellner, Douglas, 1943– II. Title.
B945 .M298 1998 v. 2
[HM585]
301′.01–dc21      00–053357

ISBN 0–415–13781–0

# CONTENTS

# FOREWORD

*Peter Marcuse*

In reading these largely unpublished manuscripts of my father's, I am struck by two things. The first has to do with the relationship of current events to long-term analysis that the selections in this volume, in particular, reveal. The second has to do, superficially, with style, but, more significantly, with the thought processes that the style reveals.

Many of these pieces were composed (some for talks, others as draft manuscripts) during the Vietnam war, as my father actively engaged himself in the day-to-day protest against it. His contribution was not particularly to marshal the arguments against the war, but rather to put it in the broader framework of developments in the economy of capitalism, in bourgeois democracy, and in the possible forms of resistance. Some of his judgments as to the *extent* of developments may seem today, with hindsight, to have been in part erroneous: the extent of formal repression, or the inability of the economic system to continue to produce. But the underlying analyses still ring very true. I would argue it is perhaps even more important today to develop a radical social critique, perhaps because the day-to-day conflicts do not seem as profound as they were then. Today, because the possibility of serious long-term change seems so remote, we tend to think less about the underlying problems and their importance, and the need for radical structural transformation.

But, as my father wrote elsewhere, utopias are no longer utopias because they can realistically be achieved today. It is thus important to consider what could be, alternative and better modes of social organization, even though, unlike then, such reflections are on the back burner today.

Above all, the theme that runs through virtually everything in this volume is the importance of the political, the fight against the depoliticization of all spheres of action, from academic economics to culture to politics itself. In later work, to be published in a subsequent volume in this series, he dealt explicitly with the political content of art in terms of a dialectic of form and content, rejecting the view that art, to be political, should be ornamented propaganda; there are hints even in the present pieces of his developing absorption in the role of art and the aesthetic dimension in the process of liberation. In the essays collected in this volume, he is concerned with the sources of social change, and sees in the growing material prosperity that capitalism has produced an increasing dehumanization that needs to be addressed in moral terms, and that means in political, rather than narrowly economic, struggle. The new 1966 preface to *Eros and Civilization* is called "Political Preface," and ends: "Today the fight for life, the fight for Eros, is the political fight." It is a moral and a political position that is grounded in a sharp theoretical analysis of current developments, and holds up well even where current developments have not gone entirely in the direction he anticipated.

As to style, I remember often, on first reading something he had published, swearing at the ambiguities of many phrases. I was trained as a lawyer, and sharpness of expression, precision, clarity, are highly prized, terms are given specific definitions, conclusions are drawn sharply and pressed one-sidedly. The result is often complex sentences, multiplication of qualifications to simple statements, difficult and inelegant reading, but, if the effort succeeds, clear and unambiguous results. Reading the Internal Revenue Code is tough going, but any lawyer would defend it as an attempt to state very precisely what is and what is not taxed, under what circumstances, with what exceptions, for what type of entity, when, and how.

My father's writing (and speaking) were, to my then professional eyes, quite the opposite. One trick he often used was to say the same thing two or three different ways, to add to a noun another noun, separated by commas, or added parentheses: "relations between things have become rational (or rather: are rationalized)." OK, but if you mean rationalized, why not say it in the first place? Because he wants first to present the appearance, then contrast it to the reality.

"American culture is still sometimes described as a 'death-denying culture' – nothing could be further from the truth. Or, rather, the neurotic death-denial hides the profound 'understanding' of death."[1] Well, which, asks my lawyerly training, is it or isn't it death-denying? Of course, the answer isn't a simple "yes" or "no"; it both is and, at another level, isn't. This is not

---

1  Historical Fate, ms. p. 22.

careless writing; it is writing that accepts contradictions, subtleties, ambiguities.

In other cases, the style exposes the content more directly: "the struggle against [aggression] . . . involves, not the suppression but the counter-activation of aggression."[2] A paradox? Yes, indeed, but a substantive paradox. An inconsistency in thinking? By no means.

Or: "modes of existence rendered possible and at the same time precluded by the given society." Both at once? Interesting; yes, that is exactly what he means and this indeed accurately describes a society that increasingly makes possible growing goods and services for all that are, however, restricted to those who can afford to pay. Or: ". . . one of the most vexing aspects of advanced industrial civilization: the rational character of its irrationality." Or: ". . . by values . . . I mean norms . . . which motivate . . . behavior . . . In this sense, . . . they express the exigencies of the established production relations . . . However, at the same time, values express the possibilities inherent in but repressed by the . . . established society." Well, asks the frustrated lawyer, who wants a word to mean one thing and one thing only, make up your mind, in which sense are you talking? The answer is: both, and the tension between them is a dialectical tension, which runs throughout the essay on values printed here.

It is a style that accepts ambiguities, that indeed sees contradictions within concepts, multiple dimensions within single acts and events; a style one might indeed call dialectical writing. For it is not, I would now say, unclear, and certainly not sloppy. Rather, it reflects the ambiguities and contradictions of reality, the fact that events in fact have multiple meanings and multiple outcomes, some inconsistent (or rather: in tension – the style is catching!) with others. Sometimes, I have the feeling, my father formulated the contradictions deliberately for their shock value: what's new in bourgeois democracy is "(a) the strength of its popular base, and (b) its militant reactionary character."[3] Sometimes the formulations are striking precisely because they appear to be oxymorons ("civilized barbarism," "profitable bondage," "repressive affluence"), or simply logically absurd ("the revocation of the Ninth Symphony," "occupation without work," "facts which are substantially incomplete"). The unusual form of the statement forces the reader to stop and think, and, with effort, the meaning becomes clear.

In part, I am led to these reflections by the very physical form of the manuscripts reprinted here. Remember, they were (almost all) unpublished;

---

2  Historical Fate, ms. p. 25. I have elided, I think not unfairly, to make the point sharper.
3  Historical Fate, ms. p. 34.

yet, even for those that were merely one lecture among a whole series of high-profile appearances, the text is written out, revised, re-revised, with cross-outs and insertions. My father never published, nor authorized the publication, of anything he did not carefully read; his work on the Meyerhoff lecture, for instance, indicates his dissatisfaction with anything but a perfected version of what he wanted to say. He often reviewed, and struggled over, translations of his articles, in German or in French, where he felt he had a sense of the nuances of the languages. He quite generally denied permission to reprint portions only of articles or books, feeling his thoughts needed to be seen in the full context of what led to them and followed from them, not in isolation or out of context. I must admit I have not followed what might well have been his wishes in allowing the publication of pieces such as those in this volume, and occasionally authorizing the publication of excerpts rather than complete pieces where I felt the context did not distort, for I feel that any reader sufficiently interested to read this volume will also be familiar with the more perfected pieces, and that the train of thought that led to those published pieces may itself be of value to others today. What was really ephemera, what my father really thought was of no value, he threw away; he was not a archivist, did not see his processes of work as having historical interest, and he tossed out drafts that today we might find to be of extraordinary interest.

But my father has become, when all is said and done, a significant figure in the history of his times, which are still our times. His ideas, including their genesis and reworking are, I think, both of historical and of real contemporary interest. In any event, that is how I justify and why I recommend the present collection.

The First Annual Hans Meyerhoff Memorial Lecture by Dr. Herbert Marcuse

"Beyond One-Dimensional Man"

Please let me know as soon as you cannot hear me. I am not on

very friendly terms with technical instruments.

I dedicate this lecture to the memory of Hans Meyerhoff not only

on personal grounds but also on very substantial and objective grounds.

Not only because I was his personal friend; he was my closest friend.

But also because I believe that the work of Hans Meyerhoff testifies to

a trend of extreme importance for understanding what is going on among

the young generation, among the intelligentsia as a whole in the

present situation. I hope to be able to show you that my presentation

will bring out the exemplary character of the work of Hans Meyerhoff.

The trend that I am alluding to I would like to characterize, in a

namely, as a

preliminary way, ~~as a very~~ strange transformation of philosophy, ~~namely,~~

which involves

~~the transformation~~ the development from philosophy to politics via

This development tends toward

literature and art. ~~It transcends of philosophy~~ a realization of

which is

philosophy, ~~which~~ quite different from the one Marx foresaw, and quite

it is often understood or rather misunderstood —

different from the way ~~it has interpretansent~~ namely, that instead

# ACKNOWLEDGMENTS

Once again, I'd like to thank Peter Marcuse for choosing me as editor of his father's collected works and for working closely with me at every stage of the production of this text. His Foreword once again provides evocative access to his father's works and provides an excellent analysis of the virtues of the infamous Marcusean style. Thanks also to Jürgen Habermas for the Afterword that provides an excellent overview of the importance of Marcuse's work. And, once again, thanks to John Abroweit for coming through in the clutch with first-rate translations of the letters and the Habermas reflections. For help in the editing of these texts, I would like to thank my loyal UCLA students Leslie Hendrickson and Hua-Lun Lee. And, finally, thanks to Tony Bruce, Muna Khogali and Liz O'Donnell at Routledge for working through the details of the production process.

Douglas Kellner, Los Angeles, October 2000

# INTRODUCTION

## Herbert Marcuse and the Vicissitudes of Critical Theory

*Douglas Kellner*

Herbert Marcuse was inextricably connected through his historical situation, his theoretical interests and undertakings, and the vicissitudes of personal life with the Institute for Social Research (*Institut für Sozialforschung*).[1] The Institute was founded at Frankfurt-am-Main in 1923 as the first Marxist-oriented research institute in Germany. In 1930, Max Horkheimer was appointed director and under his leadership the Institute became renowned for its interdisciplinary research methodology and its project of developing a critical theory of contemporary society. Horkheimer assembled a remarkable group of theorists including T. W. Adorno, Erich Fromm, Leo Löwenthal, Franz Neumann, Marcuse, Frederick Pollock, and others who theorized the new forms of monopoly state capitalism, the culture industries, the authoritarian personality, and the modes of social control that emerged in the era of fascism, communism, and state capitalism.

---

1 On the history and projects of the Institute for Social Research, also known as the "Frankfurt school," see Martin Jay, *The Dialectical Imagination*, Boston: Little, Brown and Company, 1973 (new edition, University of California Press, 1996); Helmut Dubiel, *Theory and Politics*, Cambridge: MIT Press, 1985; Douglas

In 1933, Marcuse joined the Institute and became one of the most active participants during its exile period in the United States from 1934 into the 1940s. Marcuse deeply identified with the work of the Institute and his fundamental project from the time that he joined it was developing a critical theory of society. This volume collects some later key texts of Marcuse's development of critical theory during the period of his greatest productivity and influence in the 1960s and 1970s. To set the stage for the essays that follow – many unknown and published here for the first time – I will sketch out Marcuse's work with the Institute for Social Research, his separation from the Institute when Horkheimer and Adorno returned to Germany in the late 1940s, and his own distinctive brand of critical theory which he developed from the 1940s until his death in 1979.

## MARCUSE JOINS THE INSTITUTE
## OF SOCIAL RESEARCH

Herbert Marcuse was born July 19, 1898 in Berlin, Germany. The son of Carl Marcuse, a prosperous Jewish merchant and Gertrud Kreslawsky, daughter of a wealthy German factory owner, Marcuse had a typical upper-middle class Jewish life during the first two decades of the twentieth century, in which anti-Semitism was not overt in Germany. Marcuse studied in the Mommsen Gymnasium in Berlin prior to World War I and served with the German army in the war. Transferred to Berlin early in 1918, he participated in the German revolution that drove Kaiser Wilhelm II out of Germany and established a Social Democratic government.[2]

After demobilization, Marcuse went to Freiburg to pursue his studies and received a doctorate in literature in 1922 for a dissertation on *The German Artist-Novel*. After a short career as a bookseller in Berlin, he returned to Freiburg and in 1928 began studying philosophy with Martin Heidegger, then one of the most significant thinkers in Germany.

---

Kellner, *Critical Theory, Marxism, and Modernity*, Cambridge and Baltimore: Polity Press and Johns Hopkins University Press, 1989; and Rolf Wiggershaus, *The Frankfurt School*, Cambridge and Cambridge, Mass.: Polity Press and MIT Press, 1995. For collections of basic texts, see Andrew Arato and Eike Gebhardt, *The Essential Frankfurt School Reader*, New York: Continuum, 1982, and Douglas Kellner and Stephen Eric Bronner, editors, *Critical Theory and Society. A Reader*, New York and London: Routledge, 1989.

2  For documentation, see Douglas Kellner, *Herbert Marcuse and the Crisis of Marxism*, Berkeley and London: University of California Press and Macmillan Press, 1984.

In his first published articles, written from 1928 to 1933 while he was working with Heidegger in Freiburg, Marcuse developed a synthesis of phenomenology, existentialism, and Marxism, anticipating a project which decades later would be carried out by various "existential" and "phenomenological" Marxists, such as Jean-Paul Sartre and Maurice Merleau-Ponty, as well as others in Eastern Europe and the United States in the postwar period. Marcuse contended that Marxist thought had deteriorated into a rigid orthodoxy and needed concrete "phenomenological" experience of contemporary social conditions to update and enliven the Marxian theory, which had downplayed social, cultural, and psychological analysis in favor of focus on economic and political conditions. He also believed that Marxism neglected the problem of the individual and throughout his life was concerned with personal liberation and happiness, in addition to social transformation.

Marcuse published the first major review in 1932 of Marx's recently printed *Economic and Philosophical Manuscripts of 1844*, anticipating the later tendency to revise interpretations of Marxism from the standpoint of the works of the early Marx.[3] One of the first to see the importance of the philosophical dimension of the early Marx on labor, human nature, and alienation, Marcuse believed that critical philosophical perspectives were necessary to give concrete substance to Marxism. At the same time that he was writing essays synthesizing Marxism and phenomenology, Marcuse completed a study of *Hegel's Ontology and the Theory of Historicity* (1932) which he intended as a "Habilitation" dissertation that would gain him university employment.[4] The text stressed the importance of the categories of life and history in Hegel and contributed to the revival of interest in Hegel that was taking place in Europe.

In 1932, as the Nazis came to power, the situation in Freiburg became precarious for Marcuse. As he remembers it: "Because of the political situation I desperately wanted to join the Institute. At the end of 1932 it was perfectly clear that I would never be able to qualify for a professorship (*mich habilitieren können*) under the Nazi regime."[5] Consequently, Marcuse

---

3  Herbert Marcuse, "The Foundations of Historical Materialism," in *Studies in Critical Philosophy*, Boston: Beacon Press, 1973.

4  Herbert Marcuse, *Hegel's Ontology and the Theory of Historicity*, translated by Seyla Benhabib, Cambridge, Mass.: MIT Press, 1987.

5  Herbert Marcuse, "Theory and Politics: A Discussion," *Telos* 38 (Winter 1978–1979), p. 126. For detailed documentation of the story of Marcuse's attempt to use his first Hegel book as a Habilitations-dissertation with Heidegger, see Peter-Erwin Jansen, "Marcuses Habilitationsverfahren – eine Odyssee," in Peter-Erwin Jansen, editor, *Befreiung denken – Ein politscher Imperativ*, Offenbach/Main: 2000 Verlag, 1990.

corresponded with the Institute for Social Research in Frankfurt, asking if he could work with them. They invited him for an interview, and as Leo Löwenthal recounts in a letter published in this volume, the Institute appointed him to a position (see p. 210). This was fortunate, for in 1933 Heidegger joined the Nazi party and began making speeches for them.[6] Husserl had sent the Kurator of Frankfurt University, Kurt Riezler, a letter of support, and the Institute considered petitioning the University to accept Marcuse's "Habilitation Dissertation" on Hegel, which was already published as a book, so that he could be appointed a university professor. In fact, however, Marcuse never actually worked with the Institute in Frankfurt, since they, anticipating fascist suppression, had set up a branch office in Geneva, to which Marcuse was assigned. Henceforth, despite later philosophical and political differences, Marcuse would strongly identify with what is now often called the "Frankfurt School", and would make important contributions to their projects.[7]

Marcuse's move in 1932 from the provincial philosophy department of Freiburg, dominated by Husserl and Heidegger, to association with the neo-Marxist Institute for Social Research played a crucial role in his development. Although Heideggerian influences are discernible in many of his later works, Marcuse abandoned the project of producing a synthesis of phenomenological existentialism and Marxism. Both Heidegger's "political turn" in support of Nazism, and the relentless opposition of the Institute to Heidegger's philosophy, drove Marcuse to break with Heidegger and to commit himself to a version of Hegelian Marxism which the Institute was in the process of producing. The Director of the Institute, Max Horkheimer, loathed Heidegger's oracular ontology, while his colleague Theodor Adorno, who had just finished a critical study of Kierkegaard, was writing a critique of Husserlian and Heideggerian phenomenology. For the next decade, Marcuse involved himself in the Institute's work and became one of its most important members.

Marcuse's previous studies of the Hegelian and Marxian dialectic had prepared him for work on the Institute's project of developing a dialectical social theory. However, in his collaboration with the Institute, there are important changes from his earlier writings. Methodologically, he no longer

---

6   See Martin Heidegger, *Die Selbstbehauptung der deutschen Universität*, Freiburg-im-Breslau: Korn, 1933.

7   Strictly speaking, the term "Frankfurt School" was applied to the work of the Institute for Social Research upon their return to Germany, when once again they were active in the Johann Goethe University in Frankfurt. The term stuck and has been applied to those active with the Institute both in the US exile and upon their return to Germany.

interprets Hegel and Marx as producers of an ontology of society and history, but uses their method and ideas for developing a critical theory of society. Marcuse accepts the Institute's position that the Marxian critique of political economy is the centre and foundation for critical social theory. Accordingly, he switches his focus from "concrete philosophy" and ontological analysis of such themes as "historicity" to the development of a radical social theory rooted in the Marxian critique of political economy and historical materialism oriented towards the crucial social problems of the day. There is also a political change: Marcuse abandons concepts of the "radical act" and a "catastrophic total revolution" for the milder terms "liberation" and "transformation." Part of this toning down of his revolutionary language was dictated by the decision made by the Institute that while in exile they would adopt "Aesopian language" to disguise their politics. Marcuse's shift in his political language, however, can also be attributed to the growing influence on him of Horkheimer and his associates. In view of the triumph of fascism, Stalinist tyranny and the concomitant failure of the proletariat in the West to emerge as a revolutionary agent, the Institute began to question central features of the Marxian theory of socialism and revolution.

Marcuse joined the Institute not long after Max Horkheimer took over its directorship and they began shifting their focus from empirical research and historical studies to development of an interdisciplinary social theory. Horkheimer's capacity in the Institute's affairs during the 1930s was crucial, as he was in charge of its research projects, journal, political-theoretical orientation, and overall direction. Moreover, he assumed the role of philosophical and institutional leader for the Institute during the troubled period when German fascism forced the emigration of its members throughout Western Europe and to the United States. Horkheimer was trained as a philosopher and had broad intellectual interests. He pursued a Hegelian–Marxian direction in the attempt to develop a "critical theory of society." Alfred Schmidt argues that "Horkheimer was one of the most important founders of a 'philosophically' directed interpretation of Marx, that was indeed quite different from the currently dominant tendencies" (i.e. in Marx-interpretation).[8] He rejected the orthodoxy of both the Second International and Soviet Marxism, as well as current attempts to bind

---

8  Alfred Schmidt, *Zur Idee der kritschen Theorie*, Munich: Hanser, 1974, pp. 37ff. For an excellent selection of Horkheimer's writings of the 1930s, see Max Horkheimer, *Between Philosophy and Social Science. Selected Early Writings* (Cambridge, Mass.: MIT Press, 1993); see also Seyla Benhabib, Wolfgang Bonss, and John McCole, editors, *On Max Horkheimer: New Perspectives* (Cambridge, Mass.: MIT Press, 1993).

Marxism with neo-Kantian, positivist, humanist or existentialist philosophical currents. In Schmidt's words: "for him a truly productive, progressive appropriation of dialectical materialism was necessarily bound up with a precise analysis of the historical as well as the substantive importance of Hegel and Marx."[9] Horkheimer took as fundamental Marx's statement that "Dialectic is unquestionably the last word in philosophy," and he believed that one had to liberate the dialectic from the "mystical shell" it had assumed in Hegel.[10]

During Horkheimer's directorship, the Institute developed "the critical theory of society." Their work combined theoretical construction and social criticism with empirical and theoretical research. In addition to their focus on social psychology and mass culture, the major difference in the Institute's orientation under Horkheimer was a rehabilitation of the function of philosophy in social theory. As Karl Korsch pointed out in *Marxism and Philosophy*, the ruling Marxian orthodoxies tended towards positivistic materialism and oriented theory and practice towards politics and economics, thus suppressing the philosophical components in the Marxian theory.[11] Horkheimer, Adorno and Marcuse, however, were all professional philosophers who argued for the importance of philosophy in social theory. This approach was, of course, congenial to Marcuse, who, in his pre-Institute work, had just finished a study of Hegel's ontology and had been working on a synthesis of philosophy and social theory in the service of radical social change.

Horkheimer and his colleagues published their studies in a remarkable journal, *Zeitschrift für Sozialforschung*. In a foreword to the first issue, Horkheimer indicates that the Institute's investigations would strive to develop a "theory of the contemporary society as a whole."[12] They intended to engage in historical investigations, to deal with current problems, to develop a general and comprehensive theory of contemporary society, to inquire into the "future development of the historical process," and to provide instruments for social transformation.[13] In later articles, Horkheimer and Marcuse developed the program of social research in terms of a "critical theory of society" (see the discussion in the next section).

---

9 Schmidt, op. cit., p. 41.
10 Schmidt, op. cit., p. 42.
11 Karl Korsch, *Marxism and Philosophy*, New York and London: Monthly Review Press, 1970.
12 Max Horkheimer, "Vortwort," *Zeitschrift für Sozialforschung*, Vol. 1, No. 1 (1932), p. 1.
13 Ibid., pp. 1–11.

The Frankfurt Institute's work was interrupted in 1933 by the rise of fascism. They had anticipated the fascist takeover by depositing their endowment in Holland and by establishing a branch office in Geneva. Jews and radicals, the Institute members saw that they had no future in Germany and sought institutional and existential moorings elsewhere. In the following years, the Institute suffered the uncertainties of exile, trying to set up research centers in Paris, London and New York. Marcuse went first to Geneva in 1933, then to Paris, and finally arrived in New York in July 1934, where he remained for some years in the Institute's branch located at Columbia University.

One can hardly exaggerate the importance of the Institute for Social Research in Marcuse's development. Under its influence, he broke with Heidegger and worked collectively with the members of the Institute on its projects. During Marcuse's first years of collaboration, the Institute was concerned with providing a theoretical explanation of the roots and causes of fascism. In this context, Marcuse wrote a series of essays in the 1930s which analyzed the cultural forces and tendencies that contributed to the triumph of fascism in Germany. He and his associates were certain that "the fascist state was the fascist society, and that totalitarian violence and totalitarian reason came from the structure of the existing society."[14] They accepted the orthodox Marxian theory that fascism was a product of capitalist society: its economic system, institutions, ideology and culture. The Institute assumed "the task of identifying the tendencies that linked the liberal past with its totalitarian abolition" (N, p. xii). They perceived the roots of fascism in: (a) socioeconomic crises that were given a totalitarian solution in order to protect the capitalist relations of production and to secure the control of the ruling class; (b) institutions such as the bourgeois family and repressive socialization processes which created authoritarian personalities who conformed to and accepted socially imposed domination; (c) culture and ideologies that defended, or transfigured, the existing society while mystifying social relations of domination; and (d) a totalitarian state which imposed its rule on the entire economic, social, political, and cultural system.

Marcuse's 1934 essay "The Struggle Against Liberalism in the Totalitarian View of the State" is the first Institute critique of fascism and explicates several defining positions that would characterize their distinctive analysis.[15] As Marcuse later recalls, his essay was a response to "a speech

---

14 Herbert Marcuse, "Foreword," *Negations*, Boston: Beacon Press, 1968 (hereafter N), p. xiii.
15 It is collected in *Negations*, op. cit. For more detailed explorations of Marcuse's analysis of German fascism, see *Technology, War and Fascism*, op. cit.

by Hitler, the speech at the industrial club in Dusseldorf; it became known, and Horkheimer called the colleagues together, pointed to a newspaper article and asked what was so significant about this speech that we should make it the object of a more or less independent study. We discussed it and made the decision."[16] Marcuse's argument is that the totalitarian state and its ideology respond to a new era of monopoly capitalism and provide a defense of capitalism against crises engendered by its market system and protection against opposition to the system (i.e. the working-class parties). Fascism was not seen, in this interpretation, as a monstrous rupture with the liberal past; rather, Marcuse demonstrates the continuities between liberalism and fascism and shows how liberalism's unquestioned allegiance to the capitalist economic system prepared the way for the fascist-totalitarian order and with it the abolition of liberalism itself.

Marcuse and his colleagues also engaged in empirical and theoretical studies of authoritarianism and how and why individuals submitted to totalitarian domination. The submission of the German people to fascism and their complacent acceptance of totalitarian society raised the question of what factors were responsible for developing a personality which would accept and obey even the most irrational, destructive authorities. The members of the Institute for Social Research concluded that the bourgeois family and its patriarchal structure played an important role in preparing the individual for the frightful submission to authority in fascist society. In a group project on "Authority and the Family," they studied the historical function of the family in reproducing the institutions, social practices and ideology of bourgeois society. The Institute also investigated the psychological factors involved in submission to societal domination and produced studies of authority and the family in different countries, which included a critical evaluation of the various literature on the family in these countries. The results were published in *Studien Uber Autorität und Familie*.[17]

Marcuse contributed as well a long study on "Freedom and Authority" that traced the ideas of freedom and authority through the reformation, Kant, Hegel, the counterrevolution and Marx, to recent totalitarian theories of authority.[18] In the essay he is concerned to show the dichotomy in the bourgeois concept of freedom which split the individual into two spheres:

---

16 Herbert Marcuse, "Theory and Politics," op. cit., p. 128. For Hitler's speech, see *My New Order*, New York: Reynal and Hitchcock, 1941, pp. 93ff.
17 Institute of Social Research, *Studien Uber Autorität und Familie*, Paris: Librairie Félix Alcan, two volumes.
18 Herbert Marcuse, "A Study on Authority," translated in *Studies in Critical Philosophy*, Boston: Beacon Press, 1973, pp. 49–156.

an inner realm of freedom (autonomy) and an external realm of submission and bondage (authority). The inner freedom of Protestantism and Kant, Hegel's deification of the State, and the irrational and traditionalistic doctrine of authority of the counterrevolution (Burke, de Maistre, F. J. Stahl) all contribute, Marcuse argues, to preparing the way for the totalitarian theory of authority. Marcuse's critique of the ideas that promoted the acceptance of the totalitarian theory and practice of authority is acute, and shows his ability to demonstrate connections and consequences of ideas that are often overlooked or ignored in standard intellectual history.

## TOWARDS A CRITICAL THEORY OF SOCIETY

The term "critical theory of society" was adopted by the Institute for Social Research in 1937 to describe their distinctive version of Hegelian Marxism.[19] Although the various members of the "inner circle," especially Adorno and Horkheimer, would significantly alter their 1930s conception of "critical theory," they nonetheless used the term to identify their work throughout the next several decades. In the 1930s, critical theory refers to the shared, interdisciplinary program, projects and orientation of the Institute, which advocates the primacy of an interdisciplinary social theory over individual social sciences or philosophy. Critical theory refers to the synthesis of philosophy and the social sciences in the Institute's work and the project of social critique with an orientation towards radical social change. In effect, critical theory is a code for the Institute's Marxism during its exile period, although later it would describe the distinctive brand of social theory developed by the Institute's core members, and covers a variety of types of theory from the 1930s and 1940s to the 1950s and 1960s, after the key members of the inner circle split from the Institute and pursued their own interests and projects.

In a series of essays published in the 1930s, Marcuse and Horkheimer define the program and philosophical presuppositions of the Institute's critical theory of society, while distinguishing their enterprise from other social theories and philosophies.[20] Marcuse focuses on the relation between

---

19 As Helmut Dubiel points out, in the early 1930s the Institute of Social Research used the code words "materialism" and "materialistic," or "economic theory of society," to describe their Marxian program, while only around 1936–1937 did they adopt the term "critical theory." *Theory and Politics*, op. cit.

20 See, especially, Max Horkheimer, "Critical and Traditional Theory," in *Critical Theory*, New York: Continuum, 1972, pp. 188–252, and Herbert Marcuse, "Philosophy and Critical Theory," in *Negations*, op. cit., pp. 134–58.

philosophy and critical theory, and although he criticizes bourgeois philosophy, he also defends its progressive elements: "reason, mind, morality, knowledge and happiness are not only categories of bourgeois philosophy, but concerns of humanity. As such they must be preserved, if not derived anew" (N, p. 147). Marcuse's position is that philosophy can play a progressive role in social theory by developing concepts that are subversive of the prevailing ideologies and can provide weapons of critique in the struggle for a better society.

In his 1930s essays, Marcuse is concerned at once to preserve what he regards as emancipatory elements in the bourgeois tradition, while criticizing tendencies which he concludes serve the interests of repression and domination. Often the progressive and conservative elements cannot be separated, and Marcuse's essays move from analysis of ideological and repressive features of aspects of bourgeois philosophy and culture, to depiction of their emancipatory moments. In general, he suggests that the early revolutionary ideals of the rising bourgeoisie contain aspects of a liberated society, and that their theories of freedom, rationalism, critical idealism, human rights, democracy, and materialist theories of human needs and potentialities continue to be of importance to critical social theory. Often he suggests that the bourgeoisie has failed to realize its ideals and that therefore earlier philosophies of, for example, democracy and freedom can be used to criticize their present neglect, distortion or suppression. In his view, many of the earlier bourgeois ideals could be used to criticize the current fascist suppression of liberal rights and liberties.

This is, of course, an expression of the Frankfurt School method of "immanent critique" which criticizes existing social conditions or theories from the standpoint of historically constructed ideals, principles, and institutions such as enlightenment, freedom, democracy, and human rights. Marcuse is, however, also quite critical of those tendencies in the bourgeois tradition which he claims contribute to the triumph of fascism. Hence, his essays contain ideology-critiques of liberalism, existentialism, idealism, rationalism and bourgeois culture, as well as valorization of their progressive aspects. Marcuse thinks that bourgeois philosophies and ideals tend to become ever more abstract, formal ideologies which the bourgeoisie uses to legitimate and mystify social conditions. In fact, Marcuse believes that there are conservative-conciliatory tendencies in bourgeois philosophy from the beginning which primarily function to conserve the bourgeois order of private property, possessive individualism, the unrestricted market, and the right to accumulate unlimited capital. But – and Marcuse's essays are full of these dialectical twists and turns – even some of the most ideological concepts of equality, freedom, happiness, and so on provide a "refuge" which preserves certain rational and human ideals of an emancipated humanity. Thus, the conservative and emancipatory motives are often tightly interconnected, requiring careful analysis and critique.

In this conception – shared by Marcuse and the Institute "inner circle" – there are two traditions in bourgeois culture: a progressive heritage of humanist-emancipatory elements, and a reactionary heritage of conservative, mystifying, and repressive features. In their view, the later phase of bourgeois culture is more irrational and regressive than the earlier, more progressive phase. For instance, in his 1936 essay, "The Concept of Essence," Marcuse writes:

> According to the view characteristic of the dawning bourgeois era, the critical autonomy of rational subjectivity is to establish and justify the ultimate essential truths on which all theoretical and practical truth depends. The essence of man and of things is contained in the freedom of the thinking individual, the ego cogito. At the close of this era, knowledge of essence has the function primarily of binding the critical freedom of the individual to pregiven, unconditionally valid necessities. It is no longer the spontaneity of the concept but the receptivity of intuition that serves as the organon of the doctrine of essence. Cognition culminates in recognition, where it remains fixated.

In evaluating art and ideas – their origins, nature, and social functions – Marcuse always relates cultural forms to their concrete historical situation. Moreover, in analyzing social and cultural forms, he relates his subject matter to political economy, arguing that the crucial problems of the individual and society are "to be approached from the standpoint of economics" (N, p. 134). Since critical theory "recognizes the responsibility of economic conditions for the totality of the established world," and comprehends the "social framework in which reality is organized" from the standpoint of political economy, the notion that philosophy is a special, superior discipline is rejected, as is the notion that social theory constitutes an autonomous mode of discourse on society and social life. Yet philosophy is not to be abandoned or denigrated, for critical theory is to operate with a synthesis of philosophy and the sciences, utilizing philosophical construction in conjunction with empirical research. Although Marcuse and his colleagues would accept the Marxian position that the economy is the crucial determining factor for all social life, they reject all forms of economic reductionism and attempt to describe the complex set of mediations connecting the economy, social and political institutions, culture, everyday life, and individual consciousness as parts of a reciprocally interacting social system.

Critical theory's claim "to explain the totality of human existence and its world in terms of social being" (N, pp. 134–5) contains a theory and program of social research. Critical theory argues that specific phenomena can only be comprehended as parts of a whole; hence a crucial task of social theory is to describe the structures and dynamics of the social system. Following the tenets of the Marxian theory, Marcuse stressed the importance of recognition that social and human existence are constituted by "the totality of the relations of production" (N, p. 82). As Marcuse argues in "The Concept of Essence," since the economy is the "essence" of the society, critical theory must describe the workings of the economy and how it is interconnected with and affects other forms of social life.

The critical theory of society is, Marcuse states, "linked with materialism" in accord with the "conviction of its founders" (N, p. 135). Following the Institute's strategy of not calling attention to their Marxism, Marcuse does not mention Marx once in "Philosophy and Critical Theory," although it is clear that Marx is the founder of the critical theory referred to and that the positions enunciated in the essay are the basic positions of Marxism. Marcuse does, however, propose his own interpretation of Marxian materialism: "There are two basic elements linking materialism to correct social theory: concern with human happiness and the conviction that it can be obtained only through a transformation of the material conditions of existence" (N, p. 135). Consequently, for Marcuse, "materialism" refers to a social practice and concern with human needs and happiness and not to a philosophical thesis which claims that "matter" is the primary ontological reality.

Marcuse elucidates the commitment of critical theory to human needs and their satisfaction in his essay "On Hedonism," the first detailed statement of his concern with needs, sensuality and happiness, which was to be a major focus of his later philosophy. He defends the claims of the individual to pleasure and sensuous gratification against those ascetic philosophies and systems that would repress needs and passion as being dangerous or immoral. But he also attacks those subjectivist hedonists who claim that pleasure is a purely internal affair and has no objective conditions or criteria of higher and lower, true and false pleasures. Here Marcuse shows how happiness is intimately connected with social conditions which make human happiness either possible or impossible and define its sphere and content. For example, he shows how both for the Greeks and under capitalism the labor system is essentially antagonistic to human happiness and creates two classes, one of which, the privileged class, has many more possibilities for gratification than the exploited working class, whose production makes possible the gratification of the former (N, p. 183). Under capitalism, happiness is a class phenomenon and is for the most part restricted to the sphere of consumption (N, p. 173). It is limited by the requirements of a labor system where work is for the most part boring and painful. The requirements for submission to the labor system have produced a work ethic that devalues pleasure and produces objective conditions that render happiness transitory or impossible.

Crucial to Marcuse's conception is his connection of freedom with happiness: "Happiness, as the fulfillment of all potentialities of the individual, presupposes freedom: at root, it is freedom" (N, p. 180). In Marcuse's view, without the freedom to satisfy one's needs and to act in self-fulfilling ways, true happiness is impossible. If freedom does not prevail in the material conditions of the existing system, then new social conditions must be created to make possible increased happiness and freedom. Marcuse argues that only in an association of free producers in which the economy is geared towards the satisfaction of human needs (and not profit) can individuals be truly free and happy: "Here reappears the old hedonistic definition that seeks happiness in the comprehensive gratification of needs and wants. The needs and wants to be gratified should become the regulating principle of the labour process" (N, p. 182).

The potentialities for making a fuller gratification of needs possible reside in modern technology, which could reduce alienated labor through automation and could produce the goods necessary to satisfy one's basic needs (N, p. 184). Here, for the first time, Marcuse suggests that technology could produce an environment that could provide aesthetic pleasure and sensual gratification. The fact that technology is not geared towards the satisfaction of human needs is the fault of a social system geared to profit-maximization, which is the source of untold unhappiness and suffering. This theme, adumbrated in his essay on hedonism, will increasingly concern Marcuse and will be a major focus of his later work.

In Marcuse's view, it is impossible for most people to be truly happy in the present society, not only because of the obstacles to freedom and happiness in the labor system, but because the system's dominant pleasures are false and restrictive of true happiness and freedom. From the 1930s until his death, Marcuse was convinced that reason can judge between true and false needs, pseudo and real happiness. Hence, for him, "happiness is linked to knowledge and taken out of the dimension of mere feeling" (N, p. 181). He believes that reason is "the fundamental category of human thought, the only one by means of which it has bound itself to the fate of humanity" (N, p. 135). Reason is the "critical tribunal" which puts into question the entirety of existence; it has the task of criticizing the irrationality of the social order and defining the highest human potentialities. In the materialist concept, reason is supposed to create a rational society that would liberate the individual from irrational fetters and bonds which restrict freedom, happiness and the development of individual potentialities. Reason must define true needs and the real interests of the individual and society, and must attack the prevailing false needs and repressive interests that should be abolished in the interests of the individual's happiness.

Happiness and unhappiness are thus in part social affairs that can be influenced by social practice. The enforced prolongation of the working day, the maintenance of inhuman working conditions, class division and exploitation, repressive morality, and a crisis-ridden economy: all of these social conditions are objective fetters on freedom and happiness and can only be removed

> through an economic and political process encompassing the disposal of the means of production by the community, the reorientation of the productive process towards the needs and wants of the whole society, the shortening of the working day, and the active participation of the individuals in the administration of the whole (N, p. 193).

Hence, in Marcuse's conception, individual freedom and happiness can only be secured in a project of radical social reconstruction (N, pp. 192–200). Marcuse makes clear his commitment here, albeit in muted language, to the Marxian concept of social revolution. But he does not subscribe to the restricted orthodox concept of socialism which equates socialization with nationalization of the means of production regulated by a central plan:

> Not that the labor process is regulated in accordance with a plan, but the interest determining the regulation becomes important: it is rational only if this interest is the freedom and happiness of the masses. Neglect of this element despoils the theory of one of its essential characteristics. It eradicates from the image of liberated mankind the idea of happiness that was to distinguish it from all previous mankind. Without freedom and happiness in the social relations of human beings, even the greatest increase in production and the abolition of private property in the means of production remain infected with the old injustice (N, pp. 144–5).

Marcuse here links his concept of socialism with the potentialities for freedom and happiness that are being repressed or restricted in the existing societies. He believes that this concern with the condition of human beings and their potentialities links critical theory with the great philosophies which elucidate the conditions and characteristics of human freedom, happiness and individuality. The critical theory is to define the highest human potentialities and to criticize society in terms of whether it furthers the development and realization of these potentialities, or their constriction and repression. The ultimate goal and fundamental interest of critical theory is a free and happy humanity in a rational society. What is at stake is the liberation of human beings and the development of their potentialities (N, pp. 145ff.).

This project requires radical social change; consequently all of critical theory's concepts are geared towards social practice. From a methodological point of view, critical theory is at once to comprehend the given society, criticize its contradictions and failures, and to construct alternatives. Its concepts are thus both descriptive and normative and aim at a new society. They are "constructive concepts, which comprehend not only the given reality, but simultaneously its abolition and the new reality that is to follow" (N, p. 145). The concepts of critical theory describe the structure of the given society and "already contain their own negation and transcendence: the image of a social organization without surplus value. All materialist concepts contain an accusation and an imperative" (N, p. 86). The concepts are thus multidimensional in simultaneously describing, criticizing and projecting an alternative to the given state of affairs. The paradigm of critical theory for Marcuse is Marx's project, which at once describes the alienation, exploitation, appropriation of surplus value, and capital accumulation in capitalist society, criticizes that society in sharp critical concepts, and projects the image of a society free from the oppressive features of capitalism. Since critical theory is to speak "against the facts and confront bad facticity with its better potentialities" (N, p. 143), it rejects sharp distinctions between fact and value, or descriptive and normative statements, while providing a theory which is at once descriptive, critical and geared towards social change.

In appraising the rationality or irrationality of a social order, the existing society is to be compared with its higher and better potentialities. In Marcuse's view, contradictions between "what is" and "what could be" provide an impetus for social change. For example, Marcuse continually compares the potentialities in modern technology and the accumulated social wealth with its current restrictive use, and condemns the society for its failure to use technology in more emancipatory and human ways. Critical theory is thus future-oriented (N, pp. 145, 153) and has a utopian quality. Its future projections are not to be idle daydreams, but an imaginative program of social reconstruction based on an analysis of tendencies in the present society which could be developed to construct a rational society that would increase human freedom and happiness. This project requires fantasy to bridge "the abyss between rational thought and present reality" (N, p. 154). This emphasis on the place of imagination in social theory is a constant theme of Marcuse's later works and purports to reinstate the importance of imagination that was present in such philosophers as Aristotle and Kant, but which has fallen into neglect or disrepute in modern philosophy (N, pp. 154–5). For Marcuse believes that "Without fantasy, all philosophical knowledge remains in the grip of the present or the past and severed from the future, which is the only link between philosophy and the real history of mankind" (N, p. 155).

Further, critical theory is self-reflexive and critical of the practice to which it connects itself. Marcuse writes: "Critical theory is, last but not least, critical of itself and of the social forces that make up its own basis. The philosophical element in the theory is a form of protest against the new 'Economism', which would isolate the economic struggle and separate the economic from the political sphere" (N, pp. 156–7). Here Marcuse is stating in a coded expression that critical theory should be critical of orthodox Marxism, rejecting economic reductionism (the "new Economism") and should be critical of the limitations of the working-class movement as well. Within Marxism, critical theory defends the political sphere against a narrowly conceived economic reductionism, and urges that political decisions and relations be geared to social and human goals: "the organization of the administration of social wealth in the interest of a liberated humanity" (N, p. 157). Critical theory wants to be free of illusions, and is not afraid to put its own theory and Marxism into radical question: "What . . . if the development outlined by the theory does not occur? What if the forces that were to bring about the transformation are suppressed and appear to be defeated?" (N, p. 142). Here Marcuse raises the haunting possibility that if the social forces in the working-class movement are defeated, critical theory is without a social base to realize the theory. It was precisely this predicament that would animate much of Marcuse's later writings, especially *One-Dimensional Man*, and Horkheimer's and Adorno's later work. But in the 1930s Marcuse argues that critical theory should remain faithful to its truths, despite the historical circumstances, for "critical theory preserves obstinacy as a genuine quality of philosophical thought" (N, p. 143).

In Marcuse's conception, critical theory is both to preserve philosophy's critical and emancipationary dimension and to unfold a social practice that will make possible its realization. Marx's stress on the unity of theory and practice is thus the guiding-concept of Marcuse's critical theory. He would follow this project and attempt to develop critical theory throughout his life, as the texts collected in this volume attest.

## TEN YEARS ON MORNINGSIDE HEIGHTS

Within the Institute, Marcuse became one of its most productive members. He was, in my view, a more original and sophisticated philosopher than Horkheimer and had a more solid and detailed knowledge of Hegel and Marx. Marcuse participated in the Institute's collective projects, helped formulate the concept of critical theory, produced powerful critiques of bourgeois ideology, and wrote many book reviews for the Institute's journal on topics in philosophy, sociology, history and psychology.[21] During the mid- to late 1930s, Marcuse worked especially closely with Horkheimer and their conception of critical theory at the time could be differentiated from that of Adorno and Benjamin.[22] Neither Horkheimer nor Marcuse followed Adorno's desire for the "liquidation of idealism," and both shared a version of Hegelian Marxism at odds with Adorno's early (and later!) works.[23] But with the entrance of Adorno into the group's "inner circle" in the late 1930s, Horkheimer tended to work ever more closely with Adorno, and in the 1940s their version of critical theory began to distance itself from the 1930s' program.

A text found in the Marcuse archive, "Ten Years on Morningside Heights: A Report on the Institute's History 1934–1944," provides a succinct overview of Institute activities and positions during the ten years of exile during which Marcuse was most involved with their projects. It illuminates the combination of critical social theory and philosophy that characterized the Institute approach – and Marcuse's own perspectives.

> Each study, while conforming to the highest scientific standards, should at the same time have a philosophical orientation. It should be intended as a contribution to the ultimate motives of social activity. In this sense philosophy is not separated from science by a definite line of demarcation. Science itself becomes philosophy while philosophy itself consists of more than scientific studies. It is this concept of science as philosophy, and of philosophy as science, that in our opinion has characterized the great humanistic schools of thought in Europe since the Renaissance.

---

21 See the bibliography in Kellner, *Herbert Marcuse*, op. cit.
22 On the difference between Horkheimer–Marcuse's and Adorno–Benjamin's versions of critical theory in the 1930s, see Susan Buck-Morss, *The Origin of Negative Dialectics*, New York: The Free Press, 1977.
23 On Adorno's program of the "liquidation of idealism," see Buck-Morss, op. cit., pp. 111ff; on the differences between Horkheimer and Adorno, see Stefan Breuer, "The Long Friendship: On Theoretical Differences between Adorno and Horkheimer," in *On Max Horkheimer*, op. cit., pp. 257–80.

In its studies the Institute has preserved something of this attitude. In its specifically philosophical monographs it has tried to explain this state of mind to American science and to bring it to bear on present-day issues. . . . Logical, moral and artistic problems are discussed in a critical spirit that aims to preserve the motifs of humanistic thought amidst the very decay of humanistic culture.[24]

The report stresses that: "Particular attention has been given to the fate of the individual in modern mass society, his atomization and frustration on the one hand, and the readiness of reason to surrender to methods of mass domination on the other." The summary of their "Research on Authoritarian Systems and Trends" notes how totalitarian systems are attacking the "individual in its very roots and foundation." Institute research into authority and family, fascism, and totalitarian trends suggest that "a definite consciousness of and a general belief in authority have been characteristic of modern society from the beginning." Hence, the love of freedom and reason in the Enlightenment is "from the outset a contradiction" to the main trends of bourgeois civilization.[25]

National Socialism is interpreted as "an authoritarian system in action," which is "a particularly virulent expression of tendencies and drives which can be observed all over the modern world." It is a new social order, "essentially different from all other forms of Western society." It has replaced the market economy with "a closely knit social structure based on command and obedience in a leader–follower way." In addition, National Socialism exemplifies shifts in the social function of family, private property, courts of law, and culture. In this order, parental authority is replaced by the state; authority has more objective political and social moorings; and there is a marked decline of pillars of bourgeois society such as the individual, the market, the family, religion, and traditional culture. The result is social atomization, new forms of domination, and the dissolution of all traditional societal bonds. Moreover, the fascist order exhibits features of a gangster state: the apparatus can shift at will from pseudo-legality to outright terror, autonomous groups are smashed, individuals are deprived of the means of organized resistance, reduced to monads and helplessly exposed to the combined onslaught of propaganda, corruption, and terror.[26]

"Ten Years" indicates that the Institute philosophical, political, and social studies are grounded in economic studies of "those processes which in all

---

24 Institute of Social Research, "Ten Years on Morningside Heights: A Report on the Institute's History 1934–1944," p. 11 (Herbert Marcuse archives).
25 "Ten Years," op. cit., pp. 13ff.
26 "Ten Years," op. cit., pp. 14–15. For Marcuse's own analyses of German fascism, see the papers collected in *Technology, War and Fascism*, op. cit.

highly developed countries have contributed toward a concentration of economic power." This shift from market to monopoly and state capitalism has "facilitated and partly conditioned authoritarian tendencies in other domains," transforming the role of the market and bringing about the "increased intrusion of elements of centralized control and planning into an allegedly free economy." Instead, National Socialism exhibits a "governmentally controlled economy," and a planned economy.[27]

The report also summarizes their studies in the sociology of art, prejudice and anti-Semitism, and makes clear the wide range of interdisciplinary activities which Marcuse participated in. In his postwar activity, Marcuse persisted in identifying with the project of developing a critical theory of society and throughout his life sought to integrate philosophy, political economy, social theory, and radical politics. During World War II when Horkheimer and Adorno were engaged in the philosophical studies that would become *Dialectic of Enlightenment* and were distancing themselves from Marxism and concrete politics, Marcuse was involved in both historical and political research and concrete political activity in the struggle against fascism. Moreover, Franz Neumann and Marcuse had begun developing a "theory of social change" from the present era, filling a gap in the Institute of Social Research's work[28] – a project that Marcuse would carry out in different contexts throughout his life.

Deeply influenced by the synthesis of philosophy and political economy in the early Marx, Marcuse enthusiastically devoted himself to the critical theory project of combining philosophy, social theory, and political economy, adding to classical Marxism's focus on economics and politics, the dimension of critical social theory and addressing phenomena not theorized adequately by Marx, such as the sociological, cultural and aesthetic, and psychological dimensions of human life. The result was the typically Marcusean synthesis that is on display in the studies collected in this volume.

Hence, Marcuse was not a traditional philosopher or social theorist, but a genuinely interdisciplinary and dialectical thinker for whom philosophical categories are always mediated by political economy and social theory, while philosophy provides critical perspectives on all aspects of social life. Hence, Marcuse defends the categories of philosophy, even metaphysics, for critical social theory and presents an *Aufhebung*, or sublation, of philosophy into social theory while developing a philosophical social theory with practical intent. The project involved a reconstruction and rethinking of Marxism to

---

27 "Ten Years," op. cit., pp. 15–16.
28 See Herbert Marcuse, *Technology, War and Fascism*, op. cit., pp. 93–138.

fill its lacunae and to make it more relevant to contemporary reality. This discussion sets the stage for an introduction to Marcuse's own postwar work on critical theory and the development of his distinctive version.


## MARCUSE'S CRITICAL THEORY: MARX, FREUD, AND BEYOND

Letters from Horkheimer to Marcuse in the late 1940s discuss Horkheimer's plans to return to Germany to re-establish the Institute of Social Research after several encouraging letters and invitations to return from Frankfurt University. Horkheimer, Adorno, and Horkheimer's close personal friend Friedrich Pollock did indeed return to Frankfurt in 1948, Horkheimer was elected Dean and named Rector of Frankfurt University, and what became known as the Frankfurt School was re-established in Germany. Marcuse, however, remained in the US, although he stayed in close contact with the Institute and frequently indicated interest in rejoining his former colleagues.

On October 18, 1951, Marcuse wrote to Horkheimer, whom he had recently visited in Frankfurt: "You asked me for the plan of the Freud book. As I am venturing into an area that is very risky, both privately and objectively, I have decided to write down everything that occurs to me first, and then rewrite it. So I have no plan – apart from the ideas I mentioned to you in Frankfurt."[29] Marcuse mentions here to Horkheimer the project that became *Eros and Civilization* in its earliest stages and he kept him informed of its progress and showed him the manuscript at various stages. In a September 1, 1954 letter to Adorno, Horkheimer says that it is "quite decent" and "there are so many splendid things in the book that we should accept it completely," thus recommending the study to Adorno for inclusion in a series of publications sponsored by the Institute of Social Research. Shortly thereafter, Marcuse wrote to Horkheimer: "It would be wonderful if the German edition could appear as an Institute text – it belongs to the Institute and its director."[30]

In a volume titled *Sociologica*, dedicated to Horkheimer on his sixtieth birthday, Marcuse's abridged translation of the final chapter of *Eros and*

---

29 Marcuse to Horkheimer, October 18, 1951. In Max Horkheimer, *Gesammelte Schriften*, Vol. 18, edited by Gunzelin Schmid Noerr, Frankfurt: Fischer, 1996, pp. 221–2.
30 Marcuse to Horkheimer, December 11, 1954 (letter in the Frankfurt Max Horkheimer archive).

*Civilization* appeared in the second place, immediately after Adorno's contribution,[31] but Adorno – always jealous of Marcuse and protective of his own favored relation to Horkheimer – wrote Horkheimer on August 30, 1955:

> In *Dissent* there is a long article by Herbert against the psychoanalytic revisionists, which basically contains the ideas we hold on the matter, although we are not mentioned in so much as a single word, which I find very strange. I am decisivément against one-sided solidarity, and in connection with his book, of which this article forms a chapter, I should very much like to advocate that we do *absolutely nothing*.[32]

In effect, Adorno got his way, *Eros and Civilization* was not published in the Institute book series, despite a series of letters between Marcuse, Horkheimer, Adorno, and Pollock over the issue.[33] In a letter to Marcuse, Adorno claimed that Marcuse's interpretation of Freud was too "immediate," that this was a problem of English, that German lent itself better to mediation (*Vermittlung*), and that therefore the book would be improved in German if Marcuse translated it himself so that it could take what Adorno considered an appropriate form.[34]

Marcuse was probably insulted by this response and in any case did not want to spend time on translating his own book to please Adorno; he was working on the project that became *Soviet Marxism* and allowed another German publisher to translate *Eros and Civilization* after the Institute waffling. Many critics and readers find *Eros and Civilization* to be Marcuse's

---

31 See Max Horkheimer and Theodor W. Adorno, *Sociologica I. Aufsätze zum sechziggsten Geburtstag gewidmet*. Frankfurt: Europäische Verlags-Anstalt, 1955.

32 Adorno to Horkheimer, August 30, 1955 (letter in the Max Horkheimer archive Frankfurt).

33 Wiggershaus, *The Frankfurt School*, pp. 496ff, interprets the history of the German edition of *Eros and Civilization* as a sign of distance and objective alienation between Marcuse and the Institute of Social Research. The episode also shows Adorno continuing to undermine Marcuse within the Institute of Social Research; see the letter from Adorno to Horkheimer against Marcuse that I cite in *Technology, War and Fascism*, p. 16; letters from Adorno to Horkheimer, cited above, also find him blocking a German translation of *Eros and Civilization* in the Institute series; other letters find Adorno sharply criticizing Marcuse to Horkheimer, although Adorno and Marcuse maintained a friendly correspondence with, however, some pointed criticisms by Marcuse of Horkheimer and Adorno's political attitudes and behavior in the 1960s, some of which are contained in this volume. It is fair to say that Adorno and Marcuse had a highly complex relationship, mediated by their association with Horkheimer and Adorno's desire to keep Marcuse at a distance from the man who controlled Institute purse-strings and patronage.

34 Adorno to Marcuse, July 16, 1957 (letter in the Herbert Marcuse archives, Frankfurt).

best work and one of the most important developments of critical theory.[35]
The book contains an audacious synthesis of Marx and Freud and sketches
the outlines of a non-repressive society. Although Freud argued in
*Civilization and Its Discontents* that civilization inevitably involved repression and suffering, Marcuse maintained that other elements in Freud's theory
suggested that the unconscious contained evidence of an instinctual drive
toward happiness and freedom. This material is articulated, Marcuse suggests, in daydreams, works of art, philosophy, and other cultural products.
Based on this reading of Freud and study of an emancipatory tradition of
philosophy and culture, Marcuse sketched the outlines of a non-repressive
civilization which would involve libidinal and non-alienated labor, play, free
and open sexuality, and production of a society and culture which would
further freedom and happiness. His vision of liberation anticipated many
of the values of the 1960s counterculture and helped Marcuse to become a
major intellectual and political figure during that decade.

Marcuse contended that the then current organization of society generated "surplus repression" by imposing socially unnecessary labor, excessive
restrictions on sexuality, and a social system organized around profit and
exploitation. In light of the diminution of scarcity and prospects for
increased abundance, Marcuse called for the end of repression and creation
of a new society. His radical critique of existing society and its values, his
call for a non-repressive civilization, and his critique of neo-Freudian
revisionism elicited a dispute with his former colleague Erich Fromm,
who accused him of "nihilism" (toward existing values and society) and
irresponsible hedonism. Marcuse had criticized Fromm in *Eros and
Civilization* for excessive "conformity" and "idealism" and repeated these
charges in the polemical debates over his work following the publication
of *Eros and Civilization* which heatedly discussed Marcuse's use of Freud,
his critique of existing civilization, and his proposals for an alternative
organization of society and culture.[36]

In 1956, Marcuse went to the Freud Centennial in Frankfurt cosponsored
by the Institute of Social Research, where Jürgen Habermas and other young

---

35 For my own positive evaluation, see Kellner, *Herbert Marcuse*, Chapter Six and
   my Preface to the 1998 Routledge edition of *Eros and Civilization* (London and
   New York), pp. xi–xix.
36 See Erich Fromm, "The Political Implications of Instinctual Radicalism," *Dissent*,
   II, 4 (Fall 1955), pp. 342–9 and Marcuse's response "A Reply to Erich Fromm,"
   *Dissent*, III, 1 (Winter 1956), pp. 79–81. I will discuss the Fromm–Marcuse
   relationship and their varying interpretations of Freud in more detail in the
   forthcoming Routledge Volume Five of Marcuse's *Collected Papers, Philosophy,
   Psychoanalysis, and Emancipation*.

members and students in the Institute met him for the first time and were highly impressed with an individual who seemed to embody the earlier radical currents of critical theory with a contemporary political edge missing in Horkheimer and Adorno.[37] At the conference, Marcuse presented a lecture "Progress in the Light of Psychoanalysis,"[38] which Habermas described:

> Marcuse's dialectics of progress showed that a non-repressive culture is technically possible, that the instruments of progress – science, industry, and technology – have made possible a world without poverty, repression, and material deprivation – but the current organization of society prevents this. Against Freud, Marcuse defends the possibility of a non-repressive civilization.[39]

Such a clear utopian alternative had not been articulated within the Institute and this impressed Habermas and some of his colleagues. In addition, Marcuse continued to analyze the forms of advanced industrial societies, capitalist and communist, publishing his studies of *Soviet Marxism* in 1958.[40] The distinctive Marcusean perspective of combining analyses of domination with those of liberation, stressing both the most oppressive aspects of contemporary society as well as the most utopian possibilities, was thus developing in the postwar period and his subsequent writings would stress one pole or the other – or in some cases attempt to provide a balance.

---

37 Conversation with Jürgen Habermas, Frankfurt, August 1988. Habermas told Wiggershaus that he and others did not know at the time how closely associated with Horkheimer and the Institute Marcuse had been and did not know his full background; *The Frankfurt School*, pp. 544ff. Habermas stressed to me how impressive he found Marcuse, whose progressive political attitudes, in contrast to the increasing conservativism of Horkheimer, he found appealing (discussion in Frankfurt, October 1990). A September 27, 1958 letter from Horkheimer to Adorno – over Habermas's essay in *Philosophical Rundschau* on Marx and Marxism – discloses intense hostility toward Habermas. Horkheimer claims that Habermas mentions revolution continuously, transforms critical theory into revolution theory, sublates philosophy into praxis, thus betraying (Horkheimer's and Adorno's) philosophy and critical theory. In addition, Horkheimer complains that Habermas has no sense of empirical reality, and may be a hardworking, active researcher and writer, but will bring shame to the Institute (see Horkheimer to Adorno, published in Max Horkheimer, *Gesammelte Schriften*, Vol. 18, edited by Gunzelin Schmid Noerr, Frankfurt: Fischer, 1996, pp. 437–48). Horkheimer initially blocked Habermas's promotion in the Institute of Social Research, but after he retired Adorno brought him back (see Wiggershaus, op. cit.).

38 Herbert Marcuse, "Progress and Freud's Theory of the Instincts," *Five Lectures*, Boston: Beacon Press, 1970, pp. 28–43.

39 Jürgen Habermas, "Triebschicksal als politische Schicksal," *Frankfurter Allgemeine Zeitung*, July 14, 1956.

40 For my evaluation of *Soviet Marxism*, see Kellner, *Herbert Marcuse*, Chapter Seven and my Introduction to the 1985 Columbia University Press edition (New York), pp. vii–xiii.

Marcuse's version of critical theory is thus characterized by both radical critique of forces of domination and the search for forces of opposition and liberation. Moreover, while Horkheimer and Adorno were distancing themselves from political practice, Marcuse continually sought the union of theory and practice and to make critical theory an instrument of social change. His political differences with Horkheimer and Adorno emerged clearly in the 1960s in an exchange of letters, published in this collection (see pp. 212 ff.), over what Marcuse envisaged as the increasing tendencies of Horkheimer and Adorno to engage in "cold-war ideology," to promote anti-communism while failing to adequately criticize the West. The exchange reveals Marcuse's intransigent political radicalism that would make him one of the most important critical theorists of the 1960s.

## CRITICAL THEORY AND THE FORTUNES OF HISTORY: FROM THE 1960s INTO THE 1970s

Throughout the late 1950s and early 1960s, Marcuse sought to develop his critical theory in a series of studies that formed the background and substance of *One-Dimensional Man* (1964).[41] While *Eros* contains the most detailed depiction of his vision of liberation, *One-Dimensional Man* yields Marcuse's most systematic presentation of forces of domination. In this book, he analyzed the  development of new forms of social control which were producing a "one-dimensional man" and "society without opposition." Citing trends toward conformity, Marcuse described the forms of culture and society which created "false" consumer needs that integrated individuals into the existing system of production and consumption via mass media, advertising, industrial management, and uncritical modes of thought. To "one-dimensional" thought and society, Marcuse counterposed critical and dialectical thinking which perceived a freer and happier form of culture and society, and advocated a "great refusal" of all modes of repression and domination.

*One-Dimensional Man* theorized the decline of revolutionary potential in capitalist societies and the development of new forms of social control. Marcuse claimed that "advanced industrial society" created false needs which integrated individuals into the existing system of production and

---

41 Herbert Marcuse, *One-Dimensional Man*, Boston: Beacon Press, 1964; for my evaluation of this text, see *Herbert Marcuse*, Chapter Eight and my introduction to the second Beacon Press and Routledge editions, 1991 and 1999.

consumption. Mass media and culture, advertising, industrial management, and contemporary modes of thought all reproduced the existing system and attempted to eliminate negativity, critique, and opposition. The result was a "one-dimensional" universe of thought and behavior in which the very aptitude and ability for critical thinking and oppositional behavior was withering away.

Not only had capitalism integrated the working class, the source of potential revolutionary opposition, but they had developed new techniques of stabilization through state policies and the development of new forms of social control. Thus Marcuse questioned two of the fundamental postulates of orthodox Marxism: the revolutionary proletariat and the inevitability of capitalist crisis. In contrast with the emphasis on the working class as the primary source of social change in orthodox Marxism, Marcuse championed the non-integrated forces of minorities, outsiders, and the radical intelligentsia, while attempting to nourish oppositional thought and behavior through promoting critical thinking and what he called the "great refusal."

For Marcuse, domination combined economics, politics, technology, social organization, and culture. Whereas for orthodox Marxists, domination is inscribed in capitalist relations of production and the logic of commodification, for Heideggerians, Weberians and others it is technology, technological rationality, and/or political institutions that are the major forces of societal domination. Marcuse, by contrast, synthesizes these approaches and develops a multidimensional analysis that ferrets out aspects of domination and resistance throughout the social order. Moreover, Marcuse insisted that contradictions of the system, theorized by classical Marxism as the antagonism of capital and labor, remained, albeit in altered form. Marcuse constantly cited the unity of production and destruction, the ways that creation of wealth produced systematic poverty, war, and violence. Hence, for Marcuse there was an "objective ambiguity" to even the seeming achievements of advanced industrial society which had the wealth, science, technology, and industry to alleviate poverty and suffering, but used the instruments of production to enhance domination, violence, and injustice.

Texts such as "The Problem of Social Change in the Technological Society" (1962) and "The Containment of Social Change in Industrial Society" (1965) – both collected in this volume – provide excellent analyses of what Marcuse calls "advanced industrial society." The focus in the titles of these works discloses Marcuse's abiding interest in social change – an emphasis that distinguished his work from that of Horkheimer and Adorno, who were becoming increasingly uninterested in promoting social change or political practice and transformation.

In addition to developing his general theoretical perspectives, Marcuse persistently engaged in concrete sociopolitical analysis. His text "The Individual in the Great Society" (1966), collected in this volume, provides an astute critique of the ideological pretensions of US President Lyndon Johnson's conception of a "great society" and sharp analysis of the fate of the individual in the contemporary world. Johnson called for development of a "great society" at the same time that he accelerated US involvement in Vietnam; Marcuse in turn provided a penetrating appraisal of Johnson's program, while positively evaluating its progressive elements, the realization of which Marcuse claimed would require radical change beyond the existing organization of society.

While *One-Dimensional Man* and most of Marcuse's texts of the early to mid-1960s provide often sobering and pessimistic critiques of the tendencies toward domination and increased social control, producing the containment of social change, he continued to seek agents and possibilities of social transformation which he indeed discovered in the mid-1960s in the student and anti-war movement, the emerging counterculture, and Third World liberation movements. In a "1966 Political Preface" to *Eros and Civilization* and a 1968 lecture "Beyond One-Dimensional Man," both published in this volume, Marcuse valorizes forces of opposition and revolt and the importance of aesthetic and erotic components of social rebellion. In a sense, Marcuse anticipated the counterculture and many 1960s liberation movements in *Eros and Civilization*, and when forces appeared that embodied his values of eros, love, play, and the aesthetic dimension, Marcuse defended and promoted these forces.

A previously unknown text found in the Marcuse archives that we have titled "Cultural Revolution" (n.d., around 1970), and which is included in this volume, provides Marcuse's most detailed analysis of the importance of cultural revolution for radical social transformation. The origins, genesis, and history of "Cultural Revolution" is something of a mystery. The text is highly polished and appears ready for publication, but Marcuse apparently abandoned it in favor of the project that became his 1972 book *Counterrevolution and Revolt*.[42] Continuing the revolutionary optimism of *An Essay on Liberation*, but with more qualifications, "Cultural Revolution" is in retrospect one of his best balanced works between

---

42 Some of the ideas in "Cultural Revolution" are more developed in *Counterrevolution and Revolt*, but others are more fully explicated in the former text; a few pages of text overlap and some similar themes are treated, but the valence of the concept of "cultural revolution" is different in *Counterrevolution and Revolt*. In the latter, references to "cultural revolution" are more muted, even negative, than in the more optimistic and affirmative text published here.

optimism and pessimism. It contains some of his most nuanced appraisals of the New Left, counterculture, and forces of radical opposition. He stresses the "objective ambivalence" of the forces of both the system and the opposition which combine positive and negative features, and sketches out his conception of a "new sensibility" which combines reason and the senses in an oppositional subjectivity.

We are also including in this volume another important unpublished text found in the Marcuse archive that we are calling "The Historical Fate of Bourgeois Democracy". The manuscript clearly follows *Counterrevolution and Revolt* chronologically and deepens its pessimism. Written just after Nixon's re-election in 1972 and the decisive defeat of anti-war candidate George McGovern, Marcuse carries out one of his most detailed analyses of a specific historical juncture and most sustained critiques of the contradictions of bourgeois democracy. The manuscript is polished, ready for publication and it is not clear why Marcuse did not publish this text.[43] Drawing on Erich Fromm's *Escape From Freedom* and a text co-authored by Adorno and the Institute of Social Research, *The Authoritarian Personality*, Marcuse points to what he considers "sadomasochistic" tendencies in both the underlying population and counterculture. Although the political analysis of bourgeois democracy is orthodox Marxian in places, Marcuse also valorizes the emerging women's liberation movement and ecology movement as progressive forces of change.

Marcuse's pessimism regarding the ascendancy of neo-fascist forces seemed to be put in question with the Watergate affair and the assault on Richard Nixon in both the political system and media which led to his resignation. But in a letter to the *New York Times*, published on the op-ed page as "Watergate: When Law and Morality Stand in the Way" (June 27, 1973), Marcuse claimed that the affair is being treated as an anomaly in an otherwise fair, rational, just, and functional political system. In the text, which we are including in this volume, Marcuse insists that the Watergate affair is symptomatic of a corrupt social system as a whole. Written during the period of growing revelations and media discussion of crimes in the

---

Marcuse must have become somewhat skeptical of this concept as the 1960s passed into the 1970s and he came to privilege the concept of "counterrevolution" over revolutionary forces as hegemonic around 1972. *Counterrevolution and Revolt* actually contains a sharp critique of forces of "revolt" and the "cultural revolution" as I will argue in Volume Three of the Routledge *Collected Papers* of Herbert Marcuse, *Foundations of the New Left*.

43 As with "Cultural Revolution," there are no references to the "Historical Fate of Bourgeois Democracy" in the Marcuse archives, or in letters to friends, and no one so far has been able to shed light on the origins, genesis, and history of this text.

Nixon White House in the aftermath of the Watergate burglary, it shows Marcuse resisting facile liberal optimism and continuing the sort of radical critique that is characteristic of his version of critical theory.

A distinct shift takes place between the revolutionary optimism of "Beyond One-Dimensional Man" and *An Essay on Liberation*, the more balanced positions in "Cultural Revolution," and the rather negative and pessimistic positions in *Counterrevolution and Revolt* and "Historical Fate of Bourgeois Democracy." Whereas in his writings from 1968 to the early 1970s, Marcuse focused on the forces of struggle and liberation, in his writings from around 1972 to the mid-1970s, he returns to focus on forces of domination and repression. Marcuse's critical theory was closely attuned to the political situation of the moment and his mood and analytical focus seemed to swing from optimism to pessimism depending on the prospects for the New Left and radical opposition in the current historical situation.

Throughout the 1970s, Marcuse sought to update his social and political critique and to seek new agents of social transformation – as we shall see in the next Routledge volume which treats Marcuse's interaction with the New Left. A lecture, "A Revolution in Values" (1973), included in this volume, shows how Marcuse persevered in combining philosophical with political analysis in his project of social critique and social transformation. It is significant that Marcuse continues calling for cultural revolution, in this case a revolution of values, into the 1970s. The argument presents an orthodox Marxist account of relations between values and social change and then offers a dialectical argument in which change of values anticipates social change, as, for example, the Enlightenment preceded the French revolution and the nineteenth century ideas of socialism preceded the Russian and other socialist revolutions.

While in his later years Marcuse turned from his highly political work on developing a critical theory of society and radical politics to his final work on aesthetics,[44] he also engaged feminism, ecology, and the social movements of the era, constantly updating his theoretical analysis and seeking new agents of social transformation. Hence, from the 1930s until his death in 1979, Herbert Marcuse's work can be seen as an attempt to develop a critical theory of society and radical politics for the contemporary era.

---

44 See Herbert Marcuse, *The Aesthetic Dimension*, Boston: Beacon Press, 1978. A forthcoming volume of this series will engage Marcuse's work in aesthetics.

## CONCLUDING REMARKS: MARCUSE IN
## THE NEW MILLENNIUM

The texts collected in this volume are of great importance for understanding Marcuse and the Frankfurt School. They make clear the unique synthesis of philosophy, social theory, aesthetics, and radical politics that distinguish Marcuse's critical theory and his constant updating and revision of his theory in response to political and historical change. They disclose Marcuse at his most radical, making clear his differences from Horkheimer and Adorno, and showing Marcuse to be a sharp analyst and critic of contemporary social conditions.

In conclusion, I would suggest that these texts are of more than historical interest as we need today the same sort of dialectical social theory developed by Marcuse. Although much of the controversy around Marcuse involved his critiques of contemporary capitalist societies and defense of radical social change, in retrospect, Marcuse left behind a complex and many-sided body of work comparable to the legacies of Ernst Bloch, Georg Lukacs, T. W. Adorno, and Walter Benjamin. His social theory is characterized by broad critical perspectives that attempt to capture the major sociohistorical, political and cultural features of the day. Such attempts to get at the Big Picture, to theorize the fundamental changes, developments, contradictions, and struggles of the day are more necessary than ever in an era of globalization in which the restructuring of capital and technological revolution are changing all aspects of life. Marcuse's thought thus remains pertinent because he provides a mode of global theoretical analysis and addresses issues that continue to be significant for contemporary theory and politics. His unpublished manuscripts contain much material pertinent to concerns of the present era which could provide the basis for a rebirth of interest in Marcuse's thought as we enter a new millennium and meet new theoretical and political challenges.[45]

In sum, Marcuse provides comprehensive philosophical perspectives on domination and liberation, a powerful method and framework for analyzing contemporary society, and a vision of liberation that is richer than classical Marxism, other versions of critical theory, and current forms of postmodern theory. Indeed, Marcuse presents critical philosophical perspectives on

---

45 For examples of the contemporary relevance of Marcuse, see the studies in John Bokina and Timothy J. Lukes, editors, *Marcuse. From the New Left to the Next Left*, Lawrence, Kansas: University of Kansas Press, 1994; the series of Marcuse's uncollected and unpublished writings edited by Peter-Erwin Jansen for Campus Verlag and zu klampen Verlag; and the recent books published in Brazil by Jorge Coehlo, *Marcuse. Uma Trajetoria* (Londrina: Editora UEL, 1999) and Isabel Loureiro, *Herbert Marcuse, A grande recusa hoje* (Petropolis: Editora Vozes, 1999).

human beings and their relationship to nature and society, as well as substantive social theory and radical politics. In retrospect, Marcuse's vision of liberation – of the full development of the individual in a non-repressive society – distinguishes his work, along with sharp critique of existing forms of domination and oppression, and he emerges in this narrative as a theorist of forces of domination and liberation. Deeply rooted in philosophy and the conception of social theory developed by the Institute for Social Research, Marcuse's work lacked the sustained empirical analysis in some versions of Marxist theory and the detailed conceptual analysis found in many versions of political theory. Yet he constantly showed how science, technology, and theory itself had a political dimension and produced a solid body of ideological and historical analysis of many of the dominant forms of society, culture, and thought during the turbulent era in which he lived and struggled for a better world.

Thus, I believe that Marcuse overcomes the limitations of many current varieties of philosophy and social theory and that his writings provide a viable starting-point for theoretical and political concerns of the present age. In particular, his articulations of philosophy with social theory, cultural criticism, and radical politics constitute an enduring legacy. Whereas mainstream academic divisions of labor isolate social theory from philosophy and other disciplines, Marcuse provides a robust philosophical dimension and cultural criticism to social theory, while developing his theoretical perspectives in interaction with concrete analyses of society, politics, and culture in the present age. This dialectical approach thus assigns philosophy an important position within social theory, providing critical theory with strong normative and philosophical perspectives.

In addition, Marcuse emerges as a sharp, even prescient, sociopolitical theorist. He was one of the first on the left who both developed a cogent critique of Soviet Marxism and yet foresaw the liberalizing trends in the Soviet Union.[46] After the uprisings in Poland and Hungary in 1956 were ruthlessly suppressed, many speculated that Khrushchev would have to roll back his program of de-Stalinization and crack down further. Marcuse, however, differed, writing in 1958: "The Eastern European events were likely to slow down and perhaps even reverse de-Stalinization in some fields; particularly in international strategy, a considerable 'hardening' has been apparent. However, if our analysis is correct, the fundamental trend will continue and reassert itself throughout such reversals. With respect to internal Soviet developments, this means at present continuation of 'collective leadership,' decline in the power of the secret

---

46 See Marcuse, *Soviet Marxism*, op. cit.

police, decentralization, legal reforms, relaxation in censorship, liberalization in cultural life."[47]

In part as a response to the collapse of Communism and in part as a result of new technological and economic conditions, the capitalist system has been undergoing disorganization and reorganization in a process of global restructuring. Marcuse's loyalty to Marxism always led him to analyze new conditions within capitalist societies that had emerged since Marx. Social theory today can thus build on this Marcusean tradition in developing critical theories of contemporary society grounded in analyses of the transformations of capitalism, technology, and the emergence of a new global world economic system. For Marcuse, social theory was integrally historical and must conceptualize the salient phenomena of the present age and changes from previous social formations. While the postmodern perspectives of theorists like Baudrillard and Lyotard claim to postulate a rupture in history, they fail to analyze the key constituents of the changes going on, with Baudrillard even declaring the "end of political economy."[48] Marcuse, by contrast, always attempted to analyze the changing configurations of capitalism and to relate social and cultural changes to transformations in the economy.

Moreover, Marcuse always paid special attention to the decisive position of technology in organizing contemporary societies, and with the emergence of new technologies in our time the Marcusean emphasis on the relationship between technology, the economy, culture, and everyday life is especially important. Marcuse also engaged new forms of culture and the ways that culture provided both instruments of manipulation and liberation. The proliferation of new media technologies and cultural forms in recent years also demands a Marcusean perspective to capture both their potentialities for progressive social change and the possibilities of more streamlined forms of social domination. Whereas postmodern theories also describe new technologies, Marcuse always related the economy to culture and technology, seeing both emancipatory and dominating potentials, while theorists like Baudrillard are one-dimensional, often falling prey to technological determinism and views of society and culture that fail to see positive and emancipatory potentials.

I would also argue that we are to some extent in the situation of Marcuse in the 1960s and 1970s, a highly ambiguous and fluid situation with

---

47 See Marcuse, *Soviet Marxism*, op. cit., p. 174.
48 See Steven Best and Douglas Kellner, *Postmodern Theory: Critical Interrogations*, London and New York: Macmillan and Guilford Press, 1991, and *The Postmodern Turn*, London and New York: Routledge and Guilford Press, 1998.

unpredictable results brought about by a confluence of technological revolution and a highly ambivalent political situation. The past two decades have been a period of immense change involving technological revolution and the global restructuring of capitalism. Marcuse's focus on the relations between technology, economy, and society can contribute to our understanding of the underlying factors of the great transformation that we are undergoing and his mode of thought helps us to track and appraise the dramatic changes we are living through. Great forces of transformation are being unleashed through technological revolution, especially computers and biotechnology, which contain great promise, but also threaten to intensify forces of domination and destruction. Consequently, progress and regression are embedded in the current forces of technology, society, and politics on a global scale. The current historical situation is thus fluid, open and ambiguous, requiring the mode of dialectical analysis and critique developed by Marcuse.

The ambiguities and shifts in Marcuse's texts and analysis articulate historical conflicts and transformations. A critical theory of society is always a project underway, it is always partial, historical, and subject to revision. Thus, one is always moving toward a critical theory, open to new historical experiences, phenomena, and discourses. Marcuse's life-work exhibits several decades of critical theory in action, providing copious examples of how to do critical theory, how to analyze the contradictory social forces and social changes and transformations that are a defining mark of the contemporary era.[49]

Finally, while versions of postmodern theory, like Baudrillard, have renounced radical politics, Marcuse always attempted to link his critical theory with the most radical political movements of the day and thus to politicize his philosophy and social theory. For these reasons, then, I would argue that Marcuse's thought continues to provide important resources and a stimulus for critical theory and radical politics in the present age. Marcuse himself was open to new theoretical and political currents, yet remained loyal to those theories which he believed provided inspiration

---

49 Horkheimer and Adorno, by contrast, tended to abandon development of critical theory, tending to repeat through the 1950s and 1960s many of the same theses concerning the culture industries, crisis of reason, decline of the individual, or totally administered society that they developed in the 1940s. There were also hints in some of their publications that given the fragmentation and complexity of current social conditions, it was becoming impossible to characterize contemporary society as a whole. See the Preface to Max Horkheimer and Theodor W. Adorno, *Sociologica II. Reden und Vorträge*. Frankfurt: Europäische Verlags-Anstalt, 1962.

and substance for the compelling challenges of the era. Consequently, as we confront today's theoretical and political problems, I believe that the works of Herbert Marcuse provide important resources for our current situation and that a Marcusean renaissance could provide critical social theory with new impulses and tasks.

# I

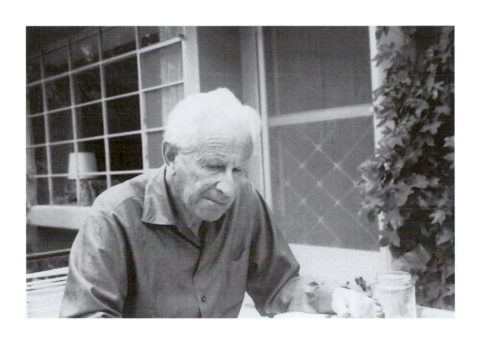

†"The Problem of Social Change in the Technological Society," was prepared as an address for a UNESCO symposium on social development that was held May 12–14, 1961. Peter-Erwin Jansen has ascertained, however, that it is probable that Marcuse did not attend the conference. While Marcuse's contribution was published in the collection of conference papers with the dual title *On Social Development* and *Le Developpement social*, edited by Raymond Aron and Bert F. Hoselitz (Paris Mouton, 1965; volume printed for limited distribution), Marcuse was not mentioned in the list of participants in the conference. Moreover, an exchange of letters with Leo Löwenthal indicates that Marcuse was planning to attend a cocktail party for Abraham Maslow on May 14 and then entertained Löwenthal at his home in Waltham, Massachusetts; shortly thereafter, Löwenthal thanked Marcuse in a May 24, 1961 letter for "a wonderful time – intellectually, emotionally and above all culinary" (see the editors' notes to Peter-Erwin Jansen, editor, Herbert Marcuse, *Das Schicksal der bürgerlichen Demokratie* (Lüneburg: zu Klampen Verlag, pp. 37–8).

Jansen notes that the topic of the UNESCO conference was analysis of social development since World War II that would seek the grounds for unequal development between the Western industrial countries and the so-called underdeveloped countries. It would also question whether moral and human progress is possible under conditions of accelerated rationalization. Marcuse's contribution, published here, analyzes social change in technological society, anticipating his theses of *One-Dimensional Man* that technological development was a threat to freedom, individualism, democracy, and other positive values – but also created the preconditions for greater freedom, equality, justice, and so on that the organization of contemporary industrial societies were blocking.

# THE PROBLEM OF SOCIAL
# CHANGE IN THE
# TECHNOLOGICAL SOCIETY†

One of the accomplishments of advanced industrial civilization[1] is the non-terroristic, democratic decline of freedom – the efficient, smooth, reasonable unfreedom which seems to have its roots in technical progress itself. What could be more rational than the suppression of individual autonomy in the mechanization and standardization of socially necessary but painful performances, the concentration of private enterprises in more effective and more productive corporations, the regulation of free competition among unequally equipped economic subjects, the curtailment of prerogatives and national sovereignties which impede the international organization of resources. The fact that this technological order involves a political and intellectual co-ordination may be a regrettable but also promising development. The rights and liberties which were such vital factors in the origins and earlier stages of industrial society yield to a higher stage of this society: they are losing their traditional rationale and content. Moreover, the capabilities of advanced industrial civilization suggest that this society may well be able to prevent and contain social change involving the basic institutions of society – as distinguished from changes *within* the given institutional framework. Social change is qualitative change if it establishes essentially different forms of human existence, with a new social division of labor, new modes of control over the productive process, a new morality, etc. Now perhaps the most singular achievement of advanced industrial society is its success in integrating and reconciling antagonistic groups and interests: bipartisan policy, acceptance of the national purpose, co-operation of business and labor testify to this achievement. To be sure,

---

1  For the purpose of this paper, defined as a society based on large mechanized industry with a growing sector of automation.

the conflicts continue and erupt violently enough, but the trend contrasts distinctly with the preceding period. Under the impact of the technical and scientific conquests, the size and efficacy of the productive apparatus, and the rising standard of living, the political opposition against the basic institutions of the established society succumbs and turns into opposition *within* the accepted conditions.

This paper aims at elucidating the historical function of these tendencies, that is to say, it aims at contributing to a critical theory of advanced industrial society in terms of its historical alternatives. From the outset, this undertaking is confronted with the question as to the ground on which such a critique can reasonably proceed. What are its criteria and standards? Evidently, they must be historical themselves, derived from demonstrable tendencies and capabilities of the established society which would render possible the emergence of more rational modes of social and individual existence. However, the latter are merely "values", ideals or abstract theoretical possibilities unless the critique can furthermore identify social groups and interests capable of transforming theory into action, values into facts. And here, the critique seems to be vitiated by the achievement of advanced industrial society in containing the internal opposition – a development which from the beginning renders the critique of the established society in terms of its historical alternatives abstract and utopian. This novel situation may be illustrated by a brief statement on the place of historical alternatives in the social theory of the preceding stages.

Prior to their realization, historical alternatives appear and disappear as "values", professed as preferential by certain groups or individuals. In social theory as well as in any other field, values are not facts and are, as values, opposed to facts; facts, as facts, are not values and are opposed to values. Their opposition can be resolved only through a historical "mediation" which reconciles the extremes by subverting their form – i.e., by establishing factual conditions (institutions and relationships) in which the values are translated into reality. Such historical mediation occurred, during the ascending period of industrial society, in the consciousness and political action of the Bourgeoisie which translated liberalism into reality; another historical mediation appeared at the mature stage of this society: in the consciousness and political action of the Proletariat. However, the subsequent development has altered the structure and function of these classes in such a way that they operate no longer as agents of historical transformation. An overriding interest in the preservation of the institutional status quo joins the former antagonists. Where the Bourgeoisie still is the ruling class, it reveals ever more openly its dependence on the containment of social change. And on the ground of the growing productivity of the

*[handwritten margin note: the tension between "values" and "facts".]*

economic-technical apparatus, that is to say, on the ground of increasing comforts under total administration, large sections of the laboring classes in the most advanced areas of industrial civilization are led from "absolute negation" to resignation and even affirmation of the system.

In the absence of demonstrable agents and agencies of social change, the critique is thrown back to a high level of abstraction: there is no ground on which theory and practice, thought and action meet. Theories of society and social change which imply objective historical tendencies and an objective evaluation of historical alternatives now appear as unrealistic speculation, and commitment to them as a matter of personal (or group) preference. Take for example Marx's idea of socialism: look at the reality of advanced capitalism and advancing communism and you must admit the unreal, wishful character of the idea. And yet, is the theory which terminated in this idea refuted by the facts of present-day capitalism and communism? These facts are substantially incomplete, ambivalent: they are elements in a larger context of historical space and time. Insulation against this context falsifies the facts and their function in the society because it insulates the facts against their negation, i.e., against the forces which make for their trancendence toward modes of existence rendered possible and at the same time precluded by the given society. If the insulation is corrected, the facts appear as other than they are in the immediate (insulated) experience. Now they are "comprehended", understood in the light of a historical reality which joins capitalism and communism, overdeveloped and underdeveloped areas, pre-technological and technological cultures, the affluent and the miserable society in one global historical structure. The latter is the empirical ground for the formation of the concepts and criteria for the critique of contemporary society. For example, concepts such as "socially necessary" and "socially wasteful", "productive" and "unproductive", "work" and "leisure", "freedom" and "enslavement" obtain, on this ground, a different content: they are redefined in terms of the material and intellectual resources available in the present period, and, in this redefinition, contrasted with the factual distribution and utilization of these resources. The historical basis is thus given for an objective evaluation of the existing societies in terms of the "optimal development" of man rendered possible by the attained stage of civilization. This "optimal development" is definable in empirical terms; in the present period, the optimum is approached to the extent to which the available resources are "rationally"[2] employed for the satisfaction of needs with a minimum of toil, that is to say, for creating the prerequisites for the

---

2  The difficulty of defining the term "rational" will be discussed presently.

free use of free time. To be sure, acceptance of these criteria still involves a decision: "value judgement" and preference inasmuch as they measure the existing societies against an optimum of life. It is perfectly possible to reject this standard and to prefer the oppression and destruction of life. Then, however, we are this side of discourse and logic, for logic and discourse developed as instruments of the effort to "save" and fulfill life.

The historical situation, understood as concrete universal, thus delimits the rationality in terms of which a critical analysis of the established society can proceed; it also delimits the alternatives of change open to the respective society. These alternatives are distinguished from each other by the degree of probability to which they approximate the "optimal" development. The tremendous uncertainty factor seems to decrease to the extent to which the technological society perfects calculability in the scientific domination of man and nature, but at the same time, the very concept of rationality, as a guide (standard) of social change, becomes questionable. A comparison of advanced industrial society with its earlier stages may clarify this new situation. During the industrial revolution, and for almost half a century thereafter, the irrational sector of the society was large and much in evidence: child labor, subhuman working conditions, the high mortality rate, pervasive poverty, blatant inequality in the distribution of social wealth testified to the irrationality of progress. It is not rendered any less irrational by pointing to the relatively low degree of material and technical productivity: even at this lower level of productivity, a reduction of toil and suffering, that is to say, a more rational organization of progress was a real possibility. At the stage of advanced industrial civilization, however, "rational" seems to defy any definition other than in terms of national or social expediency. This society is capable of "delivering the goods" on an increasingly larger scale: the permanent risk of a war of annihilation and the permanent waste and abuse of resources is no telling argument for replacing the established system by another, which may – or may not – reduce oppression and injustice. The argument for change is rendered even less telling by the development of the communist societies, which could once claim to be the historical negation of capitalism. The claim still stands, but as long as it is based on the historical calculus according to which the future liberation demands the oppressive sacrifices of the present, its higher rationality is on shaky ground.

The total character of the achievements of advanced industrial society, and the integration of opposites which is the result as well as the prerequisite of these achievements promote material and intellectual stabilization. Critical theory finds itself without the empirical basis on which it can transcend the status quo. The vacuum empties the theoretical structure itself: the categories of a critical social theory were developed during the very period in which an effective response was embodied in actual social forces; they were eminently "negative" and negating categories expressing the essential contradiction to the given state of affairs. The category "society" itself expressed the acute conflict between the social and political sphere – society as antagonistic to the State. Similarly, "individual", "class", "private", "family" denoted spheres and forces not yet integrated with the established conditions – spheres of tension and contradiction. With the growing integration of industrial society, these categories are losing their critical connotation: they tend to become descriptive, deceptive, or operational terms.

The situation of society thus inflicts upon the critique a twofold want: 1) without the ground on which thought can meet action, the critical analysis, in spite of, or perhaps because of its objective historical criteria, presents itself as mere *theory*, separated from all validating practice; 2) as social theory, the critical analysis is faced with sociological categories which seem no longer suited to comprehend the established society. An attempt to recapture the critical intent of these categories and to understand how it was "cancelled" by the social reality, that is to say, the attempt at an imminent critique of the unfolding rationality of industrial civilization appears from the outset as ideological: regression from a theory joined with practice to abstract, speculative thought, from political economy to philosophy.

The relation between ideology and reality is throughout a historical relation and as such determined by changes in the society. In the Marxian concept, "ideology" includes a consciousness which is more advanced than the reality which it confronts – advanced in the sense that it projects ideas (for example, of freedom, equality, happiness) that have been rendered possible but at the same time arrested by the societal development. Incapable of altering by itself this situation, and succumbing to the social reality, the ideological consciousness is "false consciousness", but as such it anticipates, in an idealistic form, historical possibilities contained by the established reality. However, this concept seems inapplicable to advanced industrial society. This society has surpassed its ideology by translating it into the reality of its political institutions, suburban homes, nuclear plants, supermarkets, drug-stores and psychiatric offices. In these, establishments, the ideas of reason, equality, happiness, personality etc. have obtained their value in practicable social relations. The process of translation suppressed or falsified those ideological contents which threatened to explode these relations by calling for an "end" of self-propelling productivity, namely, for a human existence where life is no longer a means and man no longer determined by the instruments of his labor. In contrast with these promises of freedom, advanced industrial society still promotes the necessity of full-time earning a living, and still perpetuates life as a means. Its productivity is in this sense self-defeating as well as self-propelling: it creates a destructive potential which shows forth not only in the arsenal of physical annihilation but also in that of internal repression: through the organized transformation of political and commercial into individual needs. And this union of growth and repression seems to characterize all contemporary forms of advanced industrial society, cutting across the most essential differences in political and economic institutions.

What is the common denominator of the liberating and the enslaving, the productive and the destructive forces? The denominator that naturally suggests itself is large-scale mechanized industry as the material, technical base of society. But this answer is at once confronted with the objection that technics are "neutral", equally susceptible to all sorts of social and political usage, and that, therefore technics cannot account for specific social and political institutions. This objection has become questionable in view of the fact that, in advanced industrial society, the technical apparatus of production and distribution functions, not as a sum total of mere instruments which can be isolated from the social and political context without losing their identity, but rather as an apparatus which determines *a priori* the product as well as the individual and social operations of servicing and extending it, that is to say, determines the socially needed demands, occupations, skills, attitudes – and thus the forms of social control and social cohesion. To be sure, the technical apparatus embodies the decisive distinction between those who control and those who serve the apparatus, but once it has become the ubiquitous base of production, i.e., of the preservation and growth of society, it imposes its exigencies on a national and international scale. The range of freedom of action at the top of society becomes smaller. For the real alternatives are indeed catastrophic: they involve not only changes *in* the established social institutions, objectives, policies but their disappearence, and this new direction of progress indeed threatens the whole. Industrial society tends towards the point of no return, which is, historically, the point of qualitative change, and it mobilizes all its resources *against* this eventuality.

There are certainly alternatives *within* the system, for contemporary capitalist as well as communist society. Thus, a welfare state, with semi-private or governmental or mixed control over production, with democratic institutions, disarmament, etc. is economically and politically possible. But such a state would retain and aggravate the main feature of its predecessor, namely, the subjection of man to the apparatus, his enslavement by his own productivity. The real alternative "beyond the welfare state" is characterized by the contrary of this feature, and this implies, for the mature technological society, progressive automation of material and routine production to the point where the traditional ratio of (necessary) working time to free time is reversed – free time becoming "full-time occupation" *at the disposal of the individual*. Such development would overthrow the repressive work morale of "earning a living" and would clash with the basic institutions of the established industrial society, i.e., with an organization of human existence for the requirements of a superimposed social (not technical!) division of labor. The point I wish to emphasize is that advanced industrial society tends toward this catastrophe to the degree to which it is *forced* to consummate technical progress: forced by the need for continuously raising productivity – a need which is in turn enforced by the necessity of internal growth and security, and by the external contest between capitalism and communism. The trend toward the catastrophe of liberation is a historical one, that is to say, it does not operate as an inexorable physical law; it can be arrested, manipulated, diverted – this is the content of the contemporary period. But even so, the trend determines the established society as the negative of its rationality, as the dissolving power of reason. Arming itself against the spectre of its own potentialities which would spell its end (in the twofold sense of limit and fulfilment), mobilizing its resources for the containment of its own power, advanced industrial society creates an expanding but closed universe, in which the increasingly effective domination of man and nature, and the increasing goods and services propel man to perpetuate the organization of the struggle for existence – quantitative progress works against qualitative change. Pursuing this course of progress, advanced industrial society is building a system of total administration: the centrifugal forces (i.e., the existing material and intellectual capabilities) are integrated into the system through the medium of technology, which appears as rationality *per se*. The historical alternatives for the realization of the existing capabilities are repelled or swallowed up by society's totalitarian achievements. Technics and technology thus operate as social and political controls which organize formerly unmastered dimensions of the private and public existence. In the centre of societal production today, the individual machine functions as part not only of a technical *ensemble* of shops, plants, branches of industries, etc., but also of a political and cultural ensemble (the chains, networks, and media of communication, the realm of the Corporation, the Trust, the Collective), which imposes its pattern of service and submission on the underlying population. The productivity and rationality of the technical-political ensemble stabilizes the social system of domination and contains progress within the framework of domination.

This type of society is still committed to its origins: it is the result of a specific experience, transformation, and organization of nature – the latest stage in the realization of the historical project of industrial civilization. Here, nature is projected as the neutral stuff of domination, as matter which offers no limits to man's theoretical and practical reason except those determined by its physico-mathematical structure. In the progress of modern physics, the very substance of nature seemed to evaporate as it appeared increasingly difficult to define objectivity independent of the subject. The scientific subject was that of observation, experiment, reasoning – it too was neutral and universal, freed from its own secondary qualities and from its particular goals. But though scientific method can abstract from particular goals and proceed as cognition for the sake of cognition, its theoretical purity remains itself derivative, preconditioned by a specific idea of *a*) what is scientific, and *b*) what is a scientific object. The development of the method and of its application both follow the guiding project which is their historical *a priori*, and this project emerges as part of and in line with the prevalent interests in the respective society. Thus the *theoretical* approach to reality in terms of mathematics becomes the authentic and effective scientific approach only if and when reality is no longer experienced (or rather: is no longer imposed upon experience) as cosmos, i.e., as a natural hierarchy of functions, time and place, values and ends. And this change in the experience of reality occurs in the *practical* approach to reality imposed by the organization of industrial society. Within this framework, science undertook the progressive formalization of nature, embarked on it as on an enterprise of knowledge: purely cognitive, endless domination. When science provided the exact mathematical concepts of matter and motion, it defined a purely theoretical object of neutral knowledge, it did not provide the contents and ends of domination: they were eliminated from the scientific conception together with all other final causes. But there is no domination *per se*. The very absence of final ends left nature as a system of universal, hypothetical instrumentalities for theoretical and practical domination – framework and medium for the goals which dominated the new society that developed the new science. The latter proceeded with a neutralization of its own: the capitalist economy reduced the concreteness of individual performances and functions to their common denominator which measured their universal exchange value; disposal over *marketable* men and things became the real content of domination. The de-naturation of nature, by which science arrived at the "true reality" of mathematical structures and relations, was paralleled in society's quantification of value. Science and society, theoretical and practical reason meet in the medium of *technology*.

This is not the place to discuss the definition of technology. I shall enter into it only insofar as it is necessary for *a*) explaining in what sense the notion of the "neutrality" of technics is untenable, and *b*) clarifying in what sense the technological society tends, with the consummation of technical progress, toward the abrogation of the conditions on which it was founded and developed.

The classical distinction between things φυσει and τέχνη [nature] points up the degree to which technics create man-made entities, by changing "natural" conditions. Moreover, such creation is "methodical", that is to say, based on the knowledge of the limits and ways in which the given natural material lends itself to transformation and even trans-substantiation. Within these limits, technics is the methodical negation of nature by human thought and action. In this negation, natural conditions and relations become instrumentalities for the preservation, enlargement, and refinement of human society; and as technics expand their role in the reproduction of society, they establish an intermediate universe between Subject (methodical, trans-forming theory and practice) and Object (nature as the stuff, material of transformation). It is in a literal sense a technological universe, in which all things and relations between things have become rational (or rather: are rationalized), that is to say, their "natural" objectivity has been re-made in accordance with the needs and interests of human society. Things have become *operational* in their very essence; technics determine their very essence, i.e., project their value and the use of their potentialities: technics constitute the Logos, the rationality of this universe. It is characterized by a new mode of mediation between Subject and Object. All objectivity is definable only in terms of a Subject, for a Subject; this relation pertains also to pre-technological rationality: even the Platonic Eidos *is*, as Idea, only for the attaining intellect. But this pre-technological intellect attains an objective reality which includes norms of existence, while the technological mediation frees objectivity from such norms. The remaining objectivity is not less but more subjective; mathematical equations are the ideational result of mental operations, and whatever "corresponds" to or is expressed by these equations is mere material for theoretical and practical transformation.

The relation between science and technics is not adequately described by calling technics applied science. Prior to any application science must be applicable by virtue of its structure rather than intent: the latter may be perfectly "pure". The structure of modern science is technological inasmuch as its basic concepts are mathematical, i.e., inasmuch as they denaturate and de-substantiate matter, thereby vastly enlarging the range within which matter can function as material for transforming operations. The more functional, the more general, symbolic, formal the scientific concept of the objective reality, the less the resistance which this reality offers to its methodical transformation by human practice, and the greater the stimulus which the reality provides for such practice. The affinity between modern science and industrial society is rooted in the very structure of the former. And in this society, technics is not one particular factor or dimension among others, but is the *a priori* of all reality and realization. The universe of discourse and action is a technological universe: the objects of thought as well as of practice are "given" as constituted by and subject to methodical transformation – negation of nature.

The technological negation of nature includes that of man as natural being. Of course, the latter transformation begins with the beginning of history. Civilization is progress not only in the mastery of nature within and without man, but also in the suppression of nature within and without man. Freud's theory of the repressive organization of the primary drives implies a historical dynamic: the subjection of the Pleasure Principle to the Reality Principle becomes universally effective only with the stage of civilization at which work has been made universal, full time, and quantifiable as social measure of value. The project of the technological object-world demands, as corollary, the technological subject: man as universal instrument (bearer of labor power). Or, to formulate a sweeping analogy which may still possess a kernel of truth: to the scientific translation of secondary into primary qualities corresponds, historically and structurally, the societal translation of concrete into abstract labor – quantification on both sides.

The preceding outline of a philosophic concept of technological society may help to elucidate the inner dialectic which this society develops in the course of its growth. It projects a universe of instruments (tools) and instrumentalities (material to be worked with tools), through which nature is subjected to the dominant social needs and interests. These are conditioned by the acquisition of exchangeable goods and services which enable their possessor to maintain and strengthen his position in the competitive struggle for existence. For the vast majority of the population, this means life-long labor in the process of material production, and on this necessity rests not only the material reproduction of this society but also its moral and political structure: the institutions of domination and their mental counterpart, the repressive work-ethics of scarcity and of earning a living. And it is precisely this necessity which technical progress threatens to render unnecessary, irrational by the double power to mechanize human labor and to conquer scarcity. The result would be the tendentious abolition of business and industrial labor, and the pacification of existence. This end is by no means inherent in technical progress. Technology can be used, and is largely used for sustaining and even increasing the quantity of socially required labor and for denying gratification and pacification. Not the rational force of technics, but the existing organization of industrial society, i.e., its vital need for constantly raising the productivity of labor drives this society toward extending automation and enlarging social wealth, thus undermining the political economy of scarcity and domination.

However, this dynamic is neither fatal nor unambivalent. I started by emphasizing the extent to which advanced industrial society is capable of containing (qualitative) social change, and I suggested that such containment is the principal content of the contemporary period. Now it is again technical progress, organized by the dominant social interests, which not only insures the efficiency of containment but also creates the new forms of containment through growth, oppression through rationalization, unfreedom through satisfaction. The new modes of domination work toward invalidating the concepts of the historical transition to a higher stage of human society which animated the critical theories of industrial society.

Technical progress evolves its own apparatus, and evolves it in accordance with the work to be done, and this work is not determined technologically: it is rather given from outside, by the social needs to be fulfilled. The latter, in turn, do not develop freely as individual needs; beyond the subsistence level, they are shaped by the prevailing social division of labor and pleasure – they must conform to its requirements, they must be socially profitable needs. In advanced industrial society, which disposes over the capability to fulfil the subsistence needs of all its members, the further development of needs is a matter of politics, which, in contrast to preceding historical stages, can now be pursued methodically, with a high degree of calculability (and with a low degree of freedom for those who make politics?); those who control the economy also control the creation of needs and the ways and means of their satisfaction. All this is external to technology. And yet, the relation between the technology and the politics of advanced industrial society is not that of an external force brought to bear upon a purely technical ensemble. By its *size*, its *internal organization*, and its *function* in the process of societal reproduction, the technical ensemble itself becomes a political ensemble – not only the medium in which the social controls are exercised in and over the individuals but also an apparatus of social controls in its own right. Technological rationality operates as political rationality. At this place, I can only indicate some of the conditions which make for the political character of technological rationality; they require detailed analysis.

*The connection between political and technological rationality*

1) Advanced industrial society reproduces itself through *mass* production. The latter is required by *a*) the growing population, *b*) the increasing productivity of mechanized labor, and *c*) the concentration of economic enterprise.

It seems that the dialectic of technical progress materializes at each of these three levels:

*a*) The growth in the population is one of the results of the greater chance of a better life, but unchecked and premature, it minimizes this chance for the individual, reduces the physical and mental space for autonomy and privacy, and perpetuates scarcity and the struggle for existence.

*b*) Rising productivity of labor within a system of domination generates the need for counteracting "premature" (in terms of the system) satisfaction and unemployment. Planned obsolescence, waste, and creation of socially profitable needs sustain toil and enslavement by the productive apparatus.

*c*) Concentration of economic enterprise enhances the technical possibilities of planning the economy for the pacification of the struggle for existence, while concentration of *private* controls vitiates these possibilities and extends subordination.

Mass production for the satisfaction of socially profitable needs demands mass distribution and mass consumption. All three must be continuously *sold* to the producers and to the consumers – sold on an enlarged scale, and an immense portion of this output is repressive of the *free* development of individual needs, and outright waste in view of the still prevailing misery. Under these circumstances, mass production takes place through an omnipresent, huge technical apparatus which integrates all spheres of the private and public existence, and integrates them in accordance with the interests which control the apparatus. But the decisive fact is that this integration does not appear as *political* act – it asserts itself as, and indeed it *is* technological integration, spreading the rationality of convenience and efficiency, the terrifying comforts and the terrifying power of the "affluent society". Producing and consuming its benefits, the individuals to whom these benefits are administered behave perfectly rationally, and no tribunal of history can justly condemn them – they have it better than before. And in acting rationally, in conforming to the technical conquest of nature which they have achieved, they support the quantitative growth and the oppressive weight of the apparatus over them.

2) This apparatus consists not only of the machinery employed in the material production but also of that which fills the offices and stores and streets and, not least, the private homes and apartments. Remarkable is the extent to which these widely distributed technical units are co-ordinated, and the degree to which their users are dependent on the co-ordinated interests of monopolistic and corporate power. The technological division of labor: scientific management and scientific rationalization intensify rather than alleviate the subjection of free labor and free relaxation to those who determine the use of labor and relaxation: intensify subjection precisely

because the technological form of the organization and its ability "to deliver the goods" lets the masters disappear behind the objective technical structure. The "capitalist bosses", the "cruel exploiters" and slave-drivers of former times have given way to "the administration", where ultimate responsibility is hardly any more definable – hatred, protest, indictment are thus being deprived of their concrete target. And in a way correctly so, for the masters themselves have become dependent on the apparatus which they have to preserve and expand – dependent in a way quite different from that in which the free entrepreneur depended on the means of his individual enterprise and on the mechanism of the free market. Now the government, the profit margin, the national interest, the East-West conflict operate as greatly independent powers over and above the corporate masters of the economy – even though the latter themselves are the decisive link in the integrating powers.

3) In the functioning of the productive and distributive apparatus, technical and political operations, technical and political controls are inexorably intertwined. Within the semi-automated plants, the workers-operators are themselves instrumentalized and mechanically adjusted to the speed and structure of a machine which is no longer their instrument and tool but (as Hegel already called it) an "independent tool". The atomization generated by this organization of work is abundantly described in the field studies of semi-automated establishments. Moreover, to the degree to which physical energy is replaced by mental energy, the latter tends to regress from conscious to semi- or subconscious processes ("day-dreaming", strictly re-active association of ideas and images engendered by the rhythm of the machine). The de-concretization characteristic of the technical universe, in which the hierarchical socio-political relations appear as the expression of objective technological rationality also occurs in the mental structure of the individuals conditioned by this rationality: unable to penetrate behind the technical curtain and to develop political consciousness, they easily adopt an un-political, technical attitude. Radical opposition to the system itself, the system which delivers the goods, seems irrational and senseless. Technological rationality and efficiency promote affirmation, positive thinking, and they spread it among the public at large. Advanced industrial society literally sells itself with the goods and services it produces, that is to say, it sells the comforts and conveniences which help to keep the people in line, to repress the real alternatives.

The decline of individual and group autonomy in technological society is not altogether negative and not altogether a token of regression. To the degree to which freedom from want, the concrete substance of all freedom becomes a real possibility, to that degree are the liberties which pertain to a state of lower productivity losing their former content. Independence of thought, autonomy, and the right to political opposition are being deprived of their basic critical function in a society which seems increasingly capable of satisfying the needs of the individuals in the way in which it is organized. Such a society may justly demand acceptance of its principles and institutions, and reduce the opposition to the discussion and promotion of alternative policies *within* the *status quo*. Under the conditions of a rising standard of living, non-conformity with the system itself appears as socially useless, and the more so when it entails tangible economic and political disadvantages and threatens the smooth operation of the whole. Indeed, at least insofar as the necessities of life are involved, there seems to be no reason why the production and distribution of goods and services should proceed through the play of individual liberties. If the individual were no longer compelled to prove himself on the market, as a free economic subject, in the "struggle for existence," in "earning a living" – the disappearance of this kind of freedom would be one of the greatest achievements of civilization.

The very possibility of such an achievement (which is the singular promise of industrial civilization) changes the social ground of freedom. The technological processes which propel mechanization and standardization of production tend to eliminate individual autonomy from a vast area in which much of its force was previously spent; and this force could be released in a yet uncharted realm of freedom beyond that of necessity. Man would then exist as an individual to the extent to which he is eliminated from the mechanized work-world; his freedom would be autonomy over the apparatus of production and distribution. This goal is within the capabilities of advanced industrial civilization; it is the "end" of technological rationality. In actual fact, however, the contrary trend operates: the apparatus imposes its economic and political requirements for defense and expansion on the labor time and the free time of man, on the material and on the intellectual culture. By virtue of the way in which it has organized its technological base, contemporary industrial society tends to be totalitarian. For totalitarian is not only a terroristic political co-ordination of society, but also non-terroristic economic-technical co-ordination which operates through the manipulation of needs by vested interests and thus precludes the emergence of an effective opposition against the whole organized by these interests. Not only a specific form of government or party rule makes for totalitarianism, but also a specific system of production and distribution which may well be compatible with a "pluralism" of parties, newspapers, "countervailing" forces, etc. In the contemporary period, political power asserts itself through the power of the machine process, which moves the technical ensemble of the productive apparatus. The government of advanced and advancing industrial societies can maintain and secure itself only when it succeeds in mobilizing, organizing, and exploiting the technical, scientific, and mechanical productivity available to industrial civilization – and this productivity tends to involve society as a whole, above and beyond any particular individual or group interests. The brute fact that the machine's physical (only physical?) power surpasses that of the individual and of any particular group of individuals makes the machine the most effective political instrument in any society whose basic organization is that of the machine process. But by virtue of the same fact, the political trend may be reversed, for the power of the machine is only the stored up and projected power of man. To the extent to which the work world is conceived of as a machine and mechanized in accordance with this conception, it becomes the *potential* basis of a new freedom.

Contemporary industrial civilization has reached the stage at which "the free society" can no longer be adequately defined in the traditional terms of economic, political, and intellectual liberties. Not because they have become insignificant, but because they are too significant to be confined within the traditional forms; they demand new modes of realization – corresponding to the capabilities of advanced industrial society. But these new modes can be indicated only in negative terms because their affirmation is the negation of the prevailing modes of freedom. Thus economic freedom would mean freedom *from* the economy, that is, man's freedom from being determined by economic forces and relationships: freedom from the daily struggle for existence, from earning a living. Political freedom would mean liberation of the individuals *from* politics over which they have no effective control – the disappearance of politics as a separate branch and function in the societal division of labor. Similarly, intellectual freedom would mean the restoration of individual thought after its absorption by mass communication and indoctrination – abolition of "public opinion" together with its makers. The unrealistic sound of these propositions is indicative, not of their utopian character, but of the predominance of forces which prevent their realization by preconditioning the material and intellectual needs which perpetuate obsolete forms of the struggle for existence.

Standardized preconditioning of needs is itself not necessarily repressive. On the contrary, the elimination of the need for stupid and wasteful varieties, for profitable and aggressive liberties may well be a prerequisite of liberation. Concentration of all efforts on the production and distribution of the necessities of life for all involves sacrifice of unnecessary choices, elimination of waste. But today, there is an overwhelming social need for the production and distribution of waste, including illusory forms of freedom in areas where it has become meaningless and deceptive. (Examples: free competition at administrative prices; free discussion after exclusion of all truly deviating opinion; a free press which censors itself better than any state-appointed censor; free choice between brands and gadgets.) Liberty can be made into a powerful instrument of domination. Not the range of choice open to the individual decides on the degree of human freedom, but *what* can be chosen and what *is* chosen by the individual. The criterion for free choice can never be an absolute one – but neither is it entirely relative. Free election of masters does not abolish the masters and the slaves; a free selection among a wide variety of goods and services does not signify freedom if, as we shall presently try to show, these goods and services sustain social controls over a life of toil and anxiety, i.e., if they sustain alienation.

The existing human needs cannot by themselves determine the range of necessary satisfaction – necessary in terms of prerequisites for the emergence of better modes of life. The only needs that carry, by virtue of their very existence, the unqualified claim for satisfaction are the vital needs, i.e., nourishment, clothing, and lodging at the attained cultural level and for all men everywhere – for their satisfaction is the prerequisite for the realization of *all* values, spiritual as well as material. Beyond this level, the human needs are historical in that their development as well as their claim for satisfaction are the product of the respective society, and, consequently, subject to political criteria and critique: subject to the question whether their satisfaction fulfills an individual, human, or "only" a social need – a need imposed upon the individual in the interest of a society dependent on the repression of freely developing needs. The fact that the satisfaction of such superimposed social needs also satisfies the individual and makes him "happier" is not a fact that has to be accepted. There are "false" and "real" needs – the former are those which serve to perpetuate toil, aggressiveness, and the powers that be (such as the need to buy a new automobile every other or third year, the need to relax before television, to work in an armament factory, to eat enriched and soggy bread, the need to "keep up with the neighbors"). In the last analysis, the question as to which are "real" needs must be answered by the individuals themselves – but only in the last analysis. As long as the individuals are indoctrinated and manipulated by a superimposed society (manipulated down to their very instincts), their answer to this question cannot be taken as their own. But by the same token, no "tribunal" can justly arrogate to itself the right to decide which needs should be developed and satisfied.

Here too, the totalitarian rationality of advanced industrial society makes the problem a purely theoretical one. The transplanting of social into individual needs is so effective that any distinction seems impossible or arbitrary. For example, can one really distinguish between the mass media as technical instruments and as instruments of manipulation, and as instruments of information and entertainment? between the automobile as nuisance and as convenience? between the horrors and the comforts of functional architecture? between industries working for national defense and for corporate gain? between the private pleasure and the commercial and political utility involved in increasing the birthrate? We are again confronted with one of the most vexing aspects of advanced industrial civilization: the rational character of its irrationality. Its productivity and efficiency, its capacity to increase and spread comforts, to turn waste into need and destruction into construction, the extent to which it subjects nature (also man's own nature) to man's power make the very notion of alienation questionable. The general misery appears as personal trouble, to be cured by the psychologist. Not that, at this stage unfreedom and domination have decreased (such interpretations would grossly distort the facts), but the transformation of political into technological controls has changed the very mechanisms which tie the individuals to their society. As the established division and control of the productive apparatus appear, by virtue of their efficiency and capacity, as the very embodiment of Reason, the political, intellectual, emotional refusal "to go along" seems neurotic and impotent. In the most advanced areas of this civilization, the social controls have been introjected into the individuals in a depth which obscures the distinction between imposed and spontaneous behavior.

But the term "introjection" perhaps no longer describes the way in which the individual by himself reproduces and perpetuates the external controls exercised by his society. "Introjection" suggests a variety of relatively spontaneous processes by which a Self (Ego) transposes the "outer" into the "inner"; thus "introjection" implies the existence of an inner dimension distinguished from and even antagonistic to the external exigencies – an individual consciousness and an individual unconscious apart from public opinion and behavior. The idea of "inner freedom" here has its reality: it designates the private space in which man may remain "himself" as against the others, with himself in his being with and for others. Now precisely this private space has been invaded and whittled down in the technological reality: mass production and mass distribution claim the *entire* individual, and industrial psychology has long since ceased to be confined to the plant. The manifold processes of introjection seem to be ossified in almost mechanical reactions. The result is, not "adjustment" but *mimesis*: an immediate identification of the individual with his society, and, through his part of society, with the society as a whole. This immediate, "spontaneous" identification (which, according to an influential sociological doctrine, distinguishes "community" from "society") reappears at the stage of high industrial civilization; however, in contrast with the primitive identification with the "community", the new "immediacy" is the product of a sophisticated and scientific process of organization and manipulation. In this process, the "inner" dimension of the mind is whittled down: the dimension in which protest and opposition to the status quo can take roots, in which the power of negative thinking is at home – Reason as the critical power of negation. The loss of this dimension becomes manifest in the weakening of the non-apologetic, non-conformist elements of the ideology, of those ill-defined values, images, ideas which were once incorporated not only in the key vocabulary of literature and philosophy but also of ordinary language in personal communion. To give some random examples: Soul and Spirit; *la raison du cœur*; the search for the absolute; *Les Fleurs du Mal*; la femme-enfant; *Ferne* and *Heimat*; fatal loyalty to oneself or another self; tragic love and the tragic hero. This essentially pretechnological vocabulary indicates existential dimensions which are obsolescent in the technological reality – they are being liquidated as the natural universe is being transformed into the scientifically mastered, administered, and manipulated technological universe. But the obsolescent dimensions were precisely those which were antagonistic to the repressive organization of life – antagonistic in that the ideas and images pertaining to this sphere were committed to modes of existence which, by their "excessive" happiness and suffering, threatened to explode the established reality. They transcended the *given* universe of discourse and behavior, not toward a Beyond and Hereafter, but toward personally experienced though normally tabooed (and yet momentarily fulfilled) possibilities. Inasmuch as these were present in the individual consciousness and effective in thought and language, human existence (and nature), were not entirely enclosed in one operational, instrumentalist universe (of work and leisure) – the given universe rather opened into another qualitatively different dimension. In contrast, the technological society tends to absorb this other dimension. Advanced industrial civilization exhibits patterns of thought and behavior according to which ideas, aspirations, and objectives which, by their content, qualitatively transcend the established state of affairs are either repelled or reduced to terms of this state of affairs. Technological rationality renders the transcendent dimension unreal or unrealistic or translates its contents into an operational context. They are incorporated into the rationality of that which *is* and that which *can be within* the given reality. The technological society is, in this sense, a *one-dimensional* universe, from which the qualitative difference, the negation is excluded. In it, Reason can no longer be designated as "the power of the negative" which destroys false consciousness and sustains the denied and defeated possibilities of progress; Reason, quite reasonably, has become co-extensive and conformist with the existing and expanding organization of man and things, and the critique itself, wide-spread and free in the democratic areas, comes to terms with this organization. In the academic establishment, this tendency shows forth in a series of intellectual liquidations which turn theoretical into behaviourist thought, for example, the liquidation of philosophy by analytic philosophy, of psychology by industrial psychology, of sociology by market research; the tendency is epitomized in the union of scholarship, corporation, and defense, and in the ideology which proclaims the end of ideology.

One-dimensional thought and behavior are systematically promoted by the makers of politics and their purveyors of information: their universe of discourse is populated by self-validating hypotheses, which, incessantly and monopolistically repeated, become hypnotic definitions or dictations. For example, "free" are the institutions which operate (and are operated on) in the countries of the Free World; other, transcending modes of freedom are either anarchism, or communism, or propaganda. "Socialistic" are all encroachments on private enterprises not undertaken by certain private enterprises (or by government contracts), such as universal and comprehensive health insurance, or the protection of nature by the establishment of National Parks, or the improvement of public services which may hurt private profit. This totalitarian dictatorship of the established facts has its Eastern counterpart. There, freedom is the way of life instituted by a communist regime, and all other transcending modes of freedom are either capitalistic, or revisionist, or leftist sectarianism. In both camps, the non-operational ideas are non-behavioral, unscientific, subversive. Reason is turned into submission to the facts of life and to the dynamic capability of producing more and bigger facts of the same sort of life. The politico-technical apparatus and its totalitarian rationality and productivity militate against change, they blunt the recognition that facts are *made*, mediated by Subjectivity (a recognition long since incorporated into scientifc method). The prevailing habit of thought does not allow itself to proceed to the assumption that the facts contain their negation: that they are what they are (how they are) because they exclude the possibilities whose realization would undo them as facts. These possibilities may be better or worse in terms of human existence – in any case, the ability to evaluate the alternatives requires the freedom to go beyond the facts and beyond the operations defined by the facts. Such freedom is not entirely an affair of the "inner man", of conscience and consciousness – it depends on societal conditions which provoke and permit dissociation from the given facts – on a political as well as private space in which genuinely free thought can develop by "testing" the facts as well as the possibilities blocked by the given facts. But this mode of thought now appears as metaphysical, irrational, illusory. It reasonably appears so because the technological society is closing the previously unconquered space which was the refuge of socially tabooed images of human fulfillment. And the closing of this space cancels the therapeutic force of operational, analytic thought: the struggle against metaphysics, the debunking of illusions and ideologies, the insistence on behavioral concepts liquidates the metaphysical *and* the historical transcendence, the illusory *and* the real possibilities – it promotes submission to that which is.

Needless to say, it is not any mode of thought and philosophy and theory which is responsible for these tendencies. Theory and practice rather have their common ground in the established structure of advanced industrial society, whose technological rationality is at the same time political rationality, which, through the domination of nature, intensifies the domination of man by man. On this common ground, theoretical and practical operationalism are fused and frozen into the pattern of one-dimensional behaviour. The achievements of progress defy ideological justification as well as indictment; before their reality, the "false consciousness" evaporates together with the true consciousness of the historical alternatives.

These historical alternatives are implied in the idea of the consummation of technical progress. I indicated the level or stage at which this progress would become incompatible with the established reality, namely, the stage when automation would reduce necessary labor time to marginal time. At this point, technical progress would transcend the realm of organized scarcity and would cease to function within the apparatus of domination and exploitation which determines technological rationality. Instead, the "end" of technology would be "deplaced" toward a free play of faculties – in the literal sense of playing with the fair capabilities of man and nature: pacification of existence. Such a qualitatively new mode of existence can never be envisaged as the mere by-product of economic and political changes, as the more or less spontaneous effect of new institutions, although the latter constitute the necessary prerequisite. The goal is, in a literal sense, the *technical a priori*. This means that qualitative change would depend on a change in the *technical* basis on which this society rests and which sustains the economic and political institutions through which the "second nature" of man is stabilized. The techniques of industrialization prejudge the goals to be achieved beyond the satisfaction of vital needs, i.e., they prejudge the possibilities of Reason and Freedom. To be sure, labor must precede the reduction of labor, and industrialization must precede the development of human needs and satisfactions. But as all freedom depends on the conquest of necessity, the realization of freedom depends on the *techniques* of this conquest. The highest productivity of labor can be used for the perpetuation of labor, and the most efficient industrialization can serve the restriction and manipulation of needs. The technology which the industrial societies have inherited and developed, and which rules our lives, is in its very roots a technology of domination. Consummation of technical progress therefore implies the determinate negation of this technology. I suggested that it is a gross oversimplification if the repressive elements of industrial society are attributed only to a specific *use* of technology, to a specific application of scientific reason. In a sense, the application was preformed by the method: there was a pre-established harmony and affinity between the idea and its realization. The explication of the inner link between technology and domination must be left to further research. But I wish to guard myself against a misunderstanding which the very suggestion of such a link seems to provoke. The critique of technology aims neither at a romantic regression nor at a spiritual restoration of "values". The oppressive features of tech-nological society are *not* due to excessive materialism and technicism. On the contrary, it seems that the causes of the trouble are rather in the *arrest* of materialism and technological rationality, that is to say, in the restraints imposed on the *materialization* of values. These restraints pertain to a particular period of civilization, to a particular organization of the struggle for existence. Their abolition, that is, the liberation of technology, would involve the entire material and intellectual culture of advanced industrial society. This culture depends, for its continued functioning (and even for its growth) on sustaining the limits which it imposes upon technology. Moreover, these limits also determine the direction in which technical progress develops within this culture. The idea of qualitatively different forms of technological rationality belongs to a new historical project.

## II

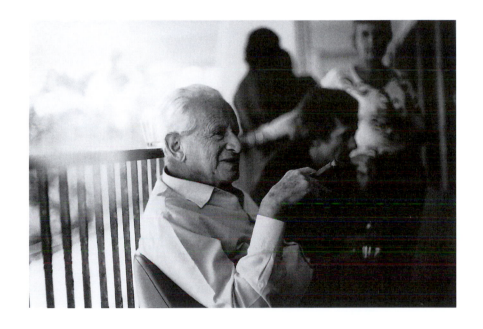

†"The Individual in the Great Society" (1966). The study was first presented in an address at Syracuse University on November 17, 1965. It was published in two parts in the underground San Diego journal *Alternatives* Vol. I, Nos. 1 and 2 (March–April 1966 and Summer 1966, pp. 21–9 and 29–35); it also appeared in *A Great Society?*, ed. Bertram M. Gross (New York: Basic Books, 1966, pp. 58–80). Marcuse's study engages President Lyndon B. Johnson's mid-1960s program of a "Great Society" in the context of actual economic, political, social and cultural trends dominant in the US and global political situation of the time. The text provides an exemplary ideology critique of Johnson's program, as well as a sharp critique of the economic system and foreign policy of the US capitalist state. Yet Marcuse is also interested in the utopian and emancipatory potential in the concept of a Great Society and how actually realizing this conception would require subversion of existing thought, practice and institutions, and radical social transformation. Thus, although the text addresses a specific situated political phenomenon, it is exemplary of the type of critical theory of society that Marcuse was developing.

# THE INDIVIDUAL IN THE
# GREAT SOCIETY †

Prior to exploring the presumed function of the "individual" in the "great society," a brief definition (or rather redefinition) of these terms is required. For I propose to proceed by placing the official and semi-official ideas and speeches about the Great Society in the context of their prospective realization, and in the context of the prevailing conditions (political, economic, intellectual) which determine their (possible or impossible) realization. Unless these factors are brought to bear on the idea, it remains mere speech, publicity, or propaganda – at best a statement of intentions. It is the responsibility of the scholar to take them seriously, that is to say, to go beyond the words or rather to stay this side of the words, in the given universe of powers, capabilities, and tendencies which defines their content.

I start with the notion of the Great Society as presented by President Johnson. I think its essentials can be summed up as follows: it is (1) a society of "unbridled growth," resting on "abundance and liberty for all," which demands an "end to poverty and racial injustice"; (2) a society in which progress is the "servant of our needs"; (3) a society in which leisure is a "welcome chance to build and reflect," and which serves "not only the needs of the body and the demands of commerce, but the desire for beauty and the hunger for community."

This picture is preceded by the statement that our society can be a place where "we will raise our families, free from the dark shadow of war and suspicion among nations." And it is followed by an enumeration of the areas where the construction of the Great Society can begin, namely: (1) the rebuilding of our cities, and of the transportation between them, in accord with the needs of the constantly growing population; (2) the reconstruction of the polluted and destroyed countryside, in order to regain "contact with nature" and to protect "America the beautiful"; (3) the improvement and enlargement of education and educational facilities. And when all this is done, we will not have reached the end of the struggle, for "most of all, the Great Society is not a safe harbor, a resting place, a final objective, a finished work. It is a challenge constantly renewed, beckoning us toward a destiny where the meaning of our lives matches the marvelous products of our labor."

## GREAT SOCIETY VS. CAPITALIST ENTERPRISE

Let me pause here and register my first dissent. I began intentionally with the most speculative, most "utopian" aspect because it is here that the basic direction of the program (and its innermost limitations) is most visible. First a slight matter of style: the meaning of our lives should "match" the "products of our labor" – shouldn't it be the other way around? In a free society, the meaning of life is determined by the free individuals, who determine the products of their labor accordingly. By itself, the phrasing may not preclude this interpretation, but in the context of the whole section it assumes special significance. Why should the Great (and Free) Society *not* be a resting place, a safe harbor? Why should it be a challenge constantly renewed? The dynamic of endlessly propelled productivity is not that of a peaceful, humane society in which the individuals have come into their own and develop their own humanity, the challenge they meet may be precisely that of protecting and preserving a "safe harbor," a "resting place" where life is no longer spent in the struggle for existence. And such a society may well reject the notion (and practice) of "unbridled growth"; it may well (I shall come back to this) restrict its technical capabilities where they threaten to increase the dependence of man on his instruments and products.

Even today, long before the start on the road to a free society, the war on poverty might be waged far more effectively by a redirection rather than by an increase of production, by the elimination of productivity from the areas of socially necessary waste, planned obsolescence, armament, publicity, manipulation. A society which couples abundance and liberty in the dynamic of unbridled growth and perpetual challenge is the ideal of a system based on the perpetuation of scarcity – more and more artificially created scarcity, namely, the need for ever more and ever new goods of abundance. For in such a system, the individuals must spend their lives in the competitive struggle for existence in order to satisfy the need for the increasing products of labor, and the products of labor must be increased because they must be sold at a profit, and the rate of profit depends on the growing productivity of labor. In less ideological language, this was called the law of the enlarged accumulation of capital. Under this aspect, the Great Society appears as the streamlined and improved continuation of the existing not-so-great society – after the latter has succeeded in cleansing itself of its sore spots and blemishes. Its ability to do so is assumed. But the scholar cannot grant the assumption without examination: we leave the speculation on the Great Society and return to the program for its construction, or rather for its preparation within the existing society.

Foremost is the war on poverty. The critical literature on it already is so large that I can be brief in my references. This war is supposed to be waged by the "affluent society" against poverty *in* the "affluent society"; thus it may turn out to be a war of this society against itself, taken of its internal contradiction. The real conquest of poverty would mean either full employment as the normal, long-range condition of the system, or unemployment and a dole sufficiently large to live the good life – also the normal, long-range condition of the system. Both achievements are within the (technical) capabilities of an advanced industrial society (paradoxically, the second may be the historical consequence of the first!). But the concept "advanced industrial society" has to be broken down into its actual main forms: capitalist and socialist. Here, we are concerned with the former only. In it, the real conquest of poverty is counteracted and "contained" by the prevailing social institutions. Full employment, as constant condition, implies a constantly high (and, with rising productivity, a constantly rising) level of real wages, not canceled by rising prices. This would be equivalent to a decline in the rate of profit below the limit tolerable to private enterprise. It is perhaps conceivable that something like full employment can be attained by an expanding war (or defense) economy, plus an expanding production of waste, status symbols, planned obsolescence, and parasitic services. But even disregarding the clear and present danger of an international explosion, such a system would produce and reproduce human beings who could by no stretch of the imagination be expected to build a free, humane society. For the construction of a Great Society depends on a "human factor" which hardly appears in the program, namely, the existence of individuals who, in their attitudes, goals, and needs, are qualitatively different from those who are educated, trained, and rewarded today: the aggression mobilized (and repressed) in the maintenance of a society geared to permanent defense militates against progress toward higher forms of freedom and rationality. To be sure, non-destructive full employment remains a real possibility: it requires nothing more, and nothing less, than the actual reconstruction outlined in the President's program – that is, the rebuilding of the cities, of the countryside, and of education. But this very program requires the elimination of the particular interests which stand in the way of its fulfillment. Today, they include capital and labor, city and countryside politics, Republicans and Democrats, and they are the powerful interests on which this Administration largely relies.

The truism must be repeated: not only the magnitude but the economic basis of the program is incompatible with these interests. The transformation of the cities into a human universe involves far more than slum clearings: it involves the literal dissolution of the cities and rebuilding according to rigidly enforced architectural plans. If undertaken for the population as a whole rather than for those who can pay, the reconstruction would be plainly unprofitable, and its public financing would mean the abrogation of some of the most powerful lobbies in the country. It would, for example, imply the establishment of a wide and efficient network of public transportation, replacing the private automobile as the main vehicle of business and leisure – the end of the motor industry as now organized. The "beautification" of the countryside would imply the (rigidly enforced) elimination of all billboards, neon signs, the reduction of the innumerable service stations, roadside stands, noise makers, and so on which have rendered impossible the desired "contact with nature." Generally, and perhaps most important, reconstruction would require the elimination of all planned obsolescence, which has become an essential prop for the system inasmuch as it ensures the necessary turnover and the competitive rat race. In all these aspects, the realization of the program seems irreconcilable with the spirit of capitalist enterprise, and this contradiction becomes perhaps most strikingly apparent in the program's insistence on beauty. Here, the words assume a false ring, the language becomes that of commercial poetry, and it comes almost as a relief when Mrs Johnson, dropping the ideological language, goes out to proclaim beauty as an economic asset: according to the *Los Angeles Times* (September 8, 1965): "Preserving the attractiveness of a city is a primary economic asset, a way to get payrolls. The city that is beautiful brings a high return on the dollar."

## ADVANCED INDUSTRIALISM'S EFFECT ON PEOPLE

I now come to the "human factor" and I shall take up education, the third area of reconstruction, in the course of my discussion. Who are the human beings, the individuals who are supposed to build the Great Society?

They live in a society where they are (for good or bad) subjected to an apparatus which, comprising production, distribution, and consumption, material and intellectual, work and leisure, politics and fun, determines their daily existence, their needs and aspirations. And this life, private, social, and rational, is enclosed in a very specific historical universe. The individuals who make up the bulk of the population in the "affluent societies" live in a universe of permanent defense and aggression. It manifests itself in the war against the Vietcong and in the struggle against the Negroes, in the huge network of industries and services which work for the military establishment and its accessories, but it also manifests itself in the violence released and made productive by science and technology, in the tenor of publicity and fun inflicted on captive audiences. Against the age-old argument that violence and aggression have always been a normal factor in all societies, I must insist on the qualitative difference. It is not only the magnitude of the destructive potential and the scope of its realization that distinguish a chariot race from an automobile race, a canon from a missile, hydraulic from nuclear energy. Similarly, it is not only the speed and range that distinguish the means of mass communication from their predecessors. The new quality is introduced by the progressing transfer of power from the human individual to the technical or bureaucratic apparatus, from living to dead labor, from personal to remote control, from a machine (or group of machines) to a whole mechanized system. I should like to reiterate that I do not (yet) evaluate this development: it may be progressive or regressive, humanizing or dehumanizing. But what actually occurs in this transfer of power is also a transfer of guilt-feeling responsibility – it releases the individual from being an autonomous person: in work and in leisure, in his needs and satisfactions, in his thought and emotions.

At the same time, however, the release is not liberation from alienated labor: the individuals must go on spending physical and mental energy in the struggle for existence, status, advantage; they must suffer, service, and enjoy the apparatus which imposes on them this necessity. The new heteronomy in the work world is not compensated by a new autonomy over the work world: alienation is intensified as it becomes transparently irrational, and it becomes unproductive as it sustains repressive productivity. And where the established society delivers the goods that raise the standard of living, alienation reaches the point at which even the consciousness of alienation is largely repressed: individuals identify themselves with their being-for-others.

In such circumstances, society calls for an Enemy against whom the prevailing conditions are to be defended and against whom the aggressive energy which cannot be channeled into the normal, daily struggle for existence can be released. The individuals who are called upon to develop the Great Society live in a society which wages war or is prepared to wage war all over the world. Any discussion which does not put the program of the Great Society into the international framework must remain ideological, propaganda. The Enemy is not one factor among others, not a contingency which an evaluation of the chances of the Great Society can ignore or to which it can refer to in passing – his existence is a determining factor at home and abroad, in business and education, in science and relaxation.

We are here concerned only with the Enemy in relation to the program of the Great Society, more specifically, with the way in which the Enemy (or rather the presentation of the Enemy and of the struggle against him) affects the individuals, the people who are supposed to change the "affluent society" into the Great Society. Thus the question is not to what degree the armament industry and its "multipliers" have become an indispensable part of the "affluent society," nor whether the present dominance and policy of the military establishment are in the "national interest" (once the national interest is defined in terms other than those of these policymakers themselves). Rather the question I want to raise is: Does the existence of the Enemy prejudge – and prejudge negatively – the capability and the capacity to build the Great Society? Before I enter into a brief discussion of the question, I must define, and redefine, "the Enemy." And I shall do so by submitting a precarious hypothesis.

Is the Enemy still communism *per se*? I think not. First, communism today exists in many forms, some in conflict and contradiction with the others. And this country does not combat all of these forms, and not only for tactical reasons. Second, capitalist trade with communist countries is constantly increasing, and precisely with those countries where communism seems to be most stable. Moreover, communism is most firmly and solidly constituted in the Soviet Union, but for quite some time the USA and the USSR have not really treated each other as Enemies (capitalized!) – in fact one even hears talk of cooperation and collusion, while the Enemy against whom the system is mobilized is presented as precluding cooperation and collusion. Third, it is difficult to regard communism as threatening this country – even on the campuses and among the Negroes. Looking at the facts, geographical and otherwise, I would say that mobilization is carried out and war is actually waged against (and among) semi-colonial and formerly colonial peoples, backward peoples, and have-nots, communist or not. This is not the old colonialism and imperialism (although in some aspects the contrast has been overdrawn: there is little essential difference between a direct government by the metropolitan power and a native government that functions only by grace of a metropolitan power). The (objective) rationale for the global struggle is, not the need for immediate capital export, resources, surplus exploitation; it is rather the danger of a subversion of the established hierarchy of master and servant, top and bottom, a hierarchy that has created and sustained the have-nations, capitalist *and* communist. There is a very primitive, very elemental threat of subversion – a slave revolt rather than a revolution, and precisely for this reason more dangerous to societies that are capable of containing or defeating revolutions. For the slaves are everywhere and countless, and they indeed have nothing to lose but their chains. To be sure, the established societies have faced the subversion of their hierarchy before: from within, by one of their own classes. This time, the threat comes from without, and precisely for this reason it threatens the system as a whole; the threat appears as a total one and those who represent it have not even a potential vested interest in the established societies. They may have no blueprint for positive reconstruction, or they may have one which would not work, but they simply do not want to be slaves any longer, and they are driven by the vital need to change intolerable conditions – and to do it differently from the old powers. This primitive rebellion, this revolt indeed implies a social program, namely, the awareness that their society cannot be constructed along the line of the have-nations which perpetuate servitude and domination. Their struggle for liberation is *objectively* anti-capitalist even if they reject socialism and want the benefits of capitalism, and their struggle is *objectively* anti-communist even if they are communists, for it aims beyond (or this side of) the established communist systems.

I used the term "objectively rational" in order to emphasize that I do not imply that the factors or tendencies just outlined are those intentionally pursued by the policy makers. I rather suggest that they are operative "behind the back" of the policy makers, and perhaps even assert themselves against the will of the policy makers – as historical tendencies which can be extrapolated from the prevailing social and political conditions. At the surface there is another, far more obvious rationale for permanent mobilization and defense, that which is expressed in the "domino theory" and the notion of the communist drive for world revolution. The notion as presented by the makers of policy and information does not correspond to the facts, but there is a kernel of truth in the domino theory. Any spectacular victory of the rebellious have-nots in any one place would activate their consciousness and their rebellion in other places as well – perhaps even at home. Moreover, for capitalism, such a victory would mean a further dangerous narrowing of the world market – a rather remote danger, which would materialize only if and when the backward countries have reached real independence, but a danger serious enough, for example, with respect to Latin America. For the Soviet Union, the economic danger does not prevail, but the threat to the established regime seems real enough. One can safely say that the attitude of the Soviet leaders toward revolution and rebellion is at best ambivalent if not hostile, as is clear in the conflict with China.

*Marcuse argues that advanced-industrial society is the most threatened by rebellion or reform because its conditions to reproduce itself are blatantly transparent.*

*Advanced-industrial society can be thus characterized by its psychopathic/ruthless pursuit of capital (greed) and its inherent insecurity about its future - that is paranoia.*

It is the most advanced industrial society which feels most directly threatened by the rebellion, because it is here that the social necessity of repression and alienation, of servitude and heteronomy is most transparently unnecessary, and unproductive in terms of human progress. This is the hidden rationale behind the cruelty and violence mobilized in the struggle against the threat, behind the monotonous regularity with which the people are made familiar with, and accustomed to, inhuman attitudes and behavior – to wholesale killing as patriotic act. What the free press achieves in this respect will perhaps later be remembered as one of the most shameful acts of civilization. Hardly a day passes when the headlines do not celebrate a victory by announcing "136 Vietcong Killed," "Marines Kill at least 156 Vietcong," "More than 240 Reds Slain." I have lived through two world wars, but I cannot recall any such brazen advertisement of slaughter. Nor can I remember – even in the Nazi press – a headline such as that which announces: "US Pleased over Lack of Protests on Tear Gas" (*Los Angeles Times*, September 9, 1965). This sort of reporting, consumed daily by millions, appeals to killers and the need for killers. And a New York judge has epitomized the situation when, in paroling two youths "who were arraigned on a charge of murdering an East Side derelict and then rearrested on a charge of killing one of their companions," he remarked, according to *The New York Times* (September 8, 1965): "They should go to Vietnam, where we need soldiers to kill Vietcong."

I have suggested that the international situation of the affluent society is in a very specific sense an expression of its internal dynamic: of the conflict between the (social, political) need to preserve the established power structure within the nation and abroad on the one hand, and the historical obsolescence of this need on the other, as dramatized in the rebellion of the backward peoples. In this conflict, society mobilizes its individuals' aggressive energy to such an extent that they seem hardly capable of becoming the builders of a *peaceful* and free society. It seems that such an undertaking, which would aim at a qualitatively different society, would mean a break, a rupture with the established one, and thus would require the emergence of "new" individuals, with qualitatively different needs and aspirations. I now propose to go one step farther and to raise the question whether the advanced industrial society has not negated the traditional notion (and possibility) of the individual in reality, while at the same time perpetuating and extolling it ideologically. In other words, does the individual still have a progressive and productive social function, or is individuality being surpassed by new advanced forms of productivity and their organization? Have individuality, personal autonomy, individual enterprise become obsolete, brakes rather than vehicles of (technical) progress? Again, I emphasize

that I propose to discuss this question without prejudice in favor of transmitted "values": it may well be that the passing of the individual can
be called "positive" in terms of human as well as technical progress. I begin
with a brief re-examination of the notion of the individual as it has become
representative of the modern period. Only a rough sketch will be attempted.

## THE EVOLVING CONCEPT OF INDIVIDUALISM

In its new historical function, the notion of the individual originates in
the Protestant Reformation. The religious and the secular, the internal and
external manifestations develop simultaneously. In this dual function, the
individual becomes the unit of the new society: in spirit, as the responsible
subject of faith, thought, and conscience; and in the spirit of capitalism, as
the responsible subject of free enterprise. The two manifestations remain
interrelated, but two trends may be distinguished which increasingly conflict
with each other as the new society advances: on the one hand there is the
development of the free moral and intellectual subject, on the other hand
the development of the subject of free enterprise in free competition.
We may also say: the individual in the struggle for himself, for moral and
intellectual autonomy, and the individual in the struggle for existence are
separated. They are still at harmony in Descartes's *ego cogito*: the individual
is the subject of science which comprehends and conquers nature in the
service of the new society, and he is the subject of methodical doubt,
of critical reason against all established prejudices. But the harmony is
fallacious: the unity of the two spheres is dissolved. The individual as subject
of the capitalist struggle for existence, economic competition, and politics
takes shape in the philosophy of Hobbes, Locke, Adam Smith, Bentham,
while the subject of individual autonomy, moral and intellectual, is
epitomized in the Enlightenment, in Leibnitz and Kant.

The conflict between the philosophical traditions reflects the unfolding
conflict in the social reality. Freedom was supposed to be the individual's
essential quality in theory and practice, thought and action; quality of the
inner and the outer man. In this sense, the individual was the corollary of
private enterprise: moral responsibility and the autonomous personality were
to have their actual basis in economic and political freedom. The individual
is *proprietor*: not merely in the sense of possessing material resources, goods,
and services necessary for the realization (demonstration, validation) of his
freedom in his society, but in the sense of having acquired these things by
virtue of his own labor or control over another's labor (already in Locke!)

and having made them his own – the material expression of his productive, creative personality. This notion, of the individual as proprietor which dominates the philosophical theory of the individual from Hobbes to Hegel, was hardly applicable, in any general sense, to the acquisitive society, in which the majority of the population remained deprived of such autonomy. But there was one class, and for a long time the ruling class, that of the agrarian and industrial entrepreneurs, of whom it could be said that they were the masters of their own enterprise: individually responsible for their decisions, choices, risks – rewarded if their decision was a good one, punished if it was bad, according to the verdict of the free, competitive market. Through the freedom of private enterprise, this class (roughly, "the bourgeoisie") developed the productive forces on an individualistic foundation – under the conditions of free capitalism which prevailed in the industrial countries until the end of the nineteenth century. And the same economic masters were autonomous individuals in their own house: determining the education of the children, the level of the household, the pattern of behavior – they enforced the Reality Principle in a rather authoritarian manner. "Masters in their house," in their business, and in their home, they could do without the government, without "public relations," without standardized mass media; thus they could be considered the living representatives of individualistic culture.

Today, no long discussion is necessary to show that the conditions under which this form of individual enterprise could flourish have disappeared. Contemporary American society has surpassed the stage of productivity where individual units of production engage in free competition with each other; with the transformation of liberalistic into organized capitalism, "individuality" in the economic sphere (and not only there!) has become obsolete, dwarfed by the rapid and overwhelming growth in the productivity of labor, and by the growth of the means and instruments for utilizing this productivity. In view of this historical development, the question arises where and how, in the advancing industrial society of our type, we can envisage the development and expression of creative individuality. But before entering into this discussion, I want to trace the vicissitudes of individuality in the dimension in which the individual is in the most authentic sense "creative": that of *literature and the arts*.

Indeed, the artistic dimension seems to have been the only real home of the individual, the only place where man could be an individual in his material as well as in his intelligible existence – not only as inner but also as outer man. In contrast to the economic individual, the artist realizes his individuality in a form of creative work which modern culture has extolled as a manifestation of higher freedom and higher value. And unlike the inner moral and spiritual autonomy attributed to the individual ("person") by the idealistic philosophy, the freedom of the artist is of more substantial stuff; it expresses itself in his *oeuvre* and in his life. The great personalities of the Renaissance could combine artistic, political, and economic individualism: Jakob Burckhardt's phrase "the state as work of art" expressed this unity. The phrase may convey a highly idealized picture, but it indicates the gap which separates the origins of individualism from its late stages. In the fully developed bourgeois society, the market value supersedes the value of individual creativity; when the latter serves to increase the former, it is the market rather than the individual which asserts itself. The individual in the full "classical" sense, as a true self, now appears possible only as *against* his society, in essential conflict with the established norms and values: he is an alien, outsider, or a member of the "inner emigration." In this society, the individual cannot fulfill himself, cannot come into his own: this is the message of the representative literature at least from the *Sturm und Drang* to Ibsen. In the inevitable struggle with society, the individual (always in the emphatic sense of the term) either perishes, or resigns – renounces that uncompromised freedom and happiness which was first the promise and goal of "development." The creative individual starts as a nonconformist; in the established society, he cannot be a "realist" without betraying himself; his autonomy is that of his imagination, which has its own rationality and truth (perhaps more valid, more rational than that of the Establishment). But as he sets out to live and to work in accordance with himself and his faculties, he recognizes that he must resign himself and find his autonomy in reason rather than imagination. In other words, the individual finds himself to the degree to which he learns to limit himself and to reconcile his happiness with being unhappy: autonomy means resignation. This is the story of the great development as illustrated by these novels: *Wilhelm Meister, Education Sentimentale, Grüne Heinrich, Récherche du Temps Perdu.*

## EDUCATION FOR DISSENT

There is, however, another form in which the individual appears in bourgeois society and which perhaps most fully actualizes individuality, namely, the *poète maudit.* He indeed lives his own life: on the margin and against his society. The individual becomes authentic as outcast, drug addict, sick, or genius. Some of this authenticity is still preserved in the "bohemian," even in the beatnik; both groups represent vaguely protected and permitted manifestations of individual freedom and happiness not enjoyed by the citizen who defines freedom and happiness in terms of his government and society rather than on his own terms.

This long digression from the Great Society seemed to me necessary in order to separate the ideology of the individual from his realization, and to point out how the creative individual has been largely localized in the "artistic dimension," that is, in the sphere which was until now far removed from the daily business of life – a sort of immaterial, more spiritual reality. Something of this is still reflected in President Johnson's emphasis on beauty, imagination (which, however, coupled with "innovation," has a technical-commercial ring), and creativity. And some observers of the contemporary scene raise explicitly the problem of the place and function of the "creative" individual in the advanced industrial society. In fact, with the growth of this society, and with the spread of automation, mass production, and standardization in the daily business of life, "individuality" is being increasingly reserved for any remaining areas of "creative" activity or receptivity – whatever "creative" may mean. In the context of the authoritative statements on the Great Society, "creative" seems to refer to the production of things, services, works, and spaces which are not only useful but also beautiful, satisfying not only material but also spiritual needs, enhancing the liberty, joy, and richness of the human existence. We must stress at the outset that this quest for the creative individual in advanced industrial society directly involves the social organization of labor. For if creativity is to be more than an individual privilege confined to an elite, then it must be a possible mode of existence for all members of the Great Society, without any discrimination other than that suggested by the different individual capacities themselves. Moreover, the embodiments of creativity either have to be produced in the material process of production (such as houses, parks, furniture, *objets d'art*), or the material process of production must provide the material basis and environment for the creation and reception of such goods. How and where can individual creativity, on a social scale, develop in a society in which material production is being increasingly mechanized, automated, standardized? The following alternatives present themselves: (1) either the material production itself changes its character fundamentally and is transformed from "alienated" to non-alienated work; (2) or material production is completely divorced from creative individuality (except for the technological intelligence and imagination brought to bear on the productive apparatus), and the individuals are creative outside the process of material production.

I shall start with the first alternative. Further progress of industrial society is tantamount to progress in mechanization and mass production. The reduction of individual energy in the production of the necessities is also progress also in human terms; the elimination of individual labor power from this production would be the greatest triumph of industry and science. Any attempt to reverse the trend on a social scale by a reintroduction of modes of work closer to handicraft and artisanship, or by reducing the mechanized apparatus while leaving intact the established social control of the productive and distributive process, would be regressive in terms of efficiency as well as human development.[1]

Thus, the emergence of the autonomous and creative individual cannot be envisaged as a gradual transformation of existing alienated into non-alienated labor. In other words, the individual will not come to life as worker, technician, engineer, or scientist who expresses his creativity in producing or attending to the established apparatus of production. The latter is and remains a technical apparatus which, in its very structure, militates against autonomy in the work process. Autonomy rather presupposes a basic change in the relations of the producers and consumers to the apparatus itself. In its prevailing form, the latter controls the individuals whom it serves: it fosters and satisfies the aggressive and, at the same time, conformist needs which reproduce the controls. Nor would a mere transfer of controls mean qualitative change unless and until the new administrators (and the people at large) experience the vital need for changing the very direction of technical progress toward the pacification of the struggle for existence. Then, the "realm of freedom" may perhaps appear in the work process itself, in the performance of socially necessary labor. The technical apparatus could then serve to create a new social and natural environment: human beings could then have their own cities, their own houses, their own space of tranquillity and joy: they could become free and learn how to live in freedom with the others. Only with the creation of such an entirely different environment (which is well within the capabilities of technology and well beyond the capabilities of the vested interests which control technology), would the words "beauty," "creativity," and "community" designate meaningful goals; the creation of such an environment would indeed be non-alienated labor.

The other alternative for the emergence of the "individual" in the advancing industrial society is expressed in the notion that the individual, as an autonomous and creative person, *develops outside* and *beyond* the material work process, outside and beyond the time and space required for

---

1 The situation is entirely different in the backward countries where the improvement and humanization of existing pre-industrial modes of work could conceivably counteract the trend toward exploitative control of industrialization by foreign or native capital – provided real national independence has been attained.

"earning a living" or producing the socially necessary foods and services. Under this general notion are subsumed two very different and even contradictory concepts: the Marxian distinction between the realm of freedom and the realm of necessity, and the modern idea of creative leisure.

Marx's "realm of freedom" presupposes a social organization of labor guided by the standards of utmost rationality in the satisfaction of individual needs for the society as a whole. Thus, it presupposes collective control of the production process by the producers themselves. But for Marx, the production process remains a "realm of necessity," that is, heteronomy, imposed on man by the continued struggle with nature, scarcity, and weakness. The time spent in this struggle would be greatly reduced, but it would still take up much of the individual's existence. The remaining time would be free time in the literal sense that it would be under the autonomy of the individual: he would be free to satisfy his own needs, to develop his own faculties, his own pleasures. Now it seems to me that contemporary industrial society has all but closed this realm of freedom, and closed it not only by virtue of its ingression into all spheres of the individual existence (thus preconditioning the free time) but also by virtue of technical progress and mass democracy. What is left to individual creativity outside the technical work process is in the way of hobbies, do-it-yourself stuff, games. There is, of course, the authentic creative expression in art, literature, music, philosophy, science – but it is hardly imaginable that this authentic creativity will, even in the best of all societies, become a general capability. The rest is sport, fun, fad. These conditions of advanced industrial society, then, seem to invalidate Marx's idea of free time. Freedom is also a matter of quantity, number, space: it demands solitude, distance, dissociation – the unoccupied, quiet space, nature not destroyed by commerce and brutality. Where these conditions do not prevail, the realm of freedom becomes a most expensive privilege. Not only the reduction of the working day and the restoration of nature but also the reduction of the birth rate would be the prerequisite.

In contradistinction to the Marxian concept, the notion of "creative leisure" is realistic and conforms to the contemporary conditions. Marx's "free time" is not "leisure time," for the realization of the all-around individual is not a matter of leisure. Free time pertains to a free society, leisure time to a repressive society. When, in the latter type of society, the working day must be greatly reduced, leisure time must be organized, even administered. For the laborer, employee, or executive enters into his leisure time equipped with the qualities, attitudes, values, behavior belonging to his station in his society; he has his being-for-others as his own; his leisure activity or passivity will simply be a prolongation or recreation of his social performance; he will not be an "individual." In the Marxian concept, man is free also in the realm of necessity to the extent to which he has organized it in accordance with his human needs, in transparent rationality; freedom thus links the two realms: the subject of the working day is also the subject of free time. In the contemporary industrial society, man is not the subject of his working day; consequently if he is to become the subject of his free time, he has to be made into such. And until the repressive organization of the working day is abolished, he will be made into a subject of leisure by exactly the same powers which govern the working day. Creativity can be learned, culture can be learned, but as long as learning and teaching do not transcend the established conditions, the result will be the enrichment, beautification, adornment of an unfree society. Instead of invoking the image of human freedom, creative culture will contribute to the absorption of this image into the status quo, which it will make more palatable.

But does not the evolution of technological civilization in its own course promote and require the development of new mental energies, of new intellectual faculties which, in turn, tend to transcend the prevailing conditions and to create liberating needs and aspirations? There is an increasing need for scientific and technological intelligence in the process of material production which will have to be satisfied; and there is also no doubt that this intelligence is creative. However, the mathematical character of modern science determines the range and direction of its creativity, and leaves the non-quantifiable qualities of *humanitas* outside the domain of exact science. The mathematical propositions about nature are held to be *the* truth about nature, and the mathematical conception and project of science are held to be the only "scientific" ones. This notion amounts to claiming universal validity for a specific historical theory and practice of science and other modes of knowledge appear as less scientific and therefore less exactly true. Or, to put it more bluntly: after having removed the non-quantifiable qualities of man and nature from scientific method, science feels the need for redemption by coming to terms with the "humanities."

The dichotomy between science and humanities (a treacherous designation: as if science did not partake of humanity!) cannot be overcome by mutual recognition and respect; its resolution would involve the ingression of humanistic goals into the formation of scientific concepts, and, vice versa, the development of humanistic goals under the guidance of such scientific concepts. Prior to this internal unification, science and the humanities will hardly be equipped to play a major role in the emergence of a free society. The humanities will be condemned to remain essentially abstract, academic, "cultural" – quite divorced from the daily work process. Science, on the other hand, will continue to shape the work process and, with it, the daily universe of work and leisure; but it will not bring about, by virtue of its own

*[handwritten margin note: Scientific and technological intelligence and the human condition]*

*[handwritten note at bottom: On educational reform ⟹]*

process, the new human freedom. The scientist may well be moved by supra-scientific goals, humane goals, but they will remain external to his science, and they will limit and even define his creativity from outside. Thus, the scientist or the technician, occupied in the designing and construction of a bridge and road net, of facilities for work and leisure, and in the planning of towns may (and indeed often does) calculate and construct something beautiful, peaceful, and humane. However, his creation will be functional in terms of the functioning of his society, and his transcending goals and values will be defined by this society. In this sense, his creativity will remain heteronomous.

The individuals who are supposed to live in the Great Society must be the individuals who build it – they must be free *for* it before they can be free in it. No other power can impose or force their society on them – not because a "despotism of freedom" *per se* contradicts liberation, but because no power, no government, no party exists which is free for such dictator-ship. So it must still be in the process of material production, of socially necessary labor and its division that the new society would have to take shape. And since individual autonomy is being eliminated from this process, the emergence of freedom and the redirection of efforts would be a matter of changing the *control* over the productive process. Moreover, the construction of the Great Society as a free society would involve more than a change in the controlling powers: it would involve the emergence of new needs and aspirations in the individuals themselves – needs and aspirations essentially different from, and even contradictory to, those sustained, satisfied, and reproduced by the established social process.

But is it not the very essence of a democratic society to allow the emergence of new needs and aspirations, even if their development threatens to demand new social institutions? Here is the fundamental task of educa-tion, the third area of reconstruction designated in the program for the Great Society. It calls for an extension and growth of education, "in quality as well as in size." Let us consider first the question of quantitative growth. Not too long ago, many voices spoke out against general education: it was considered dangerous to law and order, to culture, if the people (the lower classes) would learn how to read and write. Of course, it was the *established* law and order, the *established* culture which was to be protected from more education. Today, the situation is very different, and education is considered a desideratum for the established law and order, and for the established culture. No cultural and intellectual expression – no matter how subversive – is to be excluded from the curriculum. Marx is taught alongside Hitler; drugs are part of the equipment of existential psychology; and even the philosophy of the Marquis de Sade is sometimes respectfully treated in the classroom. Fortunately, I do not have to discuss here the question whether this achievement indicates progress in freedom and critical thought, or rather progress in the immunity and cohesion of the existing society and its values.

In any case, this cultural affluence is still better than further restriction and repression of knowledge, but it cannot *per se* be taken as progress toward a better society. Indeed, this coordination of the negative and the positive, the subversive and the conservative, reduces the qualitative difference between them; it accomplishes the flattening out of opposites, of contradiction. A change in the prevailing pattern – that is to say, a liberation of free, critical, radical thought, and of new intellectual and instinctual needs – would necessitate a break with the benevolent neutrality which embraces Marx and Hitler, Freud and Heidegger, Samuel Beckett and Mary McCarthy; it would necessitate partisanship – education to partisanship – as against a tolerance and an objectivity which in any case operate only in the realm of ideology and in areas which do not threaten the whole. However, precisely this tolerance and objectivity are the shibboleth of the democratic process in its prevailing institutions. Progressive education which could create the intellectual climate for the emergence of new individual needs, would come into conflict with many of the powers, private and public, which finance education today. Qualitative change in education is qualitative social change, and there is little chance that such a change could be organized and administered; education remains its prerequisite. The contradiction is real: the existing society must offer the possibility of education for a better society, and such education may be a threat to the existing society. Thus we cannot expect popular demand for such education, nor endorsement and support from above.

Kant stated as the goal of education that children should be educated, not in accordance with the present but with that of a future, better condition of the human race, namely, in accordance with the idea of *humanitas*. This goal still implies the subversion of the present condition of man. I wonder whether the spokesmen for education toward the Great Society are aware of this implication. To the degree to which the technical, material, and scientific resources for the development of a free society are available, the chance of its realization depends on the human, social forces who would *need* such a society – need it not only objectively (*an sich*) but also subjectively, for themselves, consciously. Today, this need is active only among a minority of the population of the "have" societies, and among the fighting people in the "have-not" areas of the world. In the technically advanced countries, education can indeed help to activate the need which "objectively" is universal, but it would be a strange, most unpopular, and unprofitable education. For example, it would include immunization of children and adults against the mass media; unhampered access to information suppressed or distorted by these media; methodical distrust of politicians and leaders, and abstention from their performances; and organization of effective protest and refusal which do not inevitably end with the martyrdom of those who protest and refuse. Such education would also aim at a basic transvaluation of values: it would require the debunking of all heroism in the service of inhumanity, of sport and fun in the service of brutality and stupidity, of the faith in the necessity of the struggle for existence and in the necessity of business. To be sure, these educational aims are negative, but the negation is the work and appearance of the positive, which first has to create the physical and mental space where it can come to life – and thus requires removal of the devastating and suffocating equipment which now occupies this space. This destruction would be the first manifestation of the new autonomy and creativity: the appearance of the free individual in the new society.

## THE INTERNAL CONTRADICTIONS OF THE GREAT SOCIETY PROGRAM

In the course of my analysis, I have tried to limit myself to topics I feel qualified to discuss. This means excluding specific administrative problems, such as the relation between federal and local authority, public and private agencies, and so on. These questions presuppose existing institutions as implementing the program for the Great Society, whereas I assume that this program would lead beyond their framework and authority.

Another problem area is that of "organization," that is, whether the ubiquitous organization characteristic of, and indispensable for, the functioning of advanced industrial society does not militate against "individual" creativity and initiative. The opposition of organization to freedom is ideological: while it is true that freedom cannot be organized, the material, technical (and perhaps even the intellectual) preconditions of freedom require organization. Not the growth of organization is to blame, but the growth of bad, exploitative organization. Against it, counter-organization is called for. For example, if the civil rights movement had an organization more powerful and more militant than the force of its opponents, it would be far more effective. A similar response could terminate the now endless debate as to the right balance between federal and local government, jurisdiction, initiative, and so forth. If the composition of the federal government indicates progressive policies, its power and authority should be made to prevail rigorously, and vice versa; otherwise, the issue is simply one of power politics, local or national.

One might also point up the international, global content of the Great Society. I note frequent acceptance of the national framework of the program: the Great Society will be an American society. But if one thing is clear, it is that the Great Society, if it should ever come about, will *not* be an American society, although this country may conceivably and initially be the leading power. Not only are some of the values which have come to be associated with the American way of life (such as the commercialization of the soul, togetherness, the sanctity of business, the science of human relations) incompatible with a free society, the warlike coexistence of the affluent society with the have-not part of the world, neo-colonialism in any form, conflicts with the very idea of a Great Society. Similarly, some of the values associated with Eastern civilization (especially its traditional aversion to "business," its emphasis on contemplation) could be revived in the new society, while other Eastern values would be incompatible with it.

To sum up: the program of the Great Society is of a substantial ambiguity which reflects the alternative prospects of the affluent society whose program it is supposed to be.

1). It can be read as a program for the extension and amelioration of the status quo: a higher standard of living for the underprivileged part of the population, abolition of discrimination and unemployment, beautification of cities and countryside, improvement of transportation, better education for all, and cultivation of leisure. Unless a policy to the contrary is proposed, it must be assumed that this development is to take place within the institutional, cultural, and mental framework of the competitive struggle for economic existence. Such a program, translated into reality, would indeed mean a vast improvement in the prevailing conditions. However, even within the given framework, the realization of the Great Society would require a permanent and considerable reduction of the military establishment and its physical and mental manifestations throughout the society – and that is to say, it would require major political and economic changes, foremost of foreign policy. Short of such change, the Great Society would be like a welfare state prepared to turn into a warfare state.

2). The program can be read as envisaging the essential transformation of the existing society which is suggested by its technological capabilities, namely, a transformation into a society where not full but marginal employment (or even unemployment) in necessarily alienated labor is the basis of growth. This would mean subversion of the prevailing organization of the economic process and subversion of the prevailing process of education: in short, it would mean a fundamental transvaluation of values and the emergence of new individual and social needs. This would also mean a radical change in the relation between the have and have-not societies – the rise of an international society beyond capitalism and communism.

Under both aspects, the traditional concept of the individual, in its classic-liberal as well as Marxist form seems to be untenable – canceled (*aufgehoben*) by the historical development of productivity. Individuality, the "person" as autonomous agent, would find increasingly less place in the work process. In the first alternative (extension and amelioration of the status quo), individuality could be (and perhaps would have to be) "artificially" maintained and fostered: some sort of organized, administered individuality expressed in external paraphernalia, gadgets, fads, hobbies, and, outside the work process, in cultivated leisure, decoration, and decor. Authentic individuality would remain the distinction of the creative artist, writer, or musician. The idea of making this creative potential general among the population at large militates against the very function and truth of the artistic creation as a form of expression – not because it must necessarily remain the privilege of a creative few, but because it implies dissociation from, and negation of, common sense and common values: ingression of a qualitatively different reality into the established one. In the case of the second alternative (fundamental transformation of the society), individuality would refer to an entirely new existential dimension: to a domain of play, experiment, and imagination which is outside the reaches of any policy and program today.

I wish to conclude on a less utopian note. Perhaps my most serious doubt concerning the Great Society is caused by the fact that American foreign policy all but invalidates the domestic program for the Great Society. The issues of coexistence, of the relations with the have-not countries, of neo-colonialism, and the military establishment are not contingent external factors – rather they determine the prospects of growth, improvement, and even the continued existence of a society, great or not so great. Declarations as to the need for extending the American program to other nations are contradicted by the brutal and dirty war in Vietnam, by the direct or indirect intervention against social change wherever it threatens vested interests, by the flowering of military bases all over the globe. For these conditions testify to the dominance of powers which are incompatible with the grand design for peace, freedom, and justice. It is the presence of these powers rather than the absence of capabilities and intentions which gives the program its ideological character. The Great Society will be a society that can exist and grow in peace, without the built-in need for defense and aggression – or it will not be at all.

# III

## The Containment of Social Change in Industrial Society*

### Herbert Marcuse

Tonight I would like to talk with you about certain tendencies in advanced industrial society. I would like to stress that it is a question of tendencies only, but tendencies which may forbode the future. I would like to start by suggesting that we are confronted with a new type, a new form, of society, to which the traditional categories — political, sociological, even psychological — no longer seem to apply. Examples: if you look at what we have today and the form of society, capitalism doesn't seem to be the same as it was not too long ago; socialism certainly doesn't seem to be what we were taught it would be, and expected it to be. In this situation there arise such bastard concepts as state capitalism, or state socialism, which don't make much sense either. Or think of what has become of democracy if West and East claim to be democratic. Think of such well established concepts as imperialism; imperialism today, where it exists, certainly is no longer the economic imperialism which may be called classic imperialism. And this applies to psychological categories too. They too don't seem to be valid any more. It seems, and I hope I can give you some illustrations of what I mean tonight, that such notions as the unconscious and sublimation have changed their meaning — if not lost their meaning altogether.

Now what is new in this form of society it seems to me, is a new relationship between rulers and ruled, between administrators on the one hand, and the administered population on the other. What we have is not adequately described as a mass society. The concept "mass society" itself is, I think, an ideological concept. It suggests that the masses really determine, at least to a considerable extent, the intellectual and material culture. What we have in fact is a highly centralized society, systematically managed from above, in all spheres of culture. The masses, which certainly exist, are the product and object of this management and of this administration; as the product and object of administration, they in turn become active and vociferous, and determine the policies which their managers and administrators want them to determine. This management is gradually reaching the scope of a total administration, a total administration which (and that again is a novel feature in history) works through the control of the huge technical and technological apparatus of production, distribution, and communication; an apparatus which is so huge and so rational that individuals, and even groups of individuals, are powerless against it.

Nor can we really call this society a technological society. A technological society would be a society which operates in accordance with the most efficient and most rational use of available resources. I submit that the term technological society again is an ideological term and does not adequately describe the society we have. I submit that advanced industrial society is not defined by technological rationality, but rather by the opposite. Namely by the blocking, by the arrest, and by the perversion of technological rationality — or, in one word, by the use of technology as an instrument of repression, an instrument of domination.

---

* This transcript of Dr. Marcuse's Tuesday Evening Lecture at Stanford on May 4, 1965, has not been read by the author. He requests that this edition be limited to distribution to students only and not be reproduced in any printed form without his approval. Fred Goff, Box 2123, Stanford.

† "The Containment of Social Change in Industrial Society" was presented as a talk at Stanford University on May 4, 1965 and appears here in print for the first time. The text is one of the last statements that emphasized forces of containment and domination as the primary feature of advanced industrial societies. Soon after, Marcuse would stress possibilities of social transformation based on his affirmation of the potential of the emerging New Left, counterculture, and global anti-war movement – an emphasis that informs the next three texts in this collection, encompassing "1966 Political Preface to *Eros and Civilization*," "Beyond One-Dimensional Man," and "Cultural Revolution." The text in the Herbert Marcuse archive has handwritten from the lefthand corner and above the title: "The Intellectual and the Establishment." On the right is handwritten: "Stanford 1965, May." The manuscript is a typescript of Marcuse's lecture and it states on the bottom of the page: "This transcript of Dr. Marcuse's Tuesday Evening Lecture at Stanford on May 4, 1965, has not been read by the author. He requests that this edition be limited to distribution to students only and not be reproduced in any printed form without his approval. Fred Goff, Box 2123, Stanford." We have chosen to print this, however, as it is one of the clearest and most concise presentations of Marcuse's views in the mid-1960s.

While working with the Institute of Social Research in the 1940s, Marcuse visited Stanford to make contact with professors there, including the Hoover Institution. During his work with the OSS in World War II, Marcuse travelled to Stanford to do research, and he maintained contacts with the University. In a May 17, 1965 letter to Leo Löwenthal, Marcuse expresses his disappointment that Löwenthal could not attend his Stanford talk because of "one of the hundred thousand faculty meetings you have out there." He then explains that he would have met Löwenthal in Berkeley, "but I had to go back the very next morning for an additional lecture at the Centre for Democratic Institutions at Santa Barbara." Marcuse's archive is full of the lectures he presented, most of which contain detailed notes that he used for his presentations and some of which, such as the lecture we are publishing here, were written up and eventually published as articles.

# THE CONTAINMENT OF SOCIAL CHANGE IN INDUSTRIAL SOCIETY†

Tonight I would like to talk with you about certain tendencies in advanced industrial society. I would like to stress that it is a question of tendencies only, but tendencies which may forbode the future. I would like to start by suggesting that we are confronted with a new type, a new form, of society, to which the traditional categories – political, sociological, even psychological – no longer seem to apply. Examples: if you look at what we have today and the form of society, capitalism doesn't seem to be the same as it was not too long ago; socialism certainly doesn't seem to be what we were taught it would be, and expected it to be. In this situation there arise such bastard concepts as state capitalism, or state socialism, which don't make much sense either. Or think of what has become of democracy if West and East claim to be democratic. Think of such well established concepts as imperialism; imperialism today, where it exists, certainly is no longer the economic imperialism which may be called classic imperialism. And this applies to psychological categories too. They too don't seem to be valid any more. It seems, and I hope I can give you some illustrations of what I mean tonight, that such notions as the unconscious and sublimation have changed their meaning – if not lost their meaning altogether.

Now what is new in this form of society it seems to me, is a new relationship between rulers and ruled, between administrators on the one hand, and the administered population on the other. What we have is not adequately described as a mass society. The concept "mass society" itself is, I think, an ideological concept. It suggests that the masses really determine, at least to a considerable extent, the intellectual and material culture. What we have in fact is a highly centralized society, systematically managed from above, in all spheres of culture. The masses, which certainly exist, are the product and object of this management and of this administration; as the product and object of administration, they in turn become active and vociferous, and determine the policies which their managers and administrators want them to determine. This management is gradually reaching the scope of a total administration, a total administration which (and that again is a novel feature in history) works through the control of the huge technical and technological apparatus of production, distribution, and communication; an apparatus which is so huge and so rational that individuals, and even groups of individuals, are powerless against it.

Nor can we really call this society a technological society. A technological society would be a society which operates in accordance with the most efficient and most rational use of available resources. I submit that the term technological society again is an ideological term and does not adequately describe the society we have. I submit that advanced industrial society is not defined by technological rationality, but rather by the opposite. Namely by the blocking, by the arrest, and by the perversion of technological rationality – or, in one word, by the use of technology as an instrument of repression, an instrument of domination.

I should like to define briefly at the outset what I mean by repression, because I do not use the term in the technical psychoanalytic sense. The degree of repression must be measured not only against the present and the past, but against the *possibilities* available to the individual and to society. Repression today is mainly characterized by the continuation of alienated labor and services in a situation in which such alienated labor could be largely abolished. Repression is further characterized by the obvious and widespread decline in individual freedom, the decline of independent thought and expression. In other words, instead of an increasing tendency toward self-determination, towards the individual's ability to determine his own existence, his own life, we have the opposite: the individual appears to be increasingly powerless, confronted with the technological and political apparatus which this society has built up. Repression is lastly and perhaps most conspicuously characterized by the fact that the struggle for existence continues, and is even intensified – again at a level of cultural progress and resources which would render possible the pacification of the struggle for existence.

Now I suggest that this use of technology, this repressive use of technology, violates and negates the inherent end and purpose of technology. And I would like to explain what I mean by it. True consummation of technological rationality and technical progress, the inherent end of technology, would imply the planful use of the available capabilities, intellectual as well as material, for the satisfaction of vital human needs on the global scale. Authentic technological rationality would be characterized by the unrestricted reduction of socially necessary labor, of toil, and of repression.

In other words, *authentic* consummation of technical progress would mean the pacification of the struggle for existence on the individual as well as national and international level. Instead we have the apparatus systematically used for intensifying the need for earning a living as a full-time occupation. And this continuation, this perpetuation, of the need for earning a living as a full-time occupation, is perpetuated by the production on a large scale of waste, planned obsolescence, destruction of resources, and by the channeling of the vast productivity of advanced industrial civilization into profitable destruction.

The question is *why* is this taking place. I suggest because the truly unrestricted and rational use of technical resources, of technical progress, would tend to what is called the abolition of labor and scarcity and to a society in which working time is reduced to marginal time and in which free time becomes full time. And such a condition would mean the collapse of the social and political institutions which are based on the permanent necessity of labor and of the struggle for existence. Even more, such a condition, which is perfectly realistic, would mean the collapse of the established civilization which is based on a morality which in turn is based on the need for life-long work, for resignation, for what Max Weber has called "inner-worldly asceticism."

Now against the supreme threat of a society which indeed could afford to abolish human labor, physical labor, in the process of production and distribution – against this supreme threat to the established institutions, and to the established morality, the present advanced industrial societies are mobilized. But in order to meet this threat the traditional forms of domination are no longer sufficient. New forms of domination, technological forms of domination and repression, are operative; namely, the administration of needs and satisfactions which reproduce the struggle for existence, and in reproducing the struggle for existence reproduce a form of society which necessitates the perpetuation of the struggle for existence. This is a new element, a new form of domination, that society has now succeeded for the first in history in perfecting. The very needs of the individual (even his instinctual needs and satisfactions) are manipulated in such a way that these needs and satisfactions at the same time strengthen the cohesion of the repressive society in which his needs are satisfied.

In having accomplished this achievement, the society has integrated the individuals to such an extent that no escape seems to be possible. Moreover, this society has achieved a condition in which individuals reproduce their own servitude; men themselves repel their own liberation. It is a voluntary servitude and, it seems, a perfectly rational servitude, because in accepting the socially preformed and preconditioned needs and satisfactions, the individuals actually live better than ever before. The growing productivity of this society provides the goods and services for a better life – a better living even for strata of the population which thus far have remained underpriviledged. It is no wonder, and it seems perfectly rational, that people submit to a society which grants them increasing satisfaction, even if the prosperity of this so-called affluent society takes place in a universe of war, misery, and destruction.

Now within this affluent society – and you may realize that I use the term "affluent society" in an ironical sense, because seriously a society cannot be called affluent if it perpetuates its affluence in the midst of poverty, misery and war – within this affluent society the permanent contradiction prevails between overflowing productivity on the one hand, and its restricted and perverted use on the other; between the historical possibility of peace and the actuality of war. But this contradiction is covered by the technological veil. The irrational in this society appears as rational because people indeed have more comforts, and more fun. Domination appears as freedom because people indeed have the choice of prefabricated goods and prefabricated candidates.

Behind the technological veil domination of man by man continues as it did before, and operates within the conception and context of free individuals.

Now to elucidate this decisive turn in the historical relationships of domination in which for the first time in history on such a large scale the dominated cooperate voluntarily and rationally with those who dominate them, I should like to illustrate it by referring to a famous passage in Hegel's *Phenomenology of Mind*, namely, the dialectic of master and servant. According to Hegel, at the origin of all domination is the life and death struggle for recognition of men as free individuals. And the primary experience, the original experience, is that of the difference between master and slave. That is to say, the one is free because he has succeeded in making another man work for him; the slave is being-for-another – for the master. The master asserts and recognizes his freedom in and through his power to obtain from the slave the objects of his, the master's needs and desires. The objects which he needs to satisfy his needs are provided him by the work of the slave, and only by the work of the slave. To these things which the master needs in order to be free the slave is chained. The master's power over things is thus the master's power over men. But, the master is free *only*, and can satisfy his needs *only* in so far as the slave does the work for him and provides him with the objects of satisfying his needs. In other words, the master finds himself dependent on the slave. Domination is thus actually the mutual dependence of master and slave. And in the same process the slave becomes conscious of his power over the master. The things which the master desires exist only because the slave has worked them into the form in which the master can use them. In other words, as Hegel puts it, the slave's labor is the very substance of the object worked.

All domination of man by man is sustained *only* through domination over things to which another man is chained by his labor. That is to say, if the human existence is no longer objectified, and no longer exhausts itself, in alien and alienable things, the way is opened for the mutual recognition of men as free individuals.

Now the actual historical development of domination seems at first to correspond to this analysis. To the degree to which labor ceased to be the work of slaves and became generalized throughout the society, to that degree domination was indeed democratized and became also generalized throughout the society – but the result was not freedom. It was not freedom because man, and not only the slave, not only the laborer, remained chained to a world of things which controlled his existence instead of being controlled by him. Man remained subordinated, and in fact increasingly subordinated to the omnipresent productive and political apparatus, which he himself had created. Science and technology had mastered the object world to the point where it could lose, and indeed did lose, its alien and hostile power, and could be transformed into the medium for human fulfillment. The master–slave relationship would be abolished and, with the conquest of scarcity there would be no longer the need for inner-worldly asceticism. But instead, domination was sustained and reproduced as the ever more contradictory basis of the established civilization, until this contradiction unfolded in the affluent society.

The "paradox" of the affluent society in this analysis is actually the very law of the existence of the affluent society; the greater the conquest of nature, the weaker man's power over his own social and private existence, the greater the conquest and knowledge of man's own nature, in psychology and sociology, the easier the human being becomes the object of total administration and management. The more the productivity of labor increases, the more is it accompanied by destructiveness and waste. For the first time in history society has the material and intellectual resources to create a life without fear, a life in peace, yet the threat of war and fear are greater than ever before.

The reasons for this development are well known, and I only sum them up here very briefly. Science and technology actually were constructed and developed within a social context which militated against the planful use of progress for the satisfaction of human needs. Such satisfaction, although it increases, was only the by-product of profitable productivity. But now the very dynamic of the society has reached the stage where its own productivity undermines its own basis. Automation undermines the basis of scarcity, toil and repression, and threatens to do away with the need for earning a living in full-time occupation. This is the final threat to domination and the very existence of the established civilization is at stake. For the established civilization depends in its entirety on the perpetuation of the need for alienated labor, on the organism as an instrument of labor rather than pleasure, and the real possibility of liberation from this repression endangers the institutions of repression.

How does contemporary society solve this contradiction? By systematically and methodically creating and reproducing the need for alienated labor, not through any terror, but through the scientific preconditioning of individual needs and the equalization of spontaneous needs and socially required needs. It solves the contradiction by closing all avenues of escape, protest, refusal and dissociation, by absorbing or defeating all effective opposition, by closing itself against qualitative social change, namely the emergence of qualitatively new forms of human existence, and by suffocating the need for social change. The achievement is the social conquest of the total existence of man, including his instinctual sphere, including his unconscious. That is one of the reasons why I stated at the beginning that these psychological categories which belonged still to the liberal face of modern society, may no longer be adequate. Can we really still speak of an unconscious (in the sense in which Freud used the term) when this unconscious has become so easily subject to social management – through the techniques of publicity, industrial psychology, or the science of human relations?

Now I would like to illustrate this novel conquest of spheres of human existence which up to now were free from social management and administration but which are now being conquered by the total society. I would like to illustrate it by the application of Freud's theory of instincts to the development of the mental structure of individuals in the affluent society. Before I do so I would like to remind you that, as in *Eros and Civilization*, I base my discussion on the final version of Freud's instinct theory, according to which there are two primary drives: Eros, the life instincts, formerly called sexuality, and the death and destruction instincts – the former governed by the pleasure principle, the latter governed by the Nirvana principle, which is to say that these instincts aim at destroying life and returning to a state before birth free of tensions. I have to add only that, according to this conception, the instinctual energy in the organism is constant, but that its distribution between the two primary drives is changeable. In other words, if you have conditions in which the energy of the erotic instincts, libido, is reduced, it means that at the same time the energy of the destructive and death instincts will increase, and vice versa. This will be important for the subsequent brief discussion.

Now first, what is happening – and I hope you will realize the entirely hypothetical character of what I have to suggest to you – what is happening to Eros, to the life instinct, in this new society which has succeeded in opening up the instinctual sphere of man and administering even his instinctual needs and satisfactions, is a repressive liberation of Eros. The shift in terminology from sexuality to Eros is more than a mere change in designation. Eros as life instinct, in contrast to sexuality, is an instinctual drive affecting the organism and cathecting the organism as a whole, while sexuality remains, compared with Eros, a localized and partial drive. You will see the importance of this distinction later on.

Now what is meant by a repressive liberation? Obviously we have a sweeping liberalization of sexuality compared with the preceding era – the Victorian and even post-Victorian. How is this liberalization of sexuality made socially tolerable, and what is involved in it? I submit that the Oedipus situation remains the basic condition in which the erotic instincts develop; the incest taboo, the struggle with the father, and the reality principle – all this remains. But, in the struggle the father now yields his function as the representative of the reality principle and as the one who imposes upon the child the necessary renunciations and restrictions. He yields this function to younger father figures outside the family, a whole series of leaders, champions, stars, team leaders, and so on, who all represent the reality principle far better and far more effectively than the father did. In fact, the progressive father today cannot fulfill the function which the authoritative father of Freud was supposed to fulfill; he certainly no longer is the threatening representative of the reality principle. The modern Daddy is rather a ridiculous figure and you would not expect that he can really perform the duty he is supposed to perform. Somehow the entire balance of power seems to have changed. And it is the younger generation that imposes the reality principle on the Daddy, and not the other way around.

Now, where actually does the reality principle impose itself upon the child? Of course mainly via the mass media. The decline in the role of the father also represents an economic change, because the father today no longer has the economic function of transmitting to the heir the family business and the family skills; all this belongs to the past. With this decline of the father the function of representing the reality principle is transferred – let us say, for brevity's sake – to the mass media and to those who represent the mass media. The super-ego as represented by the authoritative father is weakened and the moral imperatives, once imposed upon the child by the super-ego, are being replaced by the imperatives of the mass media. They tell the child and the adolescent, and without the innumerable conflicts formerly involved in the quest for identity, exactly who he is and who he is supposed to be. They even tell him what kind of soap to use, what kind of deodorant to use, what kind of hair-do to have, and so on; so this function which was formerly fulfilled in the family, and was supposed to be the result of the child's and adolescent's *own* struggle for recognition, is now performed to a great extent by the so-called media.

*Repressive Desublimation*

Now with this change of the balance of power in the puberty conflict, and with this weakening of the super-ego, we have almost naturally a weakening of sexual taboos; the taboo on virginity, the taboo on pre- and extra-marital relations, the liberalization in dress, the exhibition of the body in a way which again formerly was entirely tabooed, and so on. In other words, a genuine liberalization of sexual morality. But (and now comes the big but), this liberalization occurs within a repressive society which has succeeded in using sex as a salable commodity, thereby eliminating and subduing most of those forces and features which, according to Freud, made sexuality and Eros a really liberating and socially dangerous force. In the affluent society sex is used as a salable commodity, as a publicity stunt, as even a status symbol; this liberalization of sex is practiced by individuals who remain alienated. Sexual liberalization remains defined by alienation. Moreover, and perhaps even more important, socially facilitated sexual satisfaction becomes a vehicle of adjustment, clearly indicated by the extent to which the psychiatrist becomes an institution for self-actualization, but self-actualization which does not, and cannot, overcome alienation, but which at least makes alienation palatable to the individual.

In view of these features, I have called the liberalization of sexual morality repressive desublimation; a paradoxical concept because all de-sublimation is in itself a reduction of repression, but it is so only if it is a result of individual freedom and satisfaction. Authentic, non-repressive desublimation would be liberation of erotic, and not only sexual, energy and, most important, would manifest itself in the decline of aggressive, destructive, heteronomous needs and satisfactions. Conversely, in the ascendency of truly liberated energy we would notice a de-socialization from a repressive society, a dissociation from a repressive society. An authentic desublimation would mean that the instinctual need for privacy, for quiet, for tenderness, for solidarity, for peace, indeed gain ascendency over and above destructive and competitive instincts. For the erotic instincts are truly life instincts, prevailing upon destructiveness and aggression, prevailing upon cruelty and violence, and striving for the creation of a truly pacified and humane environment.

I think that not much evidence is required to see that today the opposite tendency prevails; namely desublimation, liberalization of sexual morality, is accompanied by a release of destructive and aggressive energy on a scale hitherto unknown. This means that desublimation is confined to sexuality as a partial drive, satisfied in a local zone of the organism, and that the erotic transcendence, the cathexis of the entire organism, and the drive to form its own peaceful and pleasureable environment, is cut off. Desublimated satisfaction remains a temporary outlet which leaves social repression unchanged. And to the degree to which society invades previously private and protected areas of existence, to the degree to which society shapes and determines even the instinctual needs and satisfactions of man, to that degree the reality principle encroaches upon the pleasure principle and upon the erotic instincts. In one word, the noticeable liberalization of sexual morality, repressive desublimation, is characterized by the contraction rather than the extension of erotic energy by its contraction to sexuality – that is to say by a contraction and reduction rather than strengthening of the life instincts.

Now if this is the case, then we would expect that the reduction in the energy of the life instincts is on the other side compensated by an increase in the energy of the death and destruction instinct, that the destruction instinct indeed is strengthened and extended.

Let us have a brief look at what is happening to the deadly partner of Eros, to the death instinct and destruction instinct, in this society. I think the growth of aggressiveness is evident enough. At the top of the society the rational calculation of total annihilation, with the prospective victims readily playing along. In the society as a whole besides the normal forms of aggression, the aggressive use of machines for the satisfaction of otherwise repressed power – machine racing in all forms as sport, the violation of nature, the violation of science. Moreover the rise in criminality with a new feature: namely, the gross and gratuitous criminality which does not have an individual and personal motive, but is simply the assertion of the only liberty which is left to the repressed individual – the liberty to kill or to hurt without being able to change his status in the society. And here again with the release of the death and destruction instinct, we have a dangerous, paradoxical situation; the liberalization of the destruction instinct is not a satisfaction of the destruction instinct by virtue of which the instinct would be alleviated. The opposite is the case. The opposite is the case because in the technological society the relaxation of controls over the death instinct decreases rather than increases individual instinctual satisfaction and therefore involves frustration, which in turn necessitates the repetition of the destruction instinct on an ever larger scale.

Why is this the case? Why, in the technological society, does the evident release of the destruction instincts not bring the instinctual satisfaction which normally in psychological terms, you should expect? Because, in technological aggression and destruction, the satisfying act is transformed from the human agent to the mechanical, electronic, or nuclear agent. That is to say, the objective power of a thing separates the human person from his target, and executes, as a thing, the satisfaction of his needs. Consequence: the weakening of individual responsibility – the apparatus did it, or the machine did it. The instrument did it and not the person. And secondly, the weakening of individual instinctual satisfaction. And to the degree to which the technical apparatus takes over, the instinctual energy remains inhibited, unspent, and unsatisfied. At the same time the fear of death, the expression of the resistance of the life instincts against the death instincts, is also alleviated.

The fear of death declines in the technological society. In the extreme case, it is easier to die while others die at the same time. It is easier to kill if you don't see the target, if the target is miles or hundreds of miles away, and if the killing is done by an instrument. Thus, inasmuch as the death instinct is sublimated, as in war, defense, machine racing, it remains destructive and it does not satisfy.

Now, one should expect, if it is really true that the energy of the death instinct is inhibited, that it would accrue to the energy of the life instincts to libido. But unfortunately, in contrast to Eros, destructive energy is not reduced. Destructive energy is allowed to transcend; it is not cut off from extension, but this extension is facilitated.

Before I conclude, I want to emphasize that it seems to me this change in the mental structure, this repressive desublimation of the life instincts and this frustrating release of destruction instincts, undermines not only the institutions of repression as I suggested, but undermines the very basis for sublimation, and thereby the very basis of civilization as such. The change in the balance of power in the instinctual dynamic in favor of destructive energy may again be a turning point in history. The universe of violence in which we live today is no longer the universe of violence which is identical with the history of mankind. The universe of Auschwitz and Buchenwald, of Hiroshima and Vietnam, of torture and over-kill as conventional techniques in international relations is no longer the historical universe of violence. Here indeed quantity turns into quality, and not only the reality, but the very idea of humanity seems invalidated today.

In conclusion, can we in any responsible way offer a more optimistic prospect than the one according to which the universe of violence is going to continue and to expand? Negatively we have to admit that there is no identification with any mass movement, with any organized movement of which you could say that this is likely to bring about a change in the direction of peace. Reality today is in open and total conflict with its own ideology and with its own promises. And it is no accident that the Orwellian language, according to which war is peace and peace is war, seems to have become the official language of politics today. We have under the domination of this language the rule of a false consciousness, a false consciousness for which it is increasingly difficult to decide what is a fact and what is not a fact; a false consciousness which increasingly represses the facts which are evident enough. But the falsehood of this consciousness is obvious enough, and the layer of falsehood is thin enough; it can fall off, it can be broken.

Which is to say that people can again learn to see and to think independently and to break the power of standardized and imposed information and indoctrination. To help people do this task, which is one of the propositions on which Western civilization was founded – independent, free thought, a self-determination of existence – to make people again see that they can learn, at least make the effort to do so, this is indeed an intellectual task. And again I think it is no accident that the first effective opposition against the tendencies I have tried to outline here is noticeable in the campuses in this country.

It is an intellectual task, but one that is so close to practice that it can easily join, and can practically at any moment join, and transcend itself into practice. I only remind you of the civil rights movement: no organization was necessary to establish here the juncture between theory and practice, between the idea – or rather between the protest against the betrayal of an idea – and the attempt to do something about it. I admit these are small junctures of theory and practice, but precisely in the grasping of these small junctures, and in the effort not to stop but to go ahead with real independence of thought – I think precisely in this there lies today the only hope for a peaceful and better life.

# IV

†"Political Preface, 1966." This text was published as a Preface to a new edition of *Eros and Civilization* (Boston: Beacon Press, 1966, pp. xi–xxv). It shows a growing activism and optimism in Marcuse's thought, as well as sympathy with the student movement and counterculture, many of whose ideas and attitudes Marcuse had anticipated in *Eros and Civilization* (1955). On January 16, 1966 a letter from Marcuse to his Beacon Press editor Arnold Tovell notes: "Enclosed is the preface to the new hard cover edition of *Eros and Civilization*. I would appreciate it if you would give it your special attention because it was written under great pressure, and I am amenable to concrete, specified suggestions." Yet there is no further correspondence in the Marcuse archive on the issue so we do not know if Marcuse did or did not further revise his 1966 "Political Preface," which contains one of the first turns to a more optimistic affirmation of forces of opposition and revolt after the publication of his opus of pessimism and domination, *One-Dimensional Man*.

# POLITICAL PREFACE
# TO *EROS AND*
# *CIVILIZATION*, 1966 †

*Eros and Civilization*: the title expressed an optimistic, euphemistic, even positive thought, namely, that the achievements of advanced industrial society would enable man to reverse the direction of progress, to break the fatal union of productivity and destruction, liberty and repression – in other words, to learn the gay science (*gaya sciencia*) of how to use the social wealth for shaping man's world in accordance with his Life Instincts, in the concerted struggle against the purveyors of Death. This optimism was based on the assumption that the rationale for the continued acceptance of domination no longer prevailed, that scarcity and the need for toil were only "artificially" perpetuated – in the interest of preserving the system of domination. (I neglected or minimized the fact that this "obsolescent" rationale had been vastly strengthened (if not replaced) by even more efficient forms of social control. The very forces which rendered society capable of pacifying the struggle for existence served to repress in the individuals the need for such a liberation. Where the high standard of living does not suffice for reconciling the people with their life and their rulers, the "social engineering" of the soul and the "science of human relations" provide the necessary libidinal cathexis. In the affluent society, the authorities are hardly forced to justify their dominion. They deliver the goods; they satisfy the sexual and the aggressive energy of their subjects. Like the unconscious, the destructive power of which they so successfully represent, they are this side of good and evil, and the principle of contradiction has no place in their logic.

As the affluence of society depends increasingly on the uninterrupted production and consumption of waste, gadgets, planned obsolescence, and means of destruction, the individuals have to be adapted to these require-ments in more than the traditional ways. The "economic whip," even in its most refined forms, seems no longer adequate to insure the continuation of the struggle for existence in today's outdated organization, nor do the laws and patriotism seem adequate to insure active popular support for the ever more dangerous expansion of the system. Scientific management of instinctual needs has long since become a vital factor in the reproduction of the system: merchandise which has to be bought and used is made into objects of the libido; and the national Enemy who has to be fought and hated is distorted and inflated to such an extent that he can activate and satisfy aggressiveness in the depth dimension of the unconscious. Mass democracy provides the political paraphernalia for effectuating this introjection of the Reality Principle; it not only permits the people (up to a point) to chose their own masters and to participate (up to a point) in the government which governs them – it also allows the masters to disappear behind the technological veil of the productive and destructive apparatus which they control, and it conceals the human (and material) costs of the benefits and comforts which it bestows upon those who collaborate. The people, efficiently manipulated and organized, are free; ignorance and impotence, introjected heteronomy is the price of their freedom.

It makes no sense to talk about liberation to free men – and we are free if we do not belong to the oppressed minority. And it makes no sense to talk about surplus repression when men and women enjoy more sexual liberty than ever before. But the truth is that this freedom and satisfaction are transforming the earth into hell. The inferno is still concentrated in certain far away places: Vietnam, the Congo, South Africa, and in the ghettos of the "affluent society": in Mississippi and Alabama, in Harlem. These infernal places illuminate the whole. It is easy and sensible to see in them only pockets of poverty and misery in a growing society capable of eliminating them gradually and without a catastrophe. This interpretation may even be realistic and correct. The question is: eliminated at what cost – not in dollars and cents, but in human lives and in human freedom?

I hesitate to use the word – freedom – because it is precisely in the name of freedom that crimes against humanity are being perpetrated. This situation is certainly not new in history: poverty and exploitation were products of economic freedom; time and again, people were liberated all over the globe by their lords and masters, and their new liberty turned out to be submission, not to the rule of law but to the rule of the law of the others. What started as subjection by force soon became "voluntary servitude," collaboration in reproducing a society which made servitude increasingly rewarding and palatable. The reproduction, bigger and better, of the same ways of life came to mean, ever more clearly and consciously, the closing of those other possible ways of life which could do away with the serfs and the masters, with the productivity of repression.

Today, this union of freedom and servitude has become "natural" and a vehicle of progress. Prosperity appears more and more as the prerequisite and by-product of a self-propelling productivity ever seeking new outlets for consumption and for destruction, in outer and inner space, while being restrained from "overflowing" into the areas of misery – at home and abroad. As against this amalgam of liberty and aggression, production and destruction, the image of human freedom is dislocated: it becomes the project of the *subversion of this sort of progress*. Liberation of the instinctual needs for peace and quiet, of the "asocial" autonomous Eros presupposes liberation from repressive affluence: a reversal in the direction of progress.

It was the thesis of *Eros and Civilization*, more fully developed in my *One-Dimensional Man*, that man could avoid the fate of a Welfare-Through-Warfare State only by achieving a new starting point where he could reconstruct the productive apparatus without that "innerworldly asceticism" which provided the mental basis for domination and exploration. This image of man was the determinate negation of Nietzsche's superman: man intelligent enough and healthy enough to dispense with all heros and heroic virtues, man without the impulse to live dangerously, to meet the challenge; man with the good conscience to make life an end-in-itself, to live in joy a life without fear. "Polymorphous sexuality" was the term which I used to indicate that the new direction of progress would depend completely on the opportunity to activate repressed or arrested *organic*, biological needs: to make the human body an instrument of pleasure rather than labor. The old formula, the development of prevailing needs and faculties, seemed to be inadequate; the emergence of new, qualitatively different needs and faculties seemed to be the prerequisite, the content of liberation.

The idea of such a new Reality Principle was based on the assumption that the material (technical) preconditions for its development were either established, or could be established in the advanced industrial societies of our time. It was self-understood that the translation of technical capabilities into reality would mean a revolution. But the very scope and effectiveness of the democratic introjection have suppressed the historical subject, the agent of revolution: free people are not in need of liberation, and the oppressed are not strong enough to liberate themselves. These conditions redefine the concept of Utopia: liberation is the most realistic, the most concrete of all historical possibilities and at the same time the most rationally and effectively repressed – the most abstract and remote possibility. No philosophy, no theory can undo the democratic introjection of the masters into their subjects. When, in the more or less affluent societies, productivity has reached a level at which the masses participate in its benefits, and at which the opposition is effectively and democratically "contained," then the conflict between master and slave is also effectively contained. Or rather it has changed its social location. It exists, and explodes, in the revolt of the backward countries against the intolerable heritage of colonialism and its prolongation by neo-colonialism. The Marxian concept stipulated that only those who were free from the blessings of capitalism could possibly change it into a free society: those whose existence was the very negation of capitalist property could become the historical agents of liberation. In the international arena, the Marxian concept regains its full validity. To the degree to which the exploitative societies have become global powers, to the degree to which the new independent nations have become the battlefield of their interests, the "external" forces of rebellion have ceased to be extraneous forces: they are the enemy within the system. This does not make these rebels the messengers of humanity. By themselves, they are not (as little as the Marxian proletariat was) the representatives of freedom. Here too, the Marxian concept applies according to which the international proletariat would get its intellectual armor from outside: the "lightning of thought" would strike the "*naiven Volksboden.*" Grandiose ideas about the union of theory and practice do injustice to the feeble beginnings of such a union. Yet the revolt in the backward countries has found a response in the advanced countries where youth is in protest against repression in affluence and war abroad.

Revolt against the false fathers, teachers, and heroes – solidarity with the wretched of the earth: is there any "organic" connection between the two facets of the protest? There seems to be an all but instinctual solidarity. The revolt at home against home seems largely impulsive, its targets hard to define: nausea caused by "the way of life," revolt as a matter of physical and mental hygiene. The body against "the machine" – not against the mechanism constructed to make life safer and milder, to attenuate the cruelty of nature, but against the machine which has taken over the mechanism: the political machine, the corporate machine, the cultural and educational machine which has welded blessing and curse into one rational whole. The whole has become too big, its cohesion too strong, its functioning too efficient – does the power of the negative concentrate in still partly unconquered, primitive, elemental forces? The body against the machine: men, women, and children fighting, with the most primitive tools, the most brutal and destructive machine of all times and keeping it in check – does guerilla warfare define the revolution of our time?

Historical backwardness may again become the historical chance of turning the wheel of progress to another direction. Technical and scientific overdevelopment stands refuted when the radar-equipped bombers, the chemicals, and the "special forces" of the affluent society are let loose on the poorest of the earth, on their shacks, hospitals, and rice fields. The "accidents" reveal the substance: they tear the technological veil behind which the real powers are hiding. The capability to overkill and to overburn, and the mental behavior that goes with it are by-products of the development of the productive forces within a system of exploitation and repression; they seem to become more productive the more comfortable the system becomes to its privileged subjects. The affluent society has now demonstrated that it is a society at war; if its citizens have not noticed it, its victims certainly have.

The historical advantage of the late-comer, of technical backwardness, may be that of skipping the stage of the affluent society. Backward peoples by their poverty and weakness may be forced to forego the aggressive and wasteful use of science and technology, to keep the productive apparatus *à la mesure de l'homme*, under his control, for the satisfaction and development of vital individual and collective needs.

For the overdeveloped countries, this chance would be tantamount to the abolition of the conditions under which man's labor perpetuates, as self-propelling power, his subordination to the productive apparatus, and, with it, the obsolete forms of the struggle for existence. The abolition of these forms is, just as it has always been, the task of political action, but there is a decisive difference in the present situation. Whereas previous revolutions brought about a larger and more rational development of the productive forces, in the overdeveloped societies of today, revolution would mean reversal of this trend: elimination of overdevelopment, and of its repressive rationality. The rejection of affluent productivity, far from being a commitment to purity, simplicity, and "nature," might be the token (and weapon) of a higher stage of human development, based on the achievements of the technological society. As the production of wasteful and destructive goods is discontinued (a stage which would mean the end of capitalism in all its forms) – the somatic and mental mutilations inflicted on man by this production may be undone. In other words, the shaping of the environment, the transformation of nature, may be propelled by the liberated rather than the repressed Life Instincts, and aggression would be subjected to their demands.

The historical chance of the backward countries is in the absence of conditions which make for repressive exploitative technology and industrialization for aggressive productivity. The very fact that the affluent warfare state unleashes its annihilating power on the backward countries illuminates the magnitude of the threat. In the revolt of the backward peoples, the rich societies meet, in an elemental and brutal form, not only a social revolt in the traditional sense, but also an instinctual revolt – biological hatred. The spread of guerilla warfare at the height of the technological century is a symbolic event: the energy of the human body rebels against intolerable repression and throws itself against the engines of repression. Perhaps the rebels know nothing about the ways of organizing a society, of constructing a socialist society; perhaps they are terrorized by their own leaders who know something about it, but the rebels' frightful existence is in total need of liberation, and their freedom is the contradiction to the overdeveloped societies.

Western civilization has always glorified the hero, the sacrifice of life for the city, the state, the nation; it has rarely asked the question of whether the established city, state, nation were worth the sacrifice. The taboo on the unquestionable prerogative of the whole has always been maintained and enforced, and it has been maintained and enforced the more brutally the more the whole was supposed to consist of free individuals. The question is now being asked – asked from without – and it is taken up by those who refuse to play the game of the affluents – the question of whether the abolition of this whole is not the precondition for the emergence of a truly human city, state, nation.

The odds are overwhelmingly on the side of the powers that be. What is romantic is not the positive evaluation of the liberation movements in the backward countries, but the positive evaluation of their prospects. There is no reason why science, technology, and money should not again do the job of destruction, and then the job of reconstruction in their own image. The price of progress is frightfully high, but we shall overcome. Not only the deceived victims but also their chief of state have said so. And yet there are photographs that show a row of half naked corpses laid out for the victors in Vietnam: they resemble in all details the pictures of the starved, emasculated corpses of Auschwitz and Buchenwald. Nothing and nobody can ever overcome these deeds, nor the sense of guilt which reacts in further aggression. But aggression can be turned against the aggressor. The strange myth according to which the unhealing wound can only be healed by the weapon that afflicted the wound has not yet been validated in history: the violence which breaks the chain of violence may start a new chain. And yet, in and against this continuum, the fight will continue. It is not the struggle of Eros against Thanatos, because the established society too has its Eros: it protects, perpetuates, and enlarges life. And it is not a bad life for those who comply and repress. But in the balance, the general presumption is that aggressiveness in defense of life is less detrimental to the Life Instincts than aggressiveness in aggression.

In defense of life: the phrase has explosive meaning in the affluent society. It involves not only the protest against neo-colonial war and slaughter, the burning of draft cards at the risk of prison, the fight for civil rights, but also the refusal to speak the dead language of affluence, to wear the clean clothes, to enjoy the gadgets of affluence, to go through the education for affluence. The new bohème, the beatniks and hipsters, the peace creeps – all these "decadents" now have become what decadence probably always was: poor refuge of defamed humanity.

Can we speak of a juncture between the erotic and political dimension?

In and against the deadly efficient organization of the affluent society, not only radical protest, but even the attempt to formulate, to articulate, to give word to protest assume a childlike, ridiculous immaturity. Thus it is ridiculous and perhaps "logical" that the Free Speech Movement at Berkeley terminated in the row caused by the appearance of a sign with the four-letter word. It is perhaps equally ridiculous and right to see deeper significance in the buttons worn by some of the demonstrators (among them infants) against the slaughter in Vietnam: MAKE LOVE, NOT WAR. On the other side, against the new youth who refuse and rebel, are the representatives of the old order who can no longer protect its life without sacrificing it in the work of destruction and waste and pollution. They now include the representatives of organized labor – correctly so to the extent to which employment within the capitalist prosperity depends on the continued defense of the established social system.

Can the outcome, for the near future, be in doubt? The people, the majority of the people in the affluent society, are on the side of that which is – not that which can and ought to be. And the established order is strong enough and efficient enough to justify this adherence and to assure its continuation. However, the very strength and efficiency of this order may become factors of disintegration. Perpetuation of the obsolescent need for full-time labor (even in a very reduced form) will require the increasing waste of resources, the creation of ever more unnecessary jobs and services, and the growth of the military or destructive sector. Escalated wars, permanent preparation for war, and total administration may well suffice to keep the people under control, but at the cost of altering the morality on which the society still depends. Technical progress, itself a necessity for the maintenance of the established society, fosters needs and faculties which are antagonistic to the social organization of labor on which the system is built. In the course of automation, the value of the social product is to an increasingly smaller degree determined by the labor time necessary for its production. Consequently, the real social need for productive labor declines, and the vacuum must be filled with unproductive activities. An ever larger amount of the work actually performed becomes superfluous, expendable, meaningless. Although these activities can be sustained and even multiplied under total administration, there seems to exist an upper limit to their augmentation. This limit would be reached when the surplus value created by productive labor no longer suffices to pay for non-production work. A progressive reduction of labor seems to be inevitable, and for this eventuality, the system has to provide for occupation without work; it has to develop needs which transcend the market economy and may even be incompatible with it.

The affluent society is in its own way preparing for this eventuality by organizing "the desire for beauty and the hunger for community," the renewal of the "contact with nature," the enrichment of the mind, and honors for "creation for its own sake." The false ring of such proclamations is indicative of the fact that, within the established system, these aspirations are translated into administered cultural activities, sponsored by the government and the big corporations – an extension of their executive arm into the soul of the masses. It is all but impossible to recognize in the aspirations thus defined those of Eros and its autonomous transformation of a repressive environment and a repressive existence. If these goals are to be satisfied without an irreconcilable conflict with the requirements of the market economy, they must be satisfied within the framework of commerce and profit. But this sort of satisfaction would be tantamount to denial, for the erotic energy of the Life Instincts cannot be freed under the dehumanizing conditions of profitable affluence. To be sure, the conflict between the necessary development of noneconomic needs which would validate the idea of the abolition of labor (life as an end in itself) on the one hand, and the necessity for maintaining the need for earning a living on the other is quite manageable (especially as long as the Enemy within and without can serve as propelling force behind the defense of the status quo). However, the conflict may become explosive if it is accompanied and aggravated by the prospective changes at the very base of advanced industrial society, namely, the gradual undermining of capitalist enterprise in the course of automation.

In the meantime, there are things to be done. The system has its weakest point where it shows its most brutal strength: in the escalation of its military potential (which seems to press for periodic actualization with ever shorter interruptions of peace and preparedness). This tendency seems reversible only under strongest pressure, and its reversal would open the danger spots in the social structure: its conversion into a "normal" capitalist system is hardly imaginable without a serious crisis and sweeping economic and political changes. Today, the opposition to war and military intervention strikes at the roots: it rebels against those whose economic and political dominion depends on the continued (and enlarged) reproduction of the military establishment, its "multipliers," and the policies which necessitate this reproduction. These interests are not hard to identify, and the war against them does not require missiles, bombs, and napalm. But it does require something that is much harder to produce – the spread of uncensored and unmanipulated knowledge, consciousness, and above all, the organized refusal to continue work on the material and *intellectual* instruments which are now being used against man – for the defense of the liberty and prosperity of those who dominate the rest.

To the degree to which organized labor operates in defense of the status quo, and to the degree to which the share of labor in the material process of production declines, *intellectual* skills and capabilities become social and political factors. Today, the organized refusal to cooperate of the scientists, mathematicians, technicians, industrial psychologists and public opinion pollsters may well accomplish what a strike, even a large-scale strike, can no longer accomplish but once accomplished, namely, the beginning of the reversal, the preparation of the ground for political action. That the idea appears utterly unrealistic does not reduce the political responsibility involved in the position and function of the intellectual in contemporary industrial society. The intellectual refusal may find support in another catalyst, the instinctual refusal among the youth in protest. It is their lives which are at stake, and if not their lives, their mental health and their capacity to function as unmutilated humans. Their protest will continue because it is a biological necessity. "By nature," the young are in the forefront of those who live and fight for Eros against Death, and against a civilization which strives to shorten the "detour to death" while controlling the means for lengthening the detour. But in the administered society, the biological necessity does not immediately issue in action; organization demands counter-organization. Today the fight for life, the fight for Eros, is the *political* fight.

# V

†"Beyond One-Dimensional Man" (1968) was found in the Marcuse archives in Frankfurt (#266.04). The text was delivered as the "First Annual Hans Meyerhoff Memorial Lecture" at UCLA on October 31, 1968. In a January 9, 1966 letter from Marcuse to T. W. Adorno, he writes: "You will have heard by now that my friends Hans Meyerhoff and Otto Kirchheimer have both died within two days of one another: Hans in an automobile accident; a student ran into him while he was sitting in a stationary car and he was crushed (he died on the operating table)."

After Meyerhoff's death, Marcuse was chosen to provide the first memorial lecture in honor of a man whom he described as his "best friend." Meyerhoff was, like Marcuse, a German refugee intellectual who emigrated in 1934 to the United States because of a Nazi edict forbidding the matriculation of Jewish students in German universities. He studied at the University of California at Berkeley and then Los Angeles, receiving a Ph.D. in philosophy at UCLA in 1942. In 1943, like Marcuse, he joined the Office of Strategic Services and, also with Marcuse, transferred to the Department of State, where he served as section chief in the Division of Research for Europe. Joining the Department of Philosophy at UCLA in 1948, he became a productive scholar and highly popular teacher, publishing books such as *Time in Literature* (1955) and editing an anthology *The Philosophy of History in Our Time* (1962). Like Marcuse, he was an early critic of US intervention in Vietnam and at the time of his death was working on a book on existentialism.

Letters from Marcuse's publisher at Beacon Press indicate that his 1969 text *An Essay on Liberation* was to be called *Beyond One-Dimensional Man*. An October 7, 1968 letter used this title, but by October 21, 1968 the reference was to *An Essay on Liberation*. Unfortunately, no letter in the Marcuse archive explains the switch, and so the title of the Meyerhoff lecture is the first text to signal that he was moving beyond the perspectives of his earlier 1960s work.

Marcuse did extensive textual revision in handwriting on the manuscript, making it difficult to transcribe. The text is one of the best expressions of Marcuse's late 1960s revolutionary optimism, which would decline under the force of circumstances in the 1970s. The lecture's provocative title implied a significant transformation in Marcuse's thought and perceptions of the contemporary historical situation. The study is indeed one of the most condensed expressions of Marcuse's synthesis of theory, politics, and art as forms of revolutionary transformation. Despite all the work on the text, it was never published, probably because Marcuse turned to work on the project that became *An Essay on Liberation* (1969). The Meyerhoff essay, however, provides one of the most concise and compressed expressions of his synthesis of philosophy, social theory, art, and politics, with special emphasis on the importance of art and culture as emancipatory forces, and is published here for the first time in the original.

# HANS MEYERHOFF

**═══════════════════**

Words Spoken at the UCLA
Memorial Service[†]
November 24, 1965

Hans concluded his last public speech at this University – in more than
one sense his last will and testament to you, to all of us – by quoting the
Bible:

> I have set before you life and death, blessing and cursing; therefore,
> choose life.

Hans had chosen life and blessing, and I want to recall what this meant to
him and to us, his friends.

Look at his publications: they are good, intelligent, sensitive, but
somehow, we feel, that is not it, that is not all of Hans, that is not Hans. He
was, not a writing but a living person – just being there, talking, helping.

For that what he wanted to say and to do, the printed communication
was too narrow, too dead; the printed word was too much abused in the
mouth of liars and deceivers. Hans had to speak, and when he spoke,
the works came alive with new meaning; they suddenly had a meaning – a
meaning inseparable from his smile, his anger, his sadness, and a meaning
very different from the academic, the ordinary one.

This is why his philosophy went beyond philosophy, into literature
and the arts – or rather recaptured the internal link between philosophy and
literature, the arts, music. Literature, art, music: not as edification, elevation,
but as a realm in which the tabooed and repressed ideas and images of the

human condition were still alive and true. They were the ideas and images which helped him to understand the world in which we live, to understand and describe it – the precarious happiness and the whole horror of this world.

He knew that if anything could be done to mitigate this horror, it had to be done by reaching the human beings who suffered and perpetrated this horror – by making them see and listen and know.

So he taught, and he loved to teach; he loved you, his students who knew that Hans stood behind his words. And these words gave you something – something that only a man could give for whom moral values were real, were empirical facts – vital needs without which one can certainly live – but not the life of a human being.

And this need to live his philosophy drove Hans to become political: to accuse, to speak out against the crimes against humanity no matter where and in what false name they were committed. Hans had made his choice: for life, for blessing. And this meant: against death and cursing. And this choice compelled him to break the silence, to fight those who had chosen death and cursing – not only for themselves but also for the others, for us.

But Hans, who had chosen life, had to die. His death was more than absurd: it was revolting, insane. And the human reaction against this death is, not in the wisdom that "there is a time to live and a time to die" but in Dylan Thomas' outcry:

> Do not go gently into that good night . . .
> Rage, rage against the dying of the light.

Like Camus, Hans was killed by the "absurdity in the modern world." But far better than Camus, Hans knew that it is a man-made absurdity, and that you, every one of us, can help to make it a little less absurd. In this knowledge, and for this goal, Hans lived and taught – without illusion, perhaps without hope, with his smile, which was cynical and loving in one. It will be very hard to forget this smile, to forget this voice and what it had to say. I hope that some of us will never succeed. . . .

Herbert Marcuse

# BEYOND
# ONE-DIMENSIONAL MAN

I dedicate this lecture to the memory of Hans Meyerhoff not only on personal grounds but also on very substantial and objective grounds. Not only because I was his personal friend; he was my closest friend. But also because I believe that the work of Hans Meyerhoff testifies to a trend of extreme importance for understanding what is going on among the young generation, among the intelligentsia as a whole in the present situation. I hope to be able to show you that my presentation will bring out the exemplary character of the work of Hans Meyerhoff.

The trend I am alluding to I would like to characterize, in a preliminary way, namely, as a strange transformation of philosophy, which involves the development from philosophy to politics via literature and art. This development tends toward a realization of philosophy, which is quite different from the one Marx foresaw, and quite different from the way it is often understood or rather misunderstood – namely, that instead of interpreting the world one should now go about changing it, an interpretation alien to the letter and the spirit of Marx.

Hans Meyerhoff's preoccupation with literature and art is, I think worth knowing. He was in the last years of his life chiefly occupied with an interpretation of existentialism, mainly with Camus and Sartre. Camus the philosopher of the absurd whose hero was the desperately happy Sisyphus; Camus, the great skeptic of the *homme revolte*, who believed "that there is but one truly serious philosophical problem, and that is suicide." The only decisive philosophical question to him was whether or not life is worth living. And Camus linked the problem of suicide with the problem of rebellion. He saw the rebel as one who attempts to solve the problem of murder: extreme violence as answer to the absurdity of the world. Is this the end of philosophy? Contrast for one minute these propositions, this definition of the decisive problems of philosophy with the beginnings of modern philosophy, with Descartes for whom the *ego cogitans*, the human subject, quite far from being absurd, helpless, suicidal or murderous was Reason itself, the rational subject which would transform the world in the interest of man: a thoroughly optimistic philosophy. Or contrast existentialism with Hegel, for whom the world was one giant realization of reason. And, now apparently the collapse of this entire universe of discourse, and the rebellion against it on all fronts, in theory and practice, in the student revolt of our days, in the Black Power Movement, in Vietnam, in Chicago. These are not some of the normal problems that beset a dynamic society, they are a questioning, an indictment and refusal of the whole. The very essence of this society has become questionable, its comforts as well as its evils. This rebellion experiences the absurdity of this society, the absurdity of its reason, the destructiveness of its productivity, and the unbearable contrast between technical and human progress. So we can almost paraphrase Hegel's famous pair of propositions in saying: the real is absurd and the absurd is rational. Hans Meyerhoff certainly knew about the absurdity of life, he fought it the greatest part of his life, and at the very time when he seemed to win his life was cut short. Absurdity triumphed again.

In the face of this prevailing absurdity, what are the possibilities of philosophy today, at least a philosophy which is committed to the human condition? I think we can distinguish three alternatives. Firstly, simply the cancellation of the commitment, namely, the transformation of philosophy into a professional technique. Secondly, a conformist empiricism and behaviorism; confinement of philosophy to the petrified universe of mutilated discourse and manipulated action. And thirdly, the radical transformation of philosophy, which, as we shall see, leads to the self-transcendence of philosophy.

I would like to discuss very briefly this last trend and again take as starting point the example of the development of existentialism. In its first phase, existentialism has a strong tone of resignation, even the reconciliation with the absurd reality – in the vision of Camus: Sisyphus in hell, condemned for eternity to roll the heavy stone up the mountain only in order to see it rolling down again once it has reached the top. Camus wants us to see this Sisyphus as "happy and free," happy and free because he has recognized the absurdity, the eternal futility to which he is condemned, and he makes this absurdity his own task and will, the act of his freedom. Then, the job becomes his own, it is no longer imposed upon him by the authority of the Gods, he himself is doing the job, and in this freedom he is happy.

Let me add to this paradoxical definition of human freedom another one: according to Sartre, human freedom is inalienable to such an extent that man remains free even in the most enslaving conditions. The Jews in the Nazi concentration camps who were driven to the gas chambers were potentially free. Because they could have refused to go – in which case they would have defined themselves freely instead of accepting the definition given to them by the others. The consequences were of course known to Sartre as they are known to us.

Today the revolt against the absurd rationality of the system has gone beyond this of existentialism; it has refused to accept this horrible definition of human freedom, which serves to sustain actual unfreedom. The obsolescence of this philosophy has become clear. It has become clear under the impact of several interrelated developments which called for a response to absurdity far more militant, far more radical than the one given by the existentialists. Two main tendencies which called for such a more radical response are first the fact that after the military defeat of Fascism and National Socialism the social systems of domination and exploitation were restored, though streamlined, technically rationalized, and made more productive. They were restored in both camps, in the West in the reform of corporate capitalism, in the East in the form of the repressive bureaucratic and authoritarian construction of socialism. The second trend is the emergence and for the time being the containment of the alternative also in both camps, namely, the possibility, and perhaps the beginning of a truly libertarian, humanistic construction of socialism. Desperate efforts in this direction are being made in Cuba and perhaps in the Chinese Cultural Revolution. A third event which radicalized the protest was the symbolic fact of Vietnam, namely, the effective, sustained and successful resistance of one of the poorest and weakest people of the earth against the greatest superpower known in history – a resistance which showed that the superpower was vulnerable, and that solidarity can be an effective weapon. Fourthly, rebellion within the superpower itself, and among social groups other than the industrial working class – a development of decisive significance for the prospects of radical change.

The representative philosopher of our time responds to this development. Jean Paul Sartre dissociates himself from his earlier writings, he has performed the symbolic act of refusing the Nobel Prize, he has stepped up direct political action as a member of the Russell war crime tribunal, he is helping to organize a congress of radical left-wing groups. But at the same time he continues his literary criticism, he writes on Flaubert and Tintoretto; the aesthetic dimension remains his concern. Radicalization here appears in a dual form: in political activism, and in the intense occupation with literature and art; immersion in the political reality on the one hand, in the realm of imagination on the other. The first way expresses the vital need to demonstrate the philosophical commitment to the human existence beyond the usual abstract and academic protest. To the degree to which the university and the cultural establishment as a whole succumb to the requirements of the status quo and its streamlined reproduction, to that degree is the critique driven beyond the classroom and beyond the study into the reality outside. Is the second way, the one into the aesthetic realm, the realm of the imagination perhaps internally related to the first, part of the political activism? Does perhaps the political effort itself, by virtue of its new goals and strategy, break open an entirely new dimension of politics?

I suggest that the efforts toward radical social change are today confronted with an entire universe of possibilities, ideas, values which have been devitalized, supersubliminated, fictionalized in the traditional culture and which now appear saturated with realism and with political content. Thus, the imagination appears as rational faculty, as catalysts of radical change. What is happening is that the real possibilities of liberation, the real possibilities of creating a free and rational society are so overwhelming, so extreme, so "impossible" in terms of the status quo, and that the powers which counteract and discredit these possibilities are so strong that the effort to translate these possibilities into reality must transcend the entire irrational rationality of the status quo. They must find their own new modes of expression, their own strategy, their own language, their own style so that they are not caught up in the rotten political universe of today and defeated before they have started. I believe that today's rebels have become conscious of this necessity, of the need for breaking with a past which is still the present.

This opening of the one-dimensional society, this prospect of a rupture with the continuum of domination and exploitation has its material basis, its emerging basis in the aggravating economic stresses of the global system of corporate capitalism, such as: inflation, international monetary crisis, intensified competition among the imperialist powers, escalation of waste and destruction in the absorption of the economic surplus in the militant opposition in its metropoles, and in the liberation movements in the Third World. And on this basis, new values, new resources, and new faculties of contestation and reconstruction make their appearance as political forces.

There is a symbolic event which, though by itself transitory and relatively quickly contained by the power structure, illuminates the historical turning point, namely, the May–June events in France. They have been abundantly written up, they have been tabled, they have been maltreated by sociologists and psychologists, and yet no analysis and no evaluation of the actual prospects for liberation are adequate without this starting point. Let me try to summarize briefly the implications of these events. They have shown that the movement toward radical change can originate outside the laboring classes, and that this outside force in turn can activate, as a catalyst, the repressed rebellious force among the laboring classes. Moreover, and this is perhaps the most important aspect of these events, strategies, goals, and values emerged which went beyond the century old conceptual and political framework of the opposition and of politics as a whole. These new strategies and goals indicate the emergence of a new consciousness, an anticipating, projecting consciousness, open and ready for the radically new extravagant prospects of freedom.

What is at stake here is indeed a transvaluation of values, a new rationality which opposes not only the rationality of capitalism in all its forms but also the rationality of Stalinist and post-Stalinist socialism. And this new consciousness expresses (and shapes) a new sensitivity and sensibility, a new experience of the established – and the repressed – reality which anchors the quest, the cry for liberation in the vital needs of man: in his "bondage". *L'homme revolté*: that is today he or she whose senses can no longer see and hear and taste what is offered to them, whose very instincts militate against oppression, cruelty, ugliness, hypocrisy and exploitation. And who also rebels on these same grounds, against the traditional higher culture of the West – rebel against it because of its affirmative, reconciling, "illusory" features. This rebellion aims at a *desublimation of culture* – revocation, *Aufhebung* of its idealizing, repressive power. It is the protest against a culture which treated freedom and equality as "inner" values: freedom of conscience, abstract equality – before God, before the Law, and thus more or less peacefully coexisting with actual unfreedom and inequality. Protest against the romantization and internalization of love, against the illusory beautification and mitigation of the horror of reality.

Now "desublimination of culture" is, according to Freud an impossible concept, in itself contradictory because all culture is sublimation, is unthinkable without sublimation and desublimation could only mean a return, a regression to uncivilized and pre-civilized stages of history. However, I suggest that the desublimation which is demanded today is not an undoing of civilization but an undoing only of the archaic exploitative aspects of civilization. Far from undoing and regressing it is rather the reintegration into civilization of human faculties, needs and satisfactions which have been reduced, mutilated and distorted in the tradition of exploitative civilization. And this mutilation has brought about, as a reaction, those prevalent frustrations which erupt in that surplus aggression and destruction so rampant in our time. In other words, this desublimation is a revolt only against the repressive aspects of a culture which fostered the false consciousness, the hypocritical morality, the administered forms of fun and elevation, the self-righteous submission to the management of human relations in our society.

The rebellion strives to extend the consciousness of man beyond the limits imposed by the requirements of domination and this means activation of the repressed imagination and sensibility of man – their use as faculties in the radical construction of reality. The imagination would recapture its creative power to project real possibilities of human freedom, not only in terms of fiction, as a poetic truth, as artistic forms, but also in terms of political goals. And the liberated sensibility, the sensitivity of man, would provide the instinctual, biological foundation in the reconstruction. This process is going on before our eyes, it is going on in the music, in the literature, in the language of protest; it is also going on in the behavior, in the apparel, in the experience, in the gestures of the rebels. The negating, destructive features are prevalent. The revolt against the sublime forms of art terminates in the rejection of the art-form itself. The integration of art into life is negation of art. There is in the work of Thomas Mann, the terrifying sentence which says, "one must revoke the Ninth Symphony"; it is perhaps the most extreme, the most radical sentence in modern literature. One must revoke the Ninth Symphony inasmuch as it is the most familiar sublime achievement of this culture: the sorrows of reality turn harmoniously into the Hymn of Joy.

Can we say that this revocation of the Ninth Symphony is already on the way? Can we say that rock n' roll has "rolled over" Beethoven? Is it true that the "living theater" of our days is the revocation of the traditional theatre? And is it true that Black Power is one of the political manifestations of the revocation, and that the Yippies practice this revocation? Common to all of them is the fight against suffocating, oppressive hypocritical spirit of seriousness and righteousness, which permeates our society. Yes, if our politicians are serious, the only adequate opposition to them seems to be defiance of this seriousness, not to accept their standards of discourse and behavior.

Obviously, the protest envisions changes of a magnitude that indeed defies the imagination, namely, a society which differs essentially not only from the established capitalist, but also from the established socialist societies, which frees not only the rational but also the sensuous capabilities of man, not only his productivity but also his receptivity, which fortifies his life instincts, Eros as against Thanatos. It would not be governed by the laws and requirements of self-propelling, competitive, profitable performances; i.e. by the laws of domination. The vision is that of the historical movement when man calls a halt to the rat race that has been his existence, when man takes stock of what he has and what he can do with it, and decides that instead of going on with the rat race, instead of producing ever more and ever bigger for those who can and must buy it, to subvert the very mode and direction of production, and thereby of their entire life. This means, to abolish poverty, and then to devote all resources to the elimination of the spiritual and material garbage with which the established societies have covered not figuratively but literally, our mental and physical space, and to construct a peaceful and beautiful universe.

The rebels are aware of the fact that this goal transcends all the reasonableness and rationality of the Establishment. Beyond the rule of Reason (this Reason) is that of the imagination. One of the slogans that appeared on the wall of the Sorbonne in May of last year read: "all power to the imagination." It has been said (and I agree with the statement) that the fourth volume of Marx' *Capital* was written on the walls of the Sorbonne; we can add that Kant's fourth *Critique* was written on the same walls, namely the critique of productive imagination.

The idea of reason, the rationality which permeates the established universe of discourse and behavior can no longer serve as a guide, is no longer qualified to define the goals and possibilities of human endeavor, of human morality, of human science, of social organization, of political action. The traditional concepts were developed and defined in a universe of domination and scarcity, where they went beyond these historical limits as in the philosophy of radical enlightenment, they remained largely abstract, or divorced from the historical practice. But then the question naturally arises: is there anything beyond the established rationality, anything other than mere fantasy, fiction, utopian speculation?

Here we have to recapture the old philosophical distinction between imagination and fantasy. The productive [imagination] is, according to Kant, the central cognitive faculty of the mind; it is the meeting ground between sensibility and understanding, percept and concept, body and mind. As cognitive faculty, the imagination is guiding the scientific projection and experimentation with the possibilities and capabilities of matter; it is playful, free, and yet bound by its material, and rooted in the historical continuum. As cognitive faculty, the imagination forms the work of art, literature, music; there it creates a reality of its own and yet *real*: in a sense more real than the given reality. Words, images, tones, gestures which deny the claim of the given reality to be all the reality and the entire reality. They deny this claim in the name of the suppressed possibilities of human relationships, of man and nature, of freedom.

Now it is perhaps clear what is meant by the political content of the slogan "all power to the imagination." The slogan expresses the militant consciousness of the suppressed possibilities, and of the degree to which they render obsolete not only the traditional theories and strategies of change but also the traditional goals of change. The leap from the rationality of scarcity and domination to the realm of freedom demands the concrete transcendence beyond this rationality, it demands new ways of seeing, hearing, feeling, touching things, a new mode of experience of corresponding to the needs of men and women who can and must fight for a free society. The historical situation thus makes the imagination into a meta-political power, and joins the playful, the creative, the sensuous aesthetic needs with the harsh political exigencies. This strange alliance has found its most striking form in the fact that the two names who appeared most frequently on the walls of the University of Paris were Karl Marx, the founder of socialism and André Breton, the founder of surrealism. And during the very night in Paris, where the fight on the barricades took place, a piano stood between the barricades, and the young pianist was playing jazz music.

These liberating forces are faced with a society which has mobilized its own imagination to full strength; it has devised forms of control which counteract liberation at its very roots in the mind of man: in the expression and communication of his needs, thoughts, and feelings. The protest movement is therefore driven to develop its own language, which must be different from that of the Establishment and yet remain understandable – a fact which contributes to the division of the movement into small self-contained groups and cliques. The linguistic rebellion struggles against the linguistic repression practiced by the Establishment: it recognizes the extent to which, in any historical period, a language expresses the given (and primarily the given) form of reality, and thus blocks the imagination and the reason of man, adjusts him to the given universe of discourse and behavior. This is the recognition that language is one of the most powerful weapons in the arsenal of the Establishment.

Today, it is a language of unprecedented brutality and sweetness in one, an Orwellian language which, holding a practical monopoly in the means of communication, stifles the consciousness, obscures and defames the alternative possibilities of existence, implants the needs of the status quo in the mind and body of men and makes them all but immune against the need for change.

But this immunization has its limits. They are inherent in the development of our society, particularly in the dynamic of the "second industrial revolution." In contrast to the first it was directly sparked by science and it is characterized by the almost immediate application of science in production and distribution. Not only application of natural sciences in mathematics but also of the social sciences, in publicity and politics, of psychology, in the frightful social science of human relations and even in literature and music as welcome stimulus, mild stimulus because you can't get too stimulated as background for business. Here you have in one reality the strange symbiosis of scientific humanistic thought and a repressive society, the symbiosis of creativity and productivity in which the intellectual culture serves the material culture, in which creativity serves productivity, in which imagination serves business. But the all but complete character of this symbiosis in which scientific and humanistic thought become engines of social control has now its own dynamic, namely the greater the achievement of science in mastering nature and exploiting its resources the greater the danger that the psychological and biological experiments in forming human behavior and in forming the life processes may get out of hand, and the wilder the capacity of the imagination in projecting ways and means of alleviating the human existence, the more obvious the contrast between these achievements and their usage. And the greater the explosive potential in the established societies. Consequently, the first form in which this explosive potential comes into consciousness [is of] the irrationalization which is going in within the established society, the political activation of minorities on the margin of integration and even perhaps loosening the cohesion of organized labor, loosening it although which way and in which direction still remains to be seen.

Now this situation brings us face to face with the question of the responsibility of the intellectual. The choice is dictated to the intellectual by the two faces of the symbiosis of science and society, imagination and domination which we find today. This choice can be formulated in the following question. Man's reason, imagination, sensibility shall they be in the service of ever more efficient and prosperous servitude or rather or shall they serve to cut this link, releasing man's faculties and his imagination and sensibility from this profitable bondage? I believe that the militant students have made this choice and they have paid dearly for it. Today the real possibilities of human freedom are so real and the crimes of the society which prevents their realization are so blatant that the philosopher, the educator can no longer avoid taking sides, and that means alliance, solidarity with those who are no longer capable and no longer willing to have their future, to have their existence determined and defined by the requirements of the status quo. Determined and defined by the powers, the very powers that have made the world the mess, the threat and the lie which it is today. We see that today students all over the globe in the East as well as in the West, in the Third World as well as in the First and Second are demonstrating this unwillingness, the refusal. If the philosopher, the educator still takes seriously his job of enlightenment he will find himself whether he wants it or not with those who want to give meaning and reality to the words and ideas he has taught during his life as educator, and not only academic meaning but a meaning to be fought for, a meaning to be lived for.

For Hans Meyerhoff this was not choice but a necessity and he has demonstrated it too. I have tried to sketch the inner logic of the way he was going, a way that was cut short in a gruesome and absurd manner. You have after his death named the free speech area on this campus after him. Let's work for the extension of free speech beyond this area.

# VI

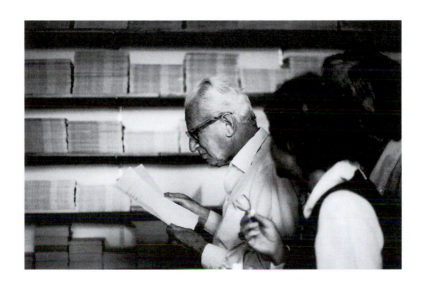

†"Cultural Revolution" (n.d., around 1970) is one of the most highly developed and interesting of the unpublished manuscripts found in the Marcuse archives in Frankfurt (# 406). The text that appears here is based on an 85-page unpublished manuscript without title or date. It is apparently written after *An Essay on Liberation* (there are references to texts published in 1969 in the notes and it appears to be a follow-up to *Essay*). It takes up many of the themes in the essay "Beyond One-Dimensional Man" and develops them further in the light of political events of the period in which it was written. The text is polished and ready for publication; there are on the manuscript, however, a number of marginal comments and some edits in the handwriting of Marcuse's third wife, Ericka (Ricky) Sherover-Marcuse whom he married in 1976; we have included edits which correct typos or add obviously missing words (which we signal in brackets), but have ignored the edits on the manuscript which alter the meanings of Marcuse's original text and are not in Marcuse's own handwriting.

It is not clear why Marcuse did not publish this text and I have been unable to find any references to it in his letters, nor have I found anyone with precise bibliographical information on the text's genesis and why it was not published. Some of the themes were taken up in *Counterrevolution and Revolt* (1972) but, as I note in this volume's introduction, the conception of cultural revolution and the more positive references to political movements of the moment were more highly developed in the unpublished manuscript that we publish here in the original for the first time. Hence, the text remains an important indicator of Marcuse's views of the significance of "cultural revolution" for radical social transformation and is perhaps his last major expression of revolutionary optimism before turning more pessimistic as the 1960s movements faded away and conservative forces once again became hegemonic.

# CULTURAL REVOLUTION†

The changes that occur before our eyes in our society, confront those who reflect on them without clichés with a disturbing phenomenon. The pattern presented by these changes does not accord with even the most sophisticated theories and projections. To mention only the most conspicuous deviations:

- the "displacement" of the radical opposition from the traditional "Left," the industrial working class, to a "New Left," loosely comprising middle class groups such as salaried employees in the basic as well as servicing industries, large sections among the youth, primarily the student movement, and oppressed racial and national minorities;
- the sustained conservatism of the masses (the not at all silent majority);
- the increasing ineffectiveness and restriction of the democratic process;
- the growing direct power of the government, especially its executive branch;
- the continued high level performance of advanced capitalism in spite of intensifying global economic difficulties.

I shall not discuss these tendencies here, but rather focus on the perhaps most outstanding feature of today's radicalism, namely, the *total* character of its claim: subversion not only of the established economic and political structure, but also (and even primarily) of the entire established *culture*, which the radicals define as "bourgeois culture." This cultural revolution ranges from the ways of dressing, selecting and preparing food, sexual behavior, language, to the denial of, and opposition to, the most celebrated works of art, literature, music. It may not be too exaggerated to say that this cultural revolution not only precedes and prepares the soil for the political revolution (including the economic changes), but that it has, at the present stage, *absorbed* the political revolution.

I believe that the total character of the rebellion (I use this term in order to indicate that it is not yet a revolution, but may issue in a revolution) corresponds to the objective conditions presented by twentieth century capitalism. Under these conditions, the basic economic institutions and relationships reproduce themselves through the extension of social management and controls to all spheres of society – including those branches of culture which were formerly left relatively free to develop according to their own inherent dynamic. This systematic integration of culture into the Establishment meets its counterpart (definite negation) in the total claim of the rebellion: "cultural revolution."

Now in its striving for totality, the cultural revolution is discovering (or rather recapturing) a neglected or suppressed basis of revolution, namely, its roots in the *individual* – more specifically, in the *sensibility* of man. In truly dialectical fashion, it is in a new individual that a new totality of life is to emerge. The new society is to originate in the individuals themselves: not as the result of a fictitious consent or contract, not as the marketplace of competing interests and votes, but as an extension, natural as well as rational, of the needs and faculties of free men. This freedom begins with the emancipation of the human senses.

The effort to anchor the social revolution in the sensibility of man resumes an old (but ruptured) tradition, which goes back to the libertarian sects of the Middle Ages, to the French Enlightenment, Fourier, the young Marx. The tradition has been defeated.

In a sense all historical revolutions have been abortive revolutions: they have replaced one form of domination, one ruling class by another. But they were also partial revolutions in still another sense: they suppressed the libertarian movements which operated in all of them which strove beyond a change in social stratification. To be sure, their failure is well explicable in terms of the immaturity of the productive forces, material and intellectual. But one aspect of this immaturity is precisely the suppression, and atrophy, of the roots of liberation in the instinctual structure of the individuals, and consequently, in their sensibility. Therefore, Freudian theory looms large in the only two radical liberation movements of the period: in the surrealist movement, and in the New Left.

In view of these facts (or rather hypotheses), I want to discuss the question whether perhaps the radical effort to free the roots of liberation in the individual opens a road to social changes in accord with the unprecedented resources of the twentieth century – whether it offers a historical chance to prevent repetition of the traditional pattern of the revolution gone sour, of the realm of freedom indefinitely postponed.

The realm of freedom has existed in history only as desired goal – it was precisely its absence which spurred the efforts toward its realization. Consequently, the latter would be a break with the continuum of history as the reality of unfreedom. But this continuum allows of no break: all revolutions start from a base within the old society, and change an existing base. Mediation of the old and the new: the process of change takes place while an identical substratum "joins" the two stages of the process together. This substratum is constituted by the attained level of the productive forces: the "system" (for it is an organized whole) of the material and intellectual resources available to society. It is the given Subject (qua substance) of change which extends the old into the new, and this extension takes place in various forms: in science, technology and technique, in the work relationships exacted by them, and in the given natural and inherited environment. And this substratum continually shapes the consciousness of men, their mental structure in its rational and subrational dimensions. The rupture, the leap into the new, takes this heritage along: it is bound to reassert itself and to make the new a prolongation (though perhaps improved) of the old – it is bound to continue the inherited unfreedom *unless* the process of change finds, in the substratum itself, a base for the total transformation. And this base must itself be the antithesis of the given reality – its definite negation. This desideratum is fulfilled in Marxism by the dual force of the proletariat, and the translation of socialist theory into practice. Being actual forces in but not *of* the existing society, they would be capable of initiating the process of qualitative change: breaking with the past and present society (the continuum of repression) and yet translating a historical alternative into reality (remaining within the historical continuum). Dialectical theory designates this relation between the old and the new as "definite negation."

But dialectical theory remains throughout committed to history: the dialectical concepts are historical constructs. This means that the base for qualitative change itself changes in the development. It must be emphasized that the Marxian base is, in both forms, a *human* base: the revolutionary class and the theory guiding its practice. They are *particular* historical forces in a *particular* historical situation; how can they possibly "embody" and represent that *universality* which is the essential feature of freedom? How can their needs and interests, and their theory claim objectively, general validity for man as man, for humanity? The dialectic of historical change here reveals itself as the dialectic of the universal and the particular. The former "exists" only *in the latter* – not as a mysterious or metaphysical entity, but as the needs and aspirations of individual men and women. This community becomes articulate in a common consciousness, operative (at various degrees of awareness) in the individual consciousness of the members of the respective social class. But the common consciousness of a class is universal only to the extent to which this class represents the interest of the society as a whole. Evidently, this universality has thus far been real only to a very limited extent. It is not necessary to restate the familiar argument by which Marx identified the proletariat as the only class whose particular interest represented the needs and aspirations of man as man, of humanity. In the Marxian conception, class consciousness is not identical with the (immediate) individual consciousness but rather is its theoretical accentuation and transformation, and a similar (even wider) discrepancy characterizes the needs and aspirations: they are not immediately identical with those of the class, that is to say, with the necessity of revolution. In his early writings, Marx assumes such a harmony between the particular interest of the proletariat, and the general interest of humanity: the vital need, the most concrete need of the proletarian is to attain a human existence, to become a human being. The inhuman, subhuman, life of the proletariat was, as it were, the brutal, impenetrable existential condition which withstood all "cooption" by the established society – the base on which the revolutionary consciousness and practice could emerge.

With the subsequent modification of this conception, Marxian theory followed, and projected, the development of the capitalist society. Exploitation and impoverishment were no longer inseparable, and the revolution was no longer predicated on the latter. To the degree to which capitalism progressed, it developed new forms of integrating the underlying population. In the advanced regions of contemporary capitalism, the needs and aspirations of the laboring classes tend to become affirmative, reproducing the society which they were to negate – reproducing it in the mental structure which was to be the individual base for generating the antithesis, the definite negation.

This does not mean that the laboring classes have ceased to be a Subject of radical change. As long as these classes continue to produce, without controlling their production, the necessities and luxuries which the established society needs, the laboring classes will be the sole power capable of redirecting and reorganizing the process of production. But here, the ambiguities begin. Redirect in what direction? Toward the improving, in efficiency or in equitable distribution of wealth, the existing society, or toward a qualitatively different society? Toward collective self-determination and solidarity, or toward another form of domination?

In the Marxian conception, this ambiguity did not prevail (though it is suggested in the recurrent alternative "socialism or barbarism"). But now, the integration of the working classes into the capitalist system of needs has vitiated the harmony between the class interest and the general interest of humanity: the integrated laboring class cannot (and does not) claim the presence of the universal in its particular practice.

The relation between the universal and the particular in the dialectic of change is a historical condition: the human base of change cannot remain identically the same when the social structure itself is changing: transformation of capitalist production *within* the framework of capitalism (Marx: disappearance of the capitalist within the framework of the capitalist mode of production).

In contemporary capitalism, such transformation is taking place. Its feature is the extension of the working class to include (as sources of surplus value and therefore as "productive labor") a very large part of the "middle classes": white collar workers, salaried employees, technicians, scientists, specialists of all sorts, even in the mere "service industries," publicity, etc.[1] This means the extension of exploitation as an objective condition (though to very different degrees of intensity) among an increasingly large part of the population. At the same time, and in the same process, the *consciousness* of this condition is diminishing or reduced among all but the victims of the most brutal exploitation: the oppressed racial and national minorities, unqualified labor, and, certainly, the laboring masses in the neo-colonial areas of the Third World. This discrepancy between existence and consciousness, between the objective and subjective condition, is far more than a psychological matter. It requires a re-examination of the human base of historical change, of the concept of "class"; it indicates a *lacuna* in dialectical theory. It seems that one decisive factor has not been conceptually incorporated into this theory, namely, the individual as the particular human being who, being the member of a class, still remains the "natural," elementary agent of change, who, no matter how much he may be "socialized," can never be "dissolved" into an aliquot part of a class: his concreteness resists abstract generalization.

Marxian theory takes into account this individual factor in the distinctions between class consciousness and individual consciousness, real needs and immediate needs. However, these distinctions do not go far enough: they do not reach into the dimension where, for good or bad, the human being constitutes itself as individual: that of his *body*, man as a "natural," "objective" (*gegenständliches*) being. To be sure, this dimension too, is historical, modified continually in the development of civilization, but it remains nevertheless an agent of change, base of change "underneath"

---

1 The extension of the sources of surplus value may well go hand in hand with the reduction of the *rate* of surplus value. See Gillman, *The Falling Rate of Profit*.

its other dimensions, "underneath" the material and intellectual culture, "underneath" even its substratum, the Marxian infrastructure. It cannot be left there, outside the main theoretical and practical concern. This neglect is part of a larger one: the minimization of the role of nature in history. Dialectical materialism has never really *aufgehoben* Feuerbach's "naturalism": it was bypassed rather than integrated into the developed theory of society.

The abundant attention paid to Marx' writings of 1844–45 has not changed this situation. Neither of the two main interpretations gets, I believe, at the roots of the problem. The first holds that these writings are the products of a metaphysical, or immature materialistic period of Marxian thought, which came to an end with the elaboration of the critique of the political economy. The second interpretation denies that there is a break between the younger and the mature Marx, and that the concepts of the former reappear, now concretized and fully developed in the mature theory.

The latter interpretation, closer to the truth, would see the earlier concepts "accomplished" in the economic-political theory: Feuerbach's naturalism, which founds the materialistic philosophy on the notion of man as "sensuous being," comes into its own (truth) in the idea of socialism as the definite negation of capitalism. If this is correct, the theoretical development would have lost precisely that dimension of individual concreteness, "nature," sensuousness, which was prevalent in the early writings, and these concepts and facts would be internally linked to the later theory only through a rather vague (and sometimes also romantic) "socialist humanism."

I suggest a third interpretation: the writings of 1844–45 must be read as if they find their theoretical (and practical) place and function *after Capital*, thus they would be an essential part of the projected transition from capitalism to socialism. In this context, they would indicate a new concept of the human base of the revolution; they would define the human agent of change in terms quite different from (though by no means invalidating and replacing) those which defined the proletariat as this agent. Is it merely the strong influence of Feuerbach which makes Marx, with passionate singlemindedness, center his conception of man as "sensuous being" on the "emancipation of the senses," on the aesthetic capability, productivity of man as "species being"? Is it only this influence, later overcome, which, in these writings, links the existence of man as *Gattungswesen* with the emancipation of the senses, and thus envisages the realization of the universal as the result of the productivity of man the sensuous being? Or has Marx here discovered the revolutionary potential in this sensuous, "aesthetic" dimension? Has he seen that exploitation, alienation, repression have their individual roots in this dimension, and that, in this dimension, the repressed individual reproduces these conditions, and, through them, his society? So that, consequently, with the abolition of capitalism, and in the construction of the socialist society, not only the consciousness of man, but also his sensibility, his senses and their activity (productivity) would radically change, and that, *vice versa*, the construction of socialism, as a qualitatively different society, would depend, would be the "product" of man as a new sensuous being. In any case, Marx states quite emphatically that the relation between man and nature, between him and the object world presuppose a qualitatively different *sensibility*: new modes of seeing, hearing, feeling. For the institution of private property has blunted, brutalized, and perverted man's sensibility, and this perverted sensibility has produced the alienated object world of class society. It is in this context that Marx develops the notion of a non-alienated mode of production, of an "aesthetic" construction of the object world, and of individual property as contrasting with private property.

These notions find their place in Marxian theory, structurally, *after Capital*, not merely because they convey the image of socialist man, but also because they presuppose Marx' full analysis of capitalist society. The dynamic of this society provides the ground, its economy constitutes the substratum on which the specific formation of the human sensibility takes place, and on which its emancipation must commence. And in the emancipated sensibility, Marx sees the roots of the "concrete universal": the realization of man as man, the existence of man as "species being": in the full development of the essentially human needs and faculties. Then, the question which I raised at the beginning: the question as to the possible objective validation of the higher Law and Order of freedom would receive an unexpected answer: the "innate ideas" turn out to be repressed claims of the human senses, and their universality, far from being a vague, rather abstract idea of humanity and humanism, would turn out to be a rather material, physiological condition. And the recollection, *Erinnerung* would be a capturing of *potentialities* of the human senses. And, to push speculation one step further, we may take the translation of Plato's concept literally and say that these potentialities are yet unrealized *Forms* of things: modes of existence of man and nature (*Dasein*) which would constitute a cosmos of *Justice* where satisfaction would be in the free human productivity in creating a good world for everyone.

The "concrete universal," freedom, humanity, can become real only with the abolition of class society. *Solidarity*, the "form" of this universal, would then be in the very senses of man, or, more precisely, in their "activity," productivity. Marx emphasizes, in opposition to the idealistic concept of the mental structure, that the senses are *active*: the eye, the ear, the nose, the hand, the tongue do not merely "receive" stimuli from outside; the senses let something happen with these stimuli: they become stimuli for acting, doing; and their sensuous, sensual quality is preserved, enters into the subsequent activity. Or, the sensuous quality would be preserved in the activity of production: free and creative in a free society, blunted and brutalized in the formation of the object world of class society. And in the medium of its object world, the blunted sensibility also enters into, shapes the relationships among men.

In the formation of the object world: the blunted sensibility learns to live with, to like, and to reproduce ("taste" as factor in the production of commodities) the things which make up the capitalist universe, its material and intellectual culture. While their use value, as exchange value, determines to a great extent their "form," the taste of the consumer enters into the determination of the form (example: *the libidinal cathexis of the automobile* and other instruments of power and efficiency becomes a factor in their production). Moreover, the senses learn to accept (as a necessity of life) and to reproduce noise, pollution, ugliness, violence – qualities which become embodied in the transformation of the natural and technical environment. They also spread through the intellectual culture: this is the repressive aspect of the destruction of classical and romantic aesthetic forms (in the arts, music, literature) which is all too readily praised as avant-gardistic. Dissonance, violence, brutality, and desublimation are not *per se* liberating; in the new arts and anti-arts too, they may well serve (as they do in the mass media) to sustain rather than weaken the existing society[2] – unless they make apparent the very opposite qualities which pertain to the universe of liberation.

The object world of this mutilated sensibility constitutes the universe of human relationships which are "a priori" antagonistic, even hostile, so that non-antagonistic relationships of solidarity can emerge and maintain themselves only by counteracting primary hostility, overcoming the barriers which separate men from each other, not as individuals, but as aliquot parts of the same universe. This means that the individuals are not set off from each other by virtue of *their own* proper needs and faculties but rather by virtue of their place and function in the pregiven social division of labor and pleasure.

In a capitalist society, the *principium individuationis* is not the realization of the universal (man as man) through the specific human faculties in the

---

2 Nothing perhaps illustrates better the utterly regressive character of avant-gardistic mass culture than the alliance between the rock 'n' roll crowds and the Hell's Angels, or the sickening glorification of murder gangs by self-styled radicals.

individuals, but rather the "law of value" which governs the exchange of commodities: the individual is "made" in accordance with his usefulness, his "value" for a society based on the production and exchange of commodities. This society must promote individuality not only on ideological grounds (against the evil collectivism of "socialism") but also as the subject of private enterprise and free competition – institutions which have long since made this subject into an object. Such a society precludes solidarity (the concrete form of the universal) in any form other than that confined to a particular group or class, organized and administered rather than spontaneous – except in sudden accidents and emergencies (and even then it seems to become increasingly shaky). Cooperation, under capitalism, is a technical necessity which in turn shapes the individual needs and faculties. Beyond and beneath, it appears as cooperation *against* the system. The individual can become individual only in its negation: his freedom is restricted to freedom *from*. This holds true particularly in that existential dimension where mine and thine, I and the other, are most immediately one: in the erotic relationships. They form a sphere of privacy against the alienated world, and in this sphere, the nuclei of a different environment, a different object world are taking shape. Erotic energy, freely sublimated, strives to create a "humanized" relationship to nature and to technique – a humanized ecology. Marx speaks of "human appropriation," of individual property (in contrast to private property) and sees in its establishment an essential feature of socialism. The emancipation of the senses is a prerequisite for the transformation of private into individual property, and the object world emerging in this transformation is that of *solidarity*, the concrete universal.

[margin handwritten note: *Marcuse and the emancipation of the senses*]

In order to understand this idea, we must go back to the notion of the senses as *active* (organs). Freed from their blunted condition, they would develop new modes of seeing, hearing, feeling; they would perceive (and imagine) new forms of the objects of their needs – new potentialities of things, natural as well as technical. Thus the "emancipation of the senses" is a transformation of the Subject *and* the Object: the new vision of the senses actively changes the object world to the degree to which the perception of the new forms of things motivates and guides the *praxis* of reconstructing the natural and technical environment.

Reconstructing in what direction? In the very context where Marx speaks of the (future, free) existence of man as "species being," he distinguishes man from animal by the specifically human faculty to form his environment "in accordance with the laws of *beauty*."[3] Together with this emphasis

---

3 *Economic-Philosophic Manuscripts of 1844*, ed. Dirk J. Struik (New York, International Publishers, 1964), p. 114.

on the emancipated sensuousness of man as token of his liberation, and on the senses as the basis of all science, this conception designates the aesthetic dimension as the "space" of socialism – "aesthetic" in the dual meaning of pertaining to the senses and pertaining to art. I believe that this conception, far from being an immature, utopian speculation, reveals an aspect of socialist theory which cannot be neglected without distorting the essence of socialism itself.

In this case, humanity, the solidarity of the species, would be rooted in the specific capability of man as a sensuous rather than rational being, or, his rationality would receive its primary impetus, and direction from his sensibility – not only epistemologically, as the first source of knowledge (understanding and reason), but also as the ground on which the *Lebenswelt* of humanity, the solidarity of reason must emerge. In other words, the sensibility of man, his body as mental-physical entity, would not only be the medium for the *principium individuationis* but also for its opposite: *universalization*, that is to say, the emergence of *humanitas*, of man as man, solidarity. And the realization of humanitas implies the establishment of a new (sensuous) relationship between man and nature. Nature would become a Subject in its own right and *Telos*: as the environment and soil of freedom, which is incompatible with the enslavement and violation of nature, its treatment as a mere object. In other words, the object would be experienced as subject to the degree to which the subject, man, makes the object world into a humane world. Realization of nature through the realization of man as "species being": for nature too, has become an object of destructive exploitation – nature too calls for liberation.

This is what Marx called the human "appropriation" of the object world: the establishment of human relationships with nature, the humanization of things. It means that the world is no longer experienced as a commodity market, nor men as buyers or sellers of labor power, nor things as the mere stuff of possession and use. What appears in this radically new experience is a use value no longer contaminated by exploitation: the experience that things, without losing their use value, exist in their own right, their own form – that they are sensitive. Exploitation is not really abolished, its heritage not really thrown off until man has established this new relationship to nature: the humanization of nature would also enable man to have the good conscience of his own nature, of himself as part of nature. This is the "second nature": it is not the world of the *bon sauvage*, but that of high civilization – the promise of freedom.

Preserved in the images of poetry, methodically explored by the surrealists, confirmed by non-conformist scientists (Bachelard) and architects, invading even Richard Wagner's magic-totalitarian music (the motive of liberated nature in the *Ring des Nibelungen*, the *Karfreitagszauber* in *Parsifal*), this promise has been consistently denounced as infantile anthropomorphism. Anthropomorphism indeed, but the Anthropos envisaged here is no other than the "socialist man": the man who is no longer caught up in the mystification of the commodity world, in the global net of exploitation freedom would transform the object as well as the subject: "recognition" of the object (dependent on man's transforming reason, and yet independent), not only material but element and "milieu" of freedom, of the life instincts rather than the destruction drives – the thing, the object *alive*. Let me formulate it in the most infantile way: unless men sense that an electric garbage disposal unit has a "soul," that there can be tenderness in an automobile, and that a bulldozer can not only pulverize but also restore nature, the repressive society will continue – no matter how different its institutions may be.

I have previously referred to Freud's theory of instincts, which, from a very different position and in a very different context, arrives at an affirmative answer. According to this theory, it is the aim of Eros to create ever larger units (of life) and to preserve them, in constant struggle with its counterpart, the death instinct, the aim of which is destruction. In contrast to sexuality, the "localized" manifestation of Eros, which is essentially "asocial" and even anti-social, Eros involves "socialization," the sublimation and extension of the instinctual aim not only to one other but to the others and to the common universe. Such extension modifies the instinct and the modes of its satisfaction: without a weakening of libidinal energy, the instinct seeks satisfaction in more than sexual relationships and objects: in cooperation, love, friendship; in the pursuit of knowledge, in the creation of a pleasurable environment, in the καλοκαγαυόν: the beautiful and the good – transformation of the sensuous into the aesthetic.

Is this development appropriately described in terms of sublimation? Evidently, in the transformation of sexuality into Eros, a change in the original aim and object takes place, a primary non-repressive, liberating sublimation. Far from destroying civilization, it strives to destroy the destructive basis of civilization. Thus it is sooner or later bound to clash with the established "reality principle." Repelled by the latter (or rather by the powers which enforce this principle, the erotic-aesthetic drive easily succumbs to another, secondary sublimation in work and leisure. And this secondary sublimation creates the traditional *culture*. It becomes generally repressive to the degree to which instinctual energy is channeled into socially necessary but alienated work, while the erotic-aesthetic component is split: Eros is reduced to sexuality; and the aesthetic needs directed to *Art* as the realm of their satisfaction. However, the separation of the "higher culture" from the work world, of intellectual and manual production does not necessarily entail the separation of Art from the latter: *vide* the artisan culture during the Middle Ages, and perhaps also classical Greece. This fact may be pertinent to the contemporary discussion of the role of Art (or anti-Art) in the transformation (and abolition) of capitalism: "living art" is not necessarily revolutionary, progressive; it might be the opposite. And the contrary notion, namely, that only the radical estrangement of Art from the living reality can free Art for its liberating function, may have its validity.

It is only in the developed exchange society that the unity of the erotic-aesthetic drive is effectively dissolved: the aesthetic is split off from the living reality and isolated (and rendered harmless!) in the creation and enjoyment of Art, while the pleasurably beautiful is gradually withdrawn from nature. As the latter is subjected to the increasing violence of capitalist industrialization, the aesthetic, here too, becomes isolated (in state parks, tourist high spots, etc.). The opposite trend prevails (or rather seems to prevail) in the work world. Here, advanced capitalism beautifies its milieu methodically and systematically: very pretty factories, shops, government centers, military installations spring up everywhere, and their living space is adorned with the most expensive and modernistic sculptures, paintings, "mildly stimulating" background music. No doubt, this is better and more desirable than the ugliness, dirt, stench of previous stages of industrialization; it anticipates the aesthetic possibilities of a society freed from the capitalist mode of production. But it is a poor anticipation, expressive of the awful dialectic which invalidates or falsifies even the good in this society. For this commercial aesthetic, like that of the beautiful girls, automobiles, and rockets advertised by the mass media, adjusts the senses to the inhuman work world, coordinates human sensibility with the destructive rationality of the system. The road forward does not curve back to ugliness and dirt, but leads to the unfolding contradiction, and the awareness thereof, between the established system and the possibilities of freedom which it prevents and distorts. And the concerted and conscious struggle for the realization of these possibilities demands not only the emancipation of the rationality of man, but also of his senses. It is the struggle for the historical, concrete realization of *humanitas*, man as man, because only on a universal scale can freedom become a reality.

Man as "species being," the universal "man as man" as autonomous being remains an abstract general concept and a helpless moral imperative until it takes shape in the emancipated sensibility of the individuals reconstructing their society in accordance with their truly human needs and faculties. This is the neglected aspect of the material basis of socialism.

Dialectical materialism finds its truth only when it recognizes the roots of socialism in the sensibility of man, when it recognizes the roots of freedom in man's sensuous needs – the necessity that the political and economic revolution be accompanied by the "emancipation of the senses." Accompanied, or even preceded? The revolution, to achieve a qualitative change in the individual and social existence, must be a vital *need* of the individuals. And this need is not always and everywhere that need for change impressed on men by conditions of misery and poverty. On the contrary, such conditions may well suffocate a need for qualitative change, or "channel" such a need into the struggle for improvements within a general system of unfreedom. Or, if this struggle leads to the replacement of the existing system by another, the needs and aspirations generated under the system of unfreedom may well be carried over into the new society and reproduce there the negative features of the old.

To take an apparently minor example: after a successful revolution in a country ruled for centuries by a reactionary ecclesiastical hierarchy, hand-maiden of political oppression, one has noticed, among the *people*, a return to the past once the initial enthusiasm is spent. Such regression is not initiated from above, nor is it the work of an organized opposition. It is rather the popular sentiment, expressed in such things as a hatred against long hair and beards, any kind of Hippie life, against homosexuals, etc. Such sentiment is bound to be a strong factor in shaping government policies along an anti-libertarian line. Or, a long tradition of accepting authority as divine or natural institution is bound to carry over into the new society, and foster a bureaucratic-authoritarian development. Such regressive tendencies are the more difficult to combat the more they have become the expression of a vital need of the people – expression of a "conservative" sensibility at the roots of political conservatism.

In contrast, the sensuous need for revolution is the expression of a sensitivity which sees, hears, smells, tastes, and touches the injustice, exploitation, ugliness, the cheat and the stupidity of the established society – not only as one's own, but also as the other's doing and suffering. And in this sensuous experience emerge the images, tones, forms of a world without these features – emerge as an evident possibility. They differ from utopian fantasies to the degree to which they are scientific, technical, economic, political concretions; already existing in the established reality as elements, rudiments, fragments, experiments of the scientific, artistic, political effort. Emergence of the new within the old, but the old is subverted in the new sensuous foundation.

We have noted that what is involved is *not* simply the liberation of instinctual drives and their sensuous manifestations. The emancipated senses are "transcendent" in a dual manner: (1) they break the prevailing, blunted universe of experience and intuit the form-elements of a universe of freedom;

(2) they enter the dimension of reason, to the degree to which they perceive a supra-individual reality as the *historical* transformation of the objects, conditions, relationships pertaining to the *established* universe. The latter, too, is a realization of reason in history. The emancipation of the senses can become a productive force (*Produktivkraft*) only if it confronts the established system on its own ground and rescues the achievements of this system by submitting it to the rationality of the collective struggle for radical social change. The new sensibility finds its own rationality (without which it remains a private affair) only in this struggle for the construction of a new world.

According to Marx, this new world emerges in a new relation of the senses to their object: they relate to the latter "for the sake of the object" (*um der Sache willen*). That is to say: they experience the object-world (including man) not as mere stuff of manipulation and use (regardless of what kind of use) but rather a human world in which the particular objects embody, in their "form," truly human needs and satisfactions, so that, in relating to an object, the senses are the realization of a human being: the individual, while being with another, is with himself: the universal in the particular. The decisive term in this conception is "human needs": it means "true," "authentic," "real" human needs, distinguished from (and contrasted with) the alienated human needs developed and satisfied in the capitalist society.

The distinction is open to serious criticism, which, in my view, can be met only by understanding individual needs as the individualization of specific social needs (requirements, imperatives). In the case of capitalism, the individual needs above the (unsublimated) biological level are shaped by the conditions of alienated labor, and by their recreation and compensation in leisure time and in inter-personal relations. Hegel (*Philosophy of Right*, pp. 189 ff.) speaks of the "system of needs" established by "civil society" (= *bürgerliche Gesellschaft*) into which the individual is born and which, as the concrete universal, operates through his particular needs. This system derives from the general competition of the individuals in (alienated) labor, and requires, for its functioning, an apparatus of *domination*. Hegel discusses under the same category the Police and the basic economic units (the *Korporation*), and sees the whole system terminating in the sovereign State and its monarchic government. It seems not inappropriate to sharpen Hegel's conception by focusing it on the repression and aggressiveness mobilized and made socially useful in this system. The needs which it generates, and satisfies, are permeated with these qualities and retain them when the social requirements are effectively introjected and become the satisfying expression of the individual's own needs and impulses. On the contrary, this false harmony between the individual and his society, between below and above, between the underlying population and its masters, formed in the mind and body of the individual, propels the increasing destructiveness and violence of capitalist productivity. The brutal satisfaction of the social need for dominating and "pacifying" ever more areas of the globe (and of outer space) also satisfies deep-rooted instinctual needs of the individual – together with his material and cultural needs.

Evidently, this harmony prevails only among the integrated classes in the advanced capitalist societies. Their cohesion is weakening, but their political weight is still heavy enough (they are the ones who elect the Presidents and Vice Presidents of aggression, and their representatives increase year by year the budget of destruction) to render rational persuasion ineffective. The trouble is *not* that they are not aware of what is going on, that they are not sufficiently informed, but that, being aware and informed, they do not and cannot respond and react. For their society has cut the instinctual and sensuous roots of that solidarity which makes the fate of the other part of one's own fate: their universe coincides with that of their nation, their government, their race, their equals in status (and superiors in status). Any universal beyond this closed living space remains abstract, intellectual, at best a moral or religious command which one can violate without much consequence. As this mental structure draws all its strength and force (political force!) from established practice and behavior, it can be shaken, and eventually broken by a definite counterpractice and counter-behavior – aiming at abolishing the conditions which gave rise to the closed mental structure.

But all the counter-practice and counter-behavior would not lead out of the established universe unless they originate on a new basis, unless their Subjects "carry" the new not only in their minds but also in their bodies. No matter how scientific socialism is to be, the senses must be the foundation of its science, that is to say, the emancipated senses and their truly human needs. We return to the distinction between real (authentic) and actual (immediate) needs. While it is possible to designate, with a degree of concreteness, the general quality of the latter, this seems to be all but impossible with respect to the former. Is there any standard, criterion for their authenticity as human needs, contrasted with the actual needs of men?

The universe of the emancipated senses is the humanized object world, in which man, as species being, has made the object world his own – medium for the development and satisfaction of his authentic needs. Strange unity of subject and object, which seems quite out of line with the basic materialist conception of the permanent struggle between man and nature! What quality unites, in this conception, subject and object: subjective need, and objective matter satisfying this need? We already quoted Marx' statement that it is a specific human quality to form the object world also in accordance with the laws of beauty; and in his discussion of the sensuous capabilities of man he emphasizes the experience of the beautiful. Kant's *Critique of Judgment* analyzes the beautiful in its dual manifestation in Art and in Nature, and Hegel's *Aesthetic* continues this tradition.

But this philosophical tradition already presupposes, without questioning, the socio-historical development which split the erotic-aesthetic unit, with the ensuing relegation of the aesthetic component to the world of the spirit, to the realm of Art. In contrast, Marx comprehends the beautiful as sensuous needs and faculty, becoming a factor in the primary formation of the object world. This productive force has been repressed and diverted by the requirements of class society – with their abolition, the aesthetic would become a creative power in the construction of a free society. By virtue of this power, the human senses become *"practical."* In this context, the "sensuous basis of all science" means something more and other than empirical verification by sense certainty: it means that the scientist, without in any way abandoning the logic and rigidity of scientific method, is guided in his research by the (emancipated) sensuous needs for the protection and amelioration of life. If the satisfaction of these needs, instead of being a mere by-product of science (a by-product which seems to become increasingly rare and feeble), would become the rationale of science, it may well lead to a different conceptual foundation of the natural and human sciences.

The reintroduction of the erotic-aesthetic component into radical theory and practice would incorporate a utopian element into scientific socialism – an element which has been a revolutionary force in heretic movements for centuries, which exploded in the Paris Commune of 1871, and found theoretical expression in Fourier. I believe that today, the utopian notion is not only a historical concept, but also a historical imperative – a categorical imperative which must serve to counteract the petrification of socialism under new forms of domination. For only if the vast capabilities of science and technology, of the scientific and artistic imagination direct the construction of a sensuous environment, only if the work world loses its alienating features and becomes the world of human relationships, only if productivity becomes creativity, are the roots of domination dried up in the individuals. No return to precapitalist, pre-industrial artisanship, but, on the contrary, perfection of the new mutilated and distorted science and technology in the formation of the object world in accordance with "the laws of beauty." And "beauty" here defines an ontological condition – not of an *oeuvre d'art* isolated from real existence, not of some people and places, but that harmony between man and his world which would shape the form of society. Not a universal reign of love and charity, not a disappearance of conflict and pain (not only an impossible but also an unbearable thought!) but a society in which pain and anxiety would be reduced to the attainable minimum, and in which conflict would be without violence and destruction.

This may do for the "utopian" projection of the emancipation of the human sensibility envisaged in the all but tabooed "utopian" notions of socialism. Prerequisite remains the change in the production relations and the mode of production. But here too, the dialectical conception remains valid: the transformation of the base incorporates the subjective factor – the human sensibility as productive force. The socialist "development of the productive forces" on the inherited technological basis is far more than technical progress: it would construct a qualitatively different, free society only to the degree to which the technological basis itself is already conquered and organized by a social group (or groups) for which "the sensibility is the basis of all science," namely the sensibility of the *emancipated* senses and *emancipated* needs. Now this new sensibility and consciousness could arise only among groups whose position and function in the productive process would generate the rebellion against the blunted consciousness and the mutilated needs prevalent in the existing society. Such rebellion transgresses beyond the dimension of vital, material needs and *given* cultural needs, that means, the transgression is possible only where the vital material and cultural needs are satisfied so that time, space, and energy are free for a dimension beyond the necessities. This "openness" of the mind implies consciousness of the blatant contradiction between the scientific-technological possibilities and their destructive and repressive realization.

Is there any realistic prospect that this consciousness, a radically political consciousness, may develop among the underlying population and thus provide the precondition for change? For the time being, there is a gap between the radicals and the masses – a gap which the former desperately try to bridge. Whether or not the juncture will take place in time, that is, before the advent of a new fascist era that will destroy democracy and civil liberty in the nation and its satellites: this is the ultimate issue of the struggle. Today, to be realistic means to be pessimistic: the concentration of power in the hands of the defenders of the status quo has never been greater; they are ready to use all available means against the increasing threat. And these means are unprecedented.

However, awareness of the brute facts, spreading in spite of, and through, the very media of the system, may and must spur the efforts to undo them. Pessimism becomes a positive force in the will not to compromise the "unrealistic" goals, to keep on working without illusions, to demonstrate the goals, to make them the desire of one's own life, to live one's own life and to make others capable of gaining their own life – rather than that imposed on them. It is this spirit that I feel active among the young radicals – not a spirit of violence and aggression, but of fighting violence and aggression in the name of something that does not yet exist: *humanity*.

The term "cultural revolution" indicates first of all an embarrassment: awareness of the fact that the radical opposition against the established system today is concentrated in apparently marginal social groups, mainly among young middle class groups, students. "Cultural" rather than political, social revolution – revolution, at present, without a mass base. Moreover, this cultural revolution is not sparked by impoverishment, not by dire material want, but rather by the historical proximity of a human freedom precluded and prevented by the established societies – no matter how productive, how benevolent they may still become. The attainment of this freedom, which would mean the emergence of a new type of human being and a new way of life, presupposes the abolition of poverty and the end of exploitation, but the transcending goals, vaguely formulated in the cultural revolution, are to become operative in the fight for the abolition of poverty and exploitation. An emancipated consciousness and an emancipated sensibility are to guide the transformation of society and nature. What is at stake is no more and no less than the development of an entirely new, sensuous culture, which would reduce and undo the surplus-repression imposed on men by the requirements of class society.

Thus, the cultural revolution envisages not only a continuous trans-formation of the cultural tradition, but its rejection – the refusal of continuity, rupture. And this refusal extends from the everyday behavior, the mores of society, to the most sublime achievements of art, literature and music; it is directed against the material as well as intellectual culture – it rejects bourgeois culture as a whole.

Rejection of "*bourgeois culture*": what is "bourgeois culture," and how can it be rejected?

Chronologically, bourgeois culture would be the culture developed by the bourgeoisie as the class whose ideas and values have become the pre-dominant ideas and values of society, shaping its mores, fashion, science, philosophy, art, literature, music. Making allowance for the very uneven development in the various countries, we should expect to find this specifi-cally bourgeois culture in the period from the sixteenth to the twentieth century. Thus, under the one category would be subsumed the artisan culture of the early urban Communes and Free Towns, the "high culture" of the nineteenth century, and the mass culture of the technological era. Is there really a common denominator specific enough, essential enough to validate the general category? For the same period of four centuries, we use the term "capitalism," comprising the very different stages of merchant, manufactural, industrial, and technological (monopoly, organized) capitalism. But for this category, there *is* a specific and essential common denominator, namely, the exchange society with private ownership of the means of production based on wage labor. During this entire period, the ruling class retains the basis of its power: control over the capitalist mode of production. This holds true (in spite of all modifications) for the present as well as the preceding stages. But is the ruling class at the present stage still that "bourgeoisie" which was the subject of bourgeois culture? Is the culture which today is under total attack still "bourgeois culture?"

The concept "bourgeois" calls for re-examination.

The New Left has retained this concept, without reflection, as it appeared in Marxian theory about a hundred years ago. Already thirty years ago, Max Horkheimer pointed out to what extent this concept has been invalidated in the advanced capitalist countries. "Bourgeoisie" was the concept of a *class*, that class which had become the ruling class since the demise of feudalism – the ruling class in the capitalist system. As such, it was the "middle class" between the still existing (and still powerful) landed aristocracy on the one side, and the proletariat on the other. It was the class which owned and controlled the means of production, and which bent the government increasingly to its interests. "Bourgeois culture" was the culture of this class: clearly distinguished from feudal culture in literature and the arts, in the mores, in the hierarchy of values. As a member of this class, the bourgeois was the free entrepreneur, the private capitalist competing with others like him, exploiting *his* workers, and appropriating and reinvesting *his* surplus value. His mores may perhaps still best be designated as those of "innerworldly asceticism" in the interest of his business: productive "savings," restraint in consumption, hard work, monogamic morality, self-imposed repression. As a corollary of private enterprise and free competition, freedom was gradually extended to the political and cultural realm: democracy with the institution of secret and universal suffrage, and civil liberties under the rule of law.

A mere glance at this brief enumeration shows to what extent these features have been outdated. The changes in the structure of capitalism, the demise of private enterprise and free competition, the capitalist "socialization" of the economic establishment are all too familiar. The merger of economic and political power did not exactly lead to the constellation outlined in classical Marxian theory. The government is more and other than the agent of capital, political responsibility is delegated to professional rackets who act increasingly independent of their constituencies, and the military exerts increasing power over the economy.[4] Rackets are also operating throughout the economy. This is still a ruling class, and its dominion still depends, in its entirety, on the defense, enlarged accumulation, and valorization of capital. But this function has ceased to be productive in any sense other than that of the ever more brutal and costly perpetuation of the established system. Their role is no longer the development of the productive forces but rather the prevention of their rational development and human progress. Within this framework, technical progress is inseparable from progress in destruction. And as the social role of this ruling class becomes increasingly unproductive, so does its system of values.

But then, what is that bourgeois culture which is disintegrating in the Establishment and, at the same time, rejected and denied in the cultural revolution?

First we must distinguish, for reasons to be explained presently, between the material and the intellectual (or "higher") culture. The former is indeed well identifiable as against the antecedent feudal culture: it is characterized by the typically bourgeois preoccupations and the "values" corresponding to them. We have already mentioned the principal ones: they are the preoccupation with money and business as the way of making a living, private competitive enterprise, the patriarchal and authoritarian family and education, the (rather abstract) equality before the law, a (rather restricted) democracy, and a (rather hypocritical) work ethic. Now precisely these preoccupations and values appear in the higher culture (art and literature but also the "art of living") denied, repelled, indicted. With notable exceptions (mainly at the earlier historical stages), a strong *anti*-bourgeois stance seems to dominate the higher culture of the bourgeois period. It is perhaps only a little exaggerated to say that the most representative (and most authentic) of its oeuvres offer the most radical critique of the bourgeoisie, the bourgeois reality.

And the once exalted bourgeois "virtues": the noble austerity, the humble but pure bourgeois daughters who, in the bourgeois drama, are seduced, deserted, victimized by the vicious members of the upper strata have long since ceased to be the embodiment of bourgeois morality. They are gone, as is the once typical interior of the bourgeois home, with its petty and ridiculous decor, its stuffiness, its laborious, "personalized" household, has

---

4  Editor's note: Marcuse's reference here to "professional rackets who act increasingly independent of their constituencies" and that "Rackets are also operating throughout the economy" is an allusion to Max Horkheimer's theory of rackets under capitalism whereby crime is the normal expression of the system and established economic and political forces themselves act like rackets.

long since been replaced by more functional and modernistic equipment – much of it still survives in working class homes.

But what has happened to the higher culture: to its celebrated features which made up the core of the cultural universe of the bourgeois period, its central ideas, its *ethos*? If there is anything that is alien to, and negated by, the cultural revolution, it is the ethos (and *pathos*) of Racine and Goethe, of the "masters" classic and romantic, it is the idea of the personality, achieving fulfillment through resignation, it is its all too sad and sublimated freedom – the *Innerlichkeit* which becomes music and song and verse, beautiful Form, but which also becomes, by virtue of these very features, reconciliation, acceptance, glorification of the miserable reality.

The idea of the person, subjectivity, is indeed the singular achievement of bourgeois intellectual culture. In its art, literature, and music, the autonomous subject, the person becomes the Archimedian Point from which the world is seen, understood, organized. And bourgeois philosophy, in its rational as well as empiricist schools, establishes the subject as epistemological foundation: from Descartes' *ego cogito* via Kant to Hegel's "the substance is subject," and from Hume's perceptionism to the "protocol statements" of the Vienna Circle.

How is this idea of the subject related to the material culture of the bourgeois period? Is it essentially ideological, repressive in its realization, or does it contain elements of liberation vital in the historical development beyond bourgeois society?

Even at a first glance, we can distinguish two contrary connotations in the notion of subjectivity:

1 subjectivity has a conformist, positivistic function: it precludes (or at least minimizes) a radical transcendence beyond the given universe of experience (metaphysical as well as historical transcendence);
2 subjectivity has an essentially negating, denying, and transcending function.

In the first case, the Subject is, as it were, empirically and theoretically enclosed in the established reality. It is taken as it appears; the difference (and conflict) between the Subject of behavior and that of thought, between the social and epistemological structure of reality is obscured, and the ingression of society into the latter is neglected. The object world appears in reified, petrified forms; the laws of motion governing it are ahistorical, and are purged of social content. In the second case, "subjectivity" is the title for the opening of another dimension of theory and practice, thought and behavior – a dimension in which the Subject comes into its own as *against* the given reality, and the determining experience moves in the antagonistic space and time uniting the given reality and its negation.

Thus, in the first case, it is (in spite of the apparent concreteness) an abstract, purified, mutilated Subject which is to express itself, to verify and validate his experience, and to organize or transform his world. It is the Subject of perception, common sense, understanding – or, in vulgar but decisive terms, the taxpayer, the object of opinion polls and questionnaires, the average voter. But it may also be the "personality" which has made its place and peace in the world through resignation and adjustment.

In the second case,[5] it is indeed a not (yet) "existing" Subject: a Subject striving to break into the existing world (and thereby breaking this world); a Subject which reveals itself through its absence, through that which is wanting. Therefore, it cannot be experienced and expressed in ordinary perception, language, common sense; the vehicle of its presentation is the *Imagination*, its medium the arts. There the negating subjectivity becomes affirmative, positive: there it creates its own world – the world constructed and organized, different from, and antagonistic to the given reality. And this antagonistic ethos is the life force of that culture which marks the bourgeois period: an ethos clearly opposed to the ethos which shaped the bourgeois *reality*, to the bourgeois himself! The dialectical paradox: the representative oeuvres of bourgeois culture are *not* bourgeois! Indeed it is meaningless to characterize the Quartets of Beethoven, the novels of Flaubert, the paintings of Cézanne, as "bourgeois" unless the argument is circular: identifying the bourgeois quality with the aesthetic Form itself.

The bourgeois is the "possessive individual," the Subject of buying and selling, whose individuality is the result of successful, aggressive competition. And precisely this bourgeois individual is indicted, ridiculed, repelled in the intellectual culture of the bourgeois period.

But then, what is the target of the cultural revolution? Is it perhaps not so much the repulsive features of the material culture (which are just as strikingly indicted in the intellectual bourgeois culture itself) as its *transcending*, "progressive" qualities – its ethos of Form and beauty? Has the cultural revolution perhaps "taken over" these qualities; is it their simple (abstract) negation, or their historical *Aufhebung*?

The cultural revolution accentuates its total rupture with the cultural tradition; it assumes the character of a cultural revolution which is to prepare the ground for the coming socialist revolution. However, its conspicuous

---

5  The two diverging modes of subjectivity may well be united in one person and oeuvre; Goethe is exemplary of this union.

ideological character should not obscure the fact that the cultural revolution itself is rooted in the contradictions of advanced capitalism, and that it is explicable only in terms of the basic changes in the capitalist mode of production. And these changes make for a genuine "displacement" of the *forms* in which the contradictions appear, and, consequently, for the displacement of the conscious revolutionary (or rather *pre*-revolutionary) Subject. I said: conscious, pre-revolutionary, because the effective, eventual Subject is still the working class *as* class, that is, the human base of the material production, the source of surplus value. But within this class, a decisive differentiation is taking place, engendered by the increasing "intellectualization" of material production – replacement of physical by mental energy. It finds expression in the (quantitative and qualitative) importance of technicians, scientists, researchers, etc. for the reproduction of capitalism. This new stratum of the working class enjoys a high degree of renumeration, security, and status; in its education, interest, and outlook it is very different from the older "labor aristocracy."

It is supposedly within this group where the contradiction between the incredible liberating potential of science and technology on the one hand, and its destructive and manipulative use on the other would become conscious to such an extent that it becomes unbearable. This experienced, immediately and constantly experienced contradiction would then be translated into political consciousness, and the latter in turn would express itself in the formulation of supra-economic, supra-trade-unionist demands, terminating in the demand for self-government in the industrial enterprises – and beyond.

Some empirical evidence for this theory is provided by the May–June events in France in 1968 – is it sufficient to indicate a radical (not to say revolutionary) trend? The basic contradiction may well generate growing malaise, discontent, frustration, and erupt in initiating strikes. But there are powerful counter-trends against a revolutionary development of this stratum of the "new working class": not only (and not primarily) its relatively high social status, but also its technocratic attitude, inherent in the predominantly *technical* (functional) *intelligence* which is required and perpetuated by the position of this class in the productive process. It is this technocratic tendency which makes for a social and political continuity between the old and the new – a continuity which is more and other than that necessitated by the progressive development of the productive forces. Continuity of domination: its technocratic rationality is still that of the Performance Principle (*Leistungsprinzip*), though a thorough rationalization of this rationality. And this continuity would militate against the qualitative difference between the old and the new, life in solidarity and freedom. True, this new quality can become real only in the construction of socialism, after the abolition of capitalism. But it is also true that, unless this quality becomes concrete in specific forms and modes of individual and group life in and against the old society, the continuity of domination is likely to assert itself in all change.

The rupture of this continuity is the aim of the cultural revolution. It is a rupture *within* the capitalist framework – and therefore no revolution. But neither is it a "reformist" movement nor an ideological fashion for it gets at the roots which produce and reproduce in the individual the rationality and sensibility, the science and the common sense of capitalist society. The strength of these cultural roots is largely responsible for the fact that the changes in the infrastructure of capitalism (from liberal to monopoly and state capitalism), which aggravate its internal contradictions to the breaking point, do not explode the popular and class consciousness; that the intermediaries are missing which translate the intolerable objective contradictions into intolerable subjective contradictions. And without this translation, the "new working class" remains – just as the old one – a revolutionary class "in itself" but not "for itself."

The missing mass base, which gives the cultural revolution its ideological, "élitist" character, indicates the extent to which the cultural revolution takes shape in a novel historical situation. While the cultural tradition of the West, throughout its long development, has been founded on *scarcity*, this foundation is now being undermined, and, on this objective ground, obsolescence is spreading from the material to the intellectual culture.

Scarcity does not only mean want of foodstuffs, material goods, low degree of technique, etc., but also the immaturity and suppression of the faculties for overcoming scarcity and its unequal, exploitative distribution. Sustained by a whole network of cultural controls (religion, morality, education), scarcity, and man's weakness in the face of the overwhelming power of nature, became an effective prop for the overwhelming power of exploitative domination. If it is true that the increasing mastery of nature also makes for an increasingly effective control of man, the reverse also seems true: the lack of understanding of nature (for centuries fostered by the ruling classes) serves to obscure the not at all "natural" roots of domination. In any case, the prevailing scarcity shaped the "higher culture" only through a complex system of intermediaries, individual and social, material and intellectual. Biological and sociological factors, the particular environment and experience, the available material (linguistic, perceptual, conceptual) operate in this system and generate the infinite variety of the cultural tradition. And yet, the foundation on scarcity remains a common denominator of this cultural universe.

First, and most familiar: the exploitative social organization of scarcity makes the higher culture a privilege of those who have the time, energy (and, though not necessarily!) education to understand, to practice, and to enjoy it. This holds true, at least partly, also for those who create this culture, for they will use the medium and level of expression prevalent among their audience. Consequently, the higher culture is, by virtue of this basis, *class* culture, and all transcendence, all "universalization" will procede from this basis. The higher culture can transcend it only in two domains: Art and Philosophy.[6] In both domains, the transcendence remains abstract, "ideal," ideological – unless and until the transcending intellectual efforts join up with revolutionary social forces: a new historical class, or its avant-garde. Philosophy has made this juncture: with the bourgeoisie in the seventeenth and eighteenth centuries and with the proletariat in the last third of the nineteenth century. Marxian theory, itself a product of "bourgeois culture," and not only in a chronological sense, has been incorporated into the cultural revolution, although in greatly modified forms. And this in spite of the fact that at least in the most advanced industrial countries, and certainly in the ritualized form imposed by the authoritarian-bureaucratic socialist regimes of today, Marxism has assumed an ideological and abstract character largely alien to the masses. And as to the other domain of cultural transcendence: the forms and values of bourgeois Art have remained "unreal," i.e., non-committal for the underlying population as well as for its rulers – a non-reality which increased to the degree to which this Art was incorporated into the daily household and business of man. No general education, no popularization, no technological improvement of communication has reduced the illusory character of bourgeois Art, its escapist traits, its "elitist" appeal.

However, the radical opposition rejects this culture not only because it is a class privilege and alien to the masses, but also because of its inherently repressive character. I quote at random from one of the "underground" papers. In an article entitled "Does 'Culture' make you think of Bach and Braque?" the author writes:

> With the emergence of a "non-repressive community" (as it is already taking shape within the existing society) there will undoubtedly develop new and better means of communication among ourselves, more spontaneous and more adequate expressions of our natural creative impulses, and a more rational, natural way of looking at ourselves and that which we perceive with our senses. Perhaps we see this already in the breaking down of the inhibitions involved with the use of certain formerly tabooed words, in a more rational attitude on

---

6 Two of Hegel's three manifestations of the "absolute spirit."

the part of many people towards certain drugs which can and do enhance
perception and sensory enjoyment, and in the development of new forms of
music more expressive of the sexual energy which is at the base, according to
Reich, of all human energy, activity and expression.

(*San Diego Free Press*, Nov. 28–Dec. 4, 1968)

At first glance, it is not quite clear in what way Bach or Beethoven inhibit
the expression of sexual energy. A good case has been made for the opposite:
in the popular Nichols and May dialogue between a not exactly inhibited
couple in bed listening to Bach; and by Tolstoi (who knew something about
sexual energy and repression) in his interpretation of the Kreutzer Sonata.
Nor is there any reason to assume that the "more natural" expression of
sexual energy would make for a better society: the self-transformation
of sexuality into Eros, which would characterize human relationships in a
free society is certainly not a "natural" process. And yet, there is a way in
which the institutionalized repression translates itself into Art and enters
into the very substance of Art which is the *Form*. I have elsewhere (*An Essay
on Liberation* and "The Future of Art") tried to identify the elements by
virtue of which the Art-Form imposes order, reconciles the irreconcilable,
mitigates prosaic injustice by poetic justice, makes sorrow beautiful. I have
also suggested that this affirmative function belongs to the very Form of
Art, that even anti-Art partakes of it, and that the affirmative character
of Art could be overcome only in the dialectical negation of Art, that is to
say, its realization in an aesthetic *Lebenswelt*. This presupposes the radical
transformation of society which would gradually reduce the separation of
individual from social production, creativity from labor, freedom from
necessity.

Prior to such transformation, the mere denial of the traditional culture
remains unpolitical. The catalysts of transformation, the forces of rebellion
are there: they are the roots of the revolution which is to come. But the anti-
authoritarian consciousness and sensibility will be capable of progressing
from rebellion to revolution only to the degree to which they rescue and
develop the radically progressive elements in bourgeois culture, their still
unfulfilled truth – this too is part of the effort to make the universal appear
in the particular: to link private and social liberation, individual and political
action. Failure to do so means that the rebellion succumbs to the coopting
and suppressing power of the system: the truly activist elements would be
brutally liquidated, while others would turn into farce, entertainment,
fashion, disease. This would be the fate of all direct sectarian action – Hippie
and non-Hippie; it would also be the fate of the "living art," the "living
theater," of the simple refusal of bourgeois forms. It would be the collapse
into "bad immediacy": a shortcut which avoids coming to grips with the

complex intermediaries between the old and the new, between the attained and the attainable. They are, in an often distorted and abortive manner, operative in the tradition: in the material culture, for example, as the "productive forces," the scientific-technical apparatus; in the political realm as the historical forms of radical-democratic organization (assemblies, councils of workers and soldiers, and other self-governing bodies).

And such intermediaries between the past and the possible future are also operative in the higher, intellectual culture: they link, in the process of change, past and present repression with the forms of freedom – link the old and the new in such a way that the liberating images and ideas contained in the old come into their truth in the new. Short of this commitment, the denial of the traditional culture is bound to be abortive, perhaps even regressive: simple but not "definite negation."

These liberating images pertain to the universe of reason and sensibility, mind and body alike. Liberation, as historical process, is never by virtue of sensibility *per se*. A free society will also be a rational society; history is indeed objective *spirit*. All liberation, no matter how sensuous, how radical, must pay tribute to the brute fact that man is a rational animal, that all his freedom and happiness depend on his consciousness of that which *is* versus that which *can* be, and that the silence of pure sensuousness is transitory: the moment before the renewed transcendence. Here too, Hegel was right: "desire" belongs to the phenomenology of the spirit. The prolongation and recurrence of the moment of pure sensuousness demand the effort of reason, of the intellect. Faust's *"verweile doch, du bist so schön"* is spoken as the imagination projects the rational *praxis* of a free society; and when *"alle Lust will Ewigkeit,"* eternity *is* only in this transcending will.

True, these radically libertarian expressions of "bourgeois culture" are themselves only moments of rupture within the old cultural tradition, but they are also the elements of a new rationality. And by virtue of this rationality, the allegedly obsolete and repressive bourgeois *Form*, its harmonizing and sublimated beauty, may turn out to be precisely the avant-gardistic element: the appearance of freedom in the realm of necessity. Or if it is true (as I believe it is) that this Form has a cathartic power, does this catharsis free the mind (and the body) for adjustment or rather for rebellion? To formulate it in a ridiculous, "undialectical," but perhaps shocking way: where is the greater negating and thus more liberating force: in Gustav Mahler or John Cage; in Yeats or Allen Ginsberg; in Cézanne or Pollock? To be sure, these examples are taken from the period when bourgeois Art itself has turned to the dissolution of the classic and romantic forms. Can we substitute, for the first series, Beethoven, Keats, Rembrandt? In any case, it would be begging the question if we simply correlate the classic, romantic, and contemporary forms to different historical stages and neglect the basic identity of the underlying social system. The capitalist system remains the foundation common to all these stages in the development of the higher culture.

Its contemporary stage, that of an anti-art, the anti-novel, rock 'n' roll, etc. is the methodical negation of the preceding stages, which were dominated by the *"tyranny of the Form."* Intolerable harmony, unbearable beauty . . . I recall Rilke's enigmatic phrase: *"Denn das Schöne ist nichts als des Schrecklichen Anfang, den wir noch grade ertragen."* (I interpret): The beautiful is the sudden appearance, the ingression of another truth into the established reality, a frightening truth which invokes those modes of perception, imagination, conception which are arrested in the established reality, and which are the a priori of liberation. We cannot say: they *invoke* liberation, they "represent" the realm of freedom. For this realm can never be "represented" in any form; it can only be shown as that which is absent. Art is no exception from this inexorable necessity to be empirical: to say "no" to the established reality while affirming its existence, to force the idea out of the given material, offered by a world of unfreedom, unhappiness, frustration.

Art forms this material in the name and image of that which is absent, and the latter has name and image because it haunts the present as an experienced possibility. It is in the needs, desires, gestures, and thoughts of men, in their senses and in their reason – for good or evil (in terms of the respective society). But:

> Hélas! qu'est-ce donc que le bien et le mal! Est-ce une même chose par laquelle nous témoignons avec rage notre impuissance, et la passion d'atteindre à l'infini par les moyens même les plus insensés?
>
> (Lautréamont)

For the realm of freedom is indeed the never attainable infinite, since man is part of nature, and nature is the essentially objective against the autonomous Subject, and even the best society would contain and reproduce this tension. No science and no technology are likely to overcome this brute fact. They may even enlarge the weight and scope of the object world, and the new society, no matter how superior its freedom, will have to cope with the vast productive apparatus of increasingly automatous things (machine systems) on which freedom will depend.

In Art, good and evil become aesthetic categories: good and bad in terms of the Form. This transmutation is the unique prerogative of Art: bad is that which violates the Form, and the latter is a transformation of reality by an intellect and a sensibility which make the realm of freedom appear in the realm of unfreedom: the epiphany of the beautiful.

Strange phenomenon, which is in a tone figure of Mozart as well as Stockhausen, in a painting of Ingres as well as Picasso, in a phrase of Flaubert as well as James Joyce, in a gesture of the Duchess of Guermantes as well as that of a Hippie! Expressions of a sensibility which repels, negates the "style" of the commodity world and of the performances and attitudes required in it – which, without "forgetting" or overlooking the commodity world, confronts it with an alien and alienating style: token of a (transitory) liberation, mastery – of a promise. A new light falls on the established reality, a light in which the brutal, destructive power of this reality seems grasped and – arrested, although the terror is ever present: in the suffering, the sorrow, the cries which enter into the Form. Modes of perception and understanding, mental and physical reactions, instincts which release men and things from the bondage of profitable and exploitable instruments: a language, an imagery, and a behavior which reveal what is being done to men and things, and what they *can* be and *can* do.

First of all: liberation of sensibility. No work of Art which does not invoke a sensuous reaction: immediate experience of the beautiful as pleasurable. But the beautiful contains the terror: Mary pertains to the image of the Crucifixion; Ophelia will be a corpse in the river; and even the most joyful finales of *Figaro* are permeated with sadness. The sensuous immediacy of the beautiful is thus "broken": it is in fact an immediacy which is the work of intellectual mediation. To the non-conformist sensibility operative in Art corresponds a non-conformist rationality. The liberating sensibility depends throughout on the liberating power of the intellect. Impossible to separate what is, in the creation (and reception) of a work of Art, the part of the intellect and that of the sensibility: the synthesis of sensuous experience is itself sensuous, and the receptive sensibility, which is qualitatively other than the "normal" one, has already become susceptible to the guidance of the intellect. Everything spontaneous, "natural," immediate in Art is a result and end of a highly organized mental activity. André Breton, the protagonist of "automatic writing," extols "the harsh discipline of the mind to which we intend purely and simply to subject everything" (*Second Manifesto of Surrealism*).[7] This mind is the power which breaks through the familiar universe of experience and establishes the points and moments in which this universe bursts open and allows a glance at a new world.

A merely *imaginary* transformation? Certainly! For what other faculty would be capable of invoking the presence of that which is *not*? A new world

---

7  *Manifestos of Surrealism*, trans. by R. Scaver and Helen R. Lane (Ann Arbor, 1969), p. 181.

which, though not existent, yet is the horizon of history – real possibility. It can be made sensuous, accessible only "indirectly": as it transfigures things in the given reality, gives them a new promise. This is the revolutionary potential of Art: it remains *outside* the actual revolutionary praxis. Courbet epitomizes this constellation. He fights on the streets of Paris, he is present at the fall of the Vendôme column, he risks his life in the struggle. But there is no direct testimony of this event in his paintings, no political content whatsoever.

> Everything happens as if he had decided that there must be some way to reflect his profound faith in the betterment of the world in everything that he tried to evoke, some way to make it appear somehow in the light he caused to fall on the horizon or on a roebuck's belly.
>
> (Breton, *Political Position of Today's Art*, 1935)[8]

And Rimbaud? He joins the Communards, he drafts a constitution for a communist society, but (as Breton points out) the tenor of the poems written under the immediate impact of the Commune "in no way differs from that of the other poems." The revolution was in his poetry from beginning to end: as a preoccupation of a "technical order, namely, to translate the world into a new language."[9]

To be sure, neither Courbet nor Rimbaud are exactly classics of bourgeois culture, and no revolution like the Commune is in the background or center of the classics. And yet, I believe that the absent realm of freedom (or the faith in the betterment of the world) is similarly reflected in their work. And reflected precisely in the way in which words are grouped and regrouped, freed from their familiar use and abuse, becoming tone and dance and cry – image and voice of protest; in the way in which shapes and colors are placed and replaced, in which harmonies open the ear to the unheard. In this way, the idea of the beautiful becomes sensuous in the organization of the material, and in the creation of a world utterly alien and yet pleasurable.

In the Form appears the latent content: the object (be it man or nature, the individual or the people, a tree or a cup or a table; the whole or a small part of it), exploited, forgotten, destroyed in the given reality; is "saved" – the established law and order collapses before the world or sound of a very material, very sensuous redemption.

The artistic transmutation works in various modes and to various degrees. Thus, in music, the object is entirely absorbed in pure Form: of sorrow, play, dance, desire. The poetic transmutation of the object occurs in the "alchemy of the word," the all but infinite ways of creating a new language, capable

---

8   Ibid., p. 219.
9   Ibid., p. 220.

of communicating the images of rejection and liberation. And painting, through ever new modes of sense perception, leads to an increasing de-structuring of the familiar object. The imaginary revolution seems to be permanent: experiencing and projecting ever new dimensions of subject and object – historical dimensions, for human reason, imagination, and sensibility remain within the continuum of history which they explode time and again. And this inexorably historical essence of Art links Art inexorably to the social, political reality.

This relation is ambivalent: by virtue of its historical situation, Art is condemned to pertain to the established society and to show the features of class society even in its most transcending achievements. ("élitism," selection of content and theme, methodical blindness to that which repulses all artistic harmonization). Yet it is only by rigidly adhering to the Form of Art, to the artistic alienation and dissociation, to the radical estrangement from the established universe of "given" facts that Art can preserve its revolutionary potential.

The cultural revolution (or rather its most spectacular protagonists) seeks this estrangement outside the Establishment, outside the market and its law of value. They know that, in the commodity universe, there can be nothing good that is not bad by virtue of its participation in the rotten whole, but they fail to realize that there is nothing outside this whole (except perhaps in a far away country), and that monopoly capitalism is a truly global system which also invades the mind and the senses – even, in rebuttal, those of its most uncompromising foes! And the truth of a work of Art is not negated by the fact that it is distributed, priced, and rewarded through the channels of the Establishment (although this truth does gently evaporate if the work becomes part of the relaxing or stimulating reproduction of market behavior) – the totally estranging work of Stockhausen or Beckett does not change a bit when the former is distributed by the big record companies, and the latter receives the Nobel Prize. It is, however, correct that Beethoven is better suited for "background" in the kitchen or shop than Stockhausen. The answer is not, to "suspend" Beethoven but to develop an understanding and a sensibility which would make Beethoven just as alien to established law and order as Stockhausen, and possibly more alien than jazz and rock 'n' roll.

"Intellectual pundits of the left" are blamed for their "revolutionary aesthetic," and a "certain coterie of talmudists" is taken to task for being more "expert in weighing the many shadings and nuances of a word than involvement in the revolutionary process."[10] Archaic anti-intellectualism

---

10 Irvin Silber, in *Guardian*, December 13, 1969.

abhors the idea that the former may be an essential part of the latter, part of that translation of the world into a new language which may communicate the radically new claims of liberation. The cultural revolution must indeed come to grips and express the legitimate claims of the working class – and most emphatically those claims which transcend all trade union policy, which transcend the system as a whole.

The radicals of proletarian ideology criticize the cultural revolution as a "middle class trip." Their philistine mind is at its very best when it proclaims that this revolution will "become meaningful" only "when it begins to understand the very real cultural meaning that a washing machine, for instance, has for a working class family with small children in diapers." And the philistine mind demands that "the artists of that revolution . . . tune in on the emotions of that family on the day, after months of debate and planning, that the washing machine is delivered . . ."[11] The philistine mind, perhaps haunted by the guilt feeling of "elitism," cannot admit that precisely these emotions around the washing machine bind the working class family to the manufacturer of the washing machine, that, in a free society, the washing machine would be normal equipment outside the family-togetherness, and that it would no longer be charged with emotions.

To be sure, the cultural revolution must recognize and subvert this atmosphere of the working class home, but this need must be present in the *absence* of this atmosphere: in the definite negation of the emotionally charged washing machine.

The ridiculed "aesthetics of the revolution" is the dialectical response to the enlargement and transformation of the potential revolutionary base in monopoly capitalism (greater weight of the so-called non-material conditions, and, consequently, gradual radicalization of non-proletarian exploited classes). The struggle against capitalism activates, in the infrastructure itself, forces and faculties which hitherto remained dormant, repressed, or the property of privileged, alienated groups (artists, poets, "decadents" of all sorts): the rebellion against the mutilation of the senses becomes a political rebellion.

The falsehood of bourgeois culture (which is rooted in its exploitative basis) can be overcome only if its radically contradictory elements (which exist only *in* this culture!) enter, as destructive forces, the mind *and* the senses of man, and there, growing like a healthy cell, make him mentally and physically incapable of performing for the Establishment. To practice this mental and physical incapacity to function for this society is an essential part

---

11 Irvin Silber, in *Guardian*, December 6, 1969, p. 17.

of the cultural revolution. Today, the variety of non-conformist behavior, including its freakish and foolish manifestations, the communes, the "underground press," is authentic to the degree to which the political goal remains transparent in the behavior and action. The all-out fight against the "*esprit de sérieux*" is an indispensable political weapon where the profitable insanity which keeps the Establishment going seems to defy all serious rational argumentation and persuasion; this is one of the reasons why the liberals (liberalism is a thoroughly rational creed) succumb so easily. It remains nevertheless true that the "sickness unto death" is not confined to the Establishment, that there is insanity and crime also among the rebels and that, if insanity has become the normal state of health, it cannot be cured by another insanity. The murder orgies of the "Manson Family"[12] are part of the Establishment for which they provide ammunition against the rebellion – feeble counterpart of the massacres in Vietnam, undertaken by clean American boys.

The cultural revolution fails where it takes the short cut of denying the radical function of the intellect, of refusing the "harsh discipline of the mind" in favor of immediate expression and realization. There is no such thing as an "unsublimated" rebellion, and there is no sensuous immediacy which is not the result of the complex intermediary function of the intellect. Nor is there a direct simple application of theory to praxis. Just as all critical theory strives, by virtue of the internal development of its concepts, toward the transformation of reality, so does this practical transformation retain and renew its theoretical foundation. Unless this relation is preserved, theory becomes empty, and praxis blind: it is without basis in the whole, and, consequently, it cannot sustain its resistance against the whole. The latter must be present and reflected, comprehended – only thus does it become the potential object of radical change. Revolutionary praxis is not simply negation but contradiction, and contradiction is a term of logic and dialectic.

Contradiction versus negation: the former rescues the liberating forces of the past culture for the future: not because of any respect for tradition, etc., but because they are part of the historical soil on which the rebellion must grow if it is itself to become a historical event. Thus, the aesthetic forms in which bourgeois culture anticipated its historical heirs reappear in the anti-bourgeois context of the cultural revolution. The hatred, rage, irony of Bob Dylan's songs of protest are again "beautiful," and whatever radical force may be in Allen Ginsberg's poetry is neither in his brutal naturalism

---

12 Their political glorification by some groups among the New Left has nothing to do with radicalism – it is the one thing a radical is not allowed to be, namely, plain silly.

nor in his Hindu chants but rather in the lovely "classical" lines which transfigure his brutal and mystical universe. It is only by virtue of this antagonistic union that defiance and destruction reflect the realm of freedom and make the entire work appear in the light of this possible freedom.

Dialectical continuity in the break also relates the transcending elements of the bourgeois *ethos* to the ethos of the rebellion. First of all the idea of subjectivity. Its autonomy, the *individuum*, the claim for self-determination reappear, freed from their possessive, competitive connotation, in the cultural revolution: in the rejection of all role-playing, in the "counter-institutions," in the communes as self-chosen associations. However, there is a strong authoritarian, manipulative, standardizing stance in and against these liberating tendencies.

It becomes manifest in many of the organized happenings, festivals, be-ins with massive release. And it is also an element in jazz, rock 'n' roll and their popular bands. By themselves, they are not the negation of bourgeois culture (Michael McClure once suggested that rock 'n' roll may just be another version of "Jingle Bells"), and the crowd at the rock festivals still seems to succumb to massive, immediate identification – not too different from the crowds at a football game, or a Billy Graham revival.[13]

Subjectivity, which is credited to the bourgeois culture as its distinguishing achievement, is indeed still the individual root of freedom – being a self, having a sphere of self-realization, of autonomy in, and against, prevailing objective conditions, social and natural.

But this subjectivity, too, has its historical denominator. The conflict between subject and object is shaped by the conditions in which men are related to each other through the exchange of commodities, through the market. This *form* of the conflict would change with the change in the society to which it is germane – without, however, attaining the identity between subject and object. For the conflict between subject and object is largely that between man and nature. It would be reproduced also in a socialist society; its alleviation, and the growth of freedom, would depend on the abolition of the ravages of the capitalist exploitation of nature, and on the construction of an aesthetic environment.

Ecology, which is today propagated by the leaders of the polluting Establishment, may well become part of a radical theory and practice if it

---

13 As against this massification, the reflex of freedom in the personal sphere: the charm of a Hippy girl reflects the new world of "make love, not war," and "make love, not babies" only when she is just herself, doing her thing quietly, standing alone, as it were, against the world in which she lives, alone with those whom she chooses (and who have chosen her).

becomes a *political* science and technology, directed toward the abolition of the very institutions which perpetuate the capitalist environment. Short of such political redirection, ecology is in danger of becoming a mere diversion. Again, the aesthetic component as revolutionary ferment – as part of the political struggle.

The fight will be won when the obscene symbiosis of opposites is broken – the symbiosis between the erotic play of the sea (its waves rolling in as conquering males, breaking by their own grace, turning female; caressing each other, and licking the rocks) and the booming death industries at its shores, between the flight of the white birds and that of the grey Airforce jets, between the silence of the night and the farts of the motorcycles. . . . Only then will man have resolved (tentatively) the contradiction between the social wealth and its abominable use, between the Fifth Avenues and the ghettoes, between procreation and genocide. In the long range, the political dimension can no longer be divorced from the aesthetic, reason from sensibility, the gesture of the barricade from that of love. To be sure, the former spells hatred – but the hatred of all that is inhuman, and this "gut hatred" is an essential ingredient of the cultural revolution.

But this is still the phase of misplaced hatred. The new sensibility is utterly unpopular; the people hate it, "the masses" despise it. Perhaps they feel that it really strikes out against the whole, against all their rotten taboos – that it endangers the necessity, the value of their performance, their fun, the prosperity around them. Prevailing is the resentment against the long hair and the beards, the sexual liberties, the feminine gesture, the contempt for the jobs of the Establishment – resentment against the rebels who permit themselves what the people have to forgo and repress.

Wilhelm Reich was right in emphasizing the roots of fascism in instinctual repression, he was wrong when he saw the mainsprings for the defeat of fascism in sexual liberation. The massification of the individuals, and their dual identification among themselves and with their leaders has a very rational basis: the leaders still deliver the goods (and, periodically, the bodies of the enemies who threaten the continued delivery of these goods). The break of this dual identification can only be the work of the masses: the rebellion, in order to prepare the ground for radical change, must indeed develop on a social scale – must indeed "seize the masses." But these will be *"new masses,"* with a new political consciousness, open to the new dimensions of freedom projected in the cultural revolution. The twentieth century revolution will be the cause of generations, for it will have to build a biological foundation in the individuals. The new society will emerge when the institutions and relationships reproduced by the existing society will have become incompatible with the life instincts of men and women who have not yet been cast (or are no longer cast) in the mold of resignation. And their instinctual rebellion will have become a political force only when it is accompanied by and guided by the rebellion of reason: the absolute refusal of the intellect (and the intelligentsia) to pact with the Establishment, to be an accessory to the crimes against humanity.

The fetishism of the commodity world, which seems to become denser every day, can be destroyed only by men and women who have torn the technological and ideological veil which conceals what is going on, which covers the insane rationality of the whole – men and women who have become free to develop their own needs, to build, in solidarity, their own world. The end of alienation and reification is the beginning of the individual: the new Subject of radical reconstruction. And the genesis of this Subject is a process which shatters the traditional framework of radical theory and practice.

The central ideas, and the goals of the cultural revolution are well founded in the historical situation: the new dimensions of freedom are contained in, and by, the existing society. This is the great promise. But its realistic, objective foundations in no way assures its fulfillment: the advent of a long period of barbarism is also a historically well-founded possibility – the threat of a second fascist era. Unless the fight against this threat is intensified, it may be lost.

The outcome depends, to a great extent, on the resolution of the young generation – not to drop out and not to accommodate, but to learn how to regroup after defeat, how to develop, with the new sensibility a new rationality, to sustain a long process of education – indispensable prerequisite for the transition to action.

There is, however, one argument against the cultural revolution which seems to me vital, and which may well vitiate its interpretation in terms of a potential revolution. At the basis of this argument is also an existential, instinctual refusal which only strengthens the rationality and truth of the argument. The gist of the argument is this: the cultural revolution diverts mental and physical energy from the arena in which the struggle against the existing society will be decided – the political arena. It transfigures economic and social into cultural conditions; it is absorbed in sexual, aesthetic, intellectual problems while the brutal force of capitalism is about to exterminate the desperate resistance movements the world over. Thus, behind the weighty title of "cultural revolution" (borrowed from a country where it is a mass movement) is nothing but a private, particular, ideological revolt: irresponsible élitism, an insult to the suffering masses.

The slogan, "let's sit down and reason together" has rightly become a joke. Can you reason with the Pentagon on any other thing than the relative effectiveness of killing machines – and their price? The Secretary of State can reason with the Secretary of the Treasury, and the latter with another Secretary and his advisers, and they all can reason with members of the Board of the great corporations. This is incestuous reasoning: they are all in agreement about the basic issue: the strengthening of the established power structure. Reasoning with it "from without" the power structure is a naive idea. They will listen only to the extent to which the voices can be translated into votes, which may perhaps bring into office another set of the same power structure with the same ultimate concern.

The argument is overwhelming. Bertolt Brecht noted that we live at a time where it seems a crime to talk about a tree. Since then, things have gotten much worse. Today, it seems a crime merely to *talk* about change while one's society is transformed into an institution of violence, terminating in Vietnam the genocide which began with the liquidation of the Indians. Is not the sheer power of this brutality immune against the spoken and written word against it? And is not the word which is directed against the practitioners of this power the same they use to defend their power? There is a level on which even the unintelligent action against them seems justified. For action smashes, though only for a moment, the closed universe of suppression, but escalation is built into the situation. For it is still true that capitalism produces its own gravediggers, and that every step into new areas of exploitation enlarges the scope of the internal contradictions and the forces of dissent and rebellion. And this dynamic necessarily propels the counter-revolution *before* the revolution ("preventative counter-revolution").

And yet, there is a time for talk and a time for action in the same social universe, and where mass action (if it occurs at all) is unpolitical in a radical sense, particular actions must be subject to *self*-limitation: they must methodically limit themselves to an educational function. That is to say, they must reveal, publicize, communicate the protest against particular injustices and crimes which telescope the injustice and criminality of the whole.

Today, education which counteracts the professional training for effective performance for the Establishment – counter-education is the indispensable weapon of political radicalization. By now it has become clear that the "final crisis" of capitalism is a global process on all levels of development, and that it may take a century. And this process may bring to the fore quite "unorthodox" modes of disintegration, corresponding to the important role of the instinctual controls. They have their own ambivalence. On the one hand, the instinctual intensification of social controls fortifies the established society by severely reducing effective rational discourse and action while allowing the system to escalate its profitable destructiveness. On the other hand, the instinctual dynamic unleashed by this system is likely to make for an increasing disintegration of the moral fiber which is still an essential factor of social cohesion. This disintegration may reach the point where the normal functioning of the economic and administrative process is seriously disrupted: a sort of generalization of wildcat strikes, group and individual refusal to work in protest against prevailing conditions (and not only material conditions). The rebellion may at first be "unpolitical" and insurrectional in terms of traditional union policy, but may assume political weight as it spreads among the population. A historical event may illustrate this possibility:

> L'été 1953 voit un phénomène unique dans l'histoire de France et dans l'histoire du mouvement ouvrier international: la grève spontanée de plusieurs millions de travailleurs qui, en quelques jours, paralyse tout un pays.
>
> Il ne s'agit pas d'une grève politique, encore moins d'une grève insurrectionnelle, mais plutôt, si l'expression ne choque pas, d'une grève de tristesse. On s'arrête de travailler parce que rien ne va. On a le sentiment d'être pris dans une masse: on ne vois pas d'issue. On en a assez. De quoi? De tout et de rien. Et brusquement, c'est l'explosion à laquelle il n'est pas d'explication logique. Jamais encore une grève générale n'a éclaté l'été, durant les congés payés: jamais encore une grève n'a pris ce caractère: tout un peuple qui s'assied moralement au bord de la route et se croise les bras, attendant . . . L'ensemble du pays approuve les grévistes: du moment ils sont mécontents, ils ont raison. (In the middle of August: 4 millions were on strike.)
>
> Ça et là, des ouvriers, des garçons de café, des coiffeurs 'débrayant' seuls pour suivre l'exemple. 'Moi aussi j'en ai assez de travailler.' Il fait beau, on se met en congé non payé.
>
> Chaque jour renforce le caractère insolite de la grève . . . Mendès-France interroge les grévistes de sa ville:
>
> – Que demandez-vous exactement?
> – Cela ne peut continuer.
> – Vous voulez une augmentation de vos salaires?
> – Oui, on en veut toujours quand on fait la grève.
> – Mais si vous l'obtenez, les prix monteront, cela ne vous aura servi à rien.
> – Oui.
> – Mais alors?
> – On ne peut pas continuer comme ça![14]

---

14 Georgette Elgey, *Histoire de la IVième République: La République des Contradictions. 1951–1954.* (Paris, Fayard, 1968), pp. 149, 155, 156, 159.

Translation:
The summer of 1953 saw a unique phenomenon in the history of France and in the history of the international workers' movement: the spontaneous

It would be senseless to speculate any further. We know from history that a society can continue to reproduce itself for a long period at a stage of moral (and even economic) disintegration. And a society operating with technological controls and a huge military apparatus can indulge in a long, protracted barbarism. Even an extreme release of primary destructiveness, if effectively channelled to serve an established regime, can be "conservative," that is, sustain the regime. Fascism is a good example, and enough signs point to a neo-fascist phase of capitalism. The instinctual dynamic operating in present-day industrial society, the structure beneath the infrastructure, is by itself no force capable of counteracting the neo-fascist development. Where the cultural revolution activates and transforms the instinctual structure (as in the Hippie and Yippie movements), it partakes of its ambivalence: the interaction of radical and "conservative" forces, the impossibility of protecting the former from the ingression of the latter, be it through absorption by the market, be it through a blind "actionism" which delivers the rebels as easy game to the hunting forces of law and order.

---

strike of several million workers who, within a few days, paralyzed an entire nation.

It was not a political strike, and still less an insurrection, but rather, if the expression isn't too shocking, a strike of sadness. People stopped working because nothing was right. People had the feeling of being swept up into the masses: no one could see any solution. They had had enough. Enough of what? Enough of everything and of nothing. And suddenly, there was an explosion without a logical explanation. Never before had a general strike broken out during the summer, during a paid vacation: never before had a strike taken on this character: an entire people who, morally, sat down in the streets and crossed their arms, waiting . . . The whole nation approved of the strikers' action: from the moment they became dissatisfied, they were right.

Here and there, workers, waiters, barbers "walking out" alone – following the general example. "I, also, have had enough of working." The weather was beautiful, and people began an unpaid vacation.

Each day reinforced the unprecedented character of the strike . . . Mendès-France questioned the strikers in his town:

– What, exactly, are you asking for?
– This can't go on.
– Do you want a raise in salary?
– Yes, you always want that when you go on strike.
– But if you get it, and prices go up, it won't have done you any good.
– True.
– Well then?
– We can't continue like this!

A similar ambivalence haunts the "communes." On the one hand, their isolation from the society (precondition for their radical function) leads to a premature "personalization": preoccupation with "private" problems, which are, without intermediaries, interpreted in political terms. This, in turn, tends to weaken individual responsibility: "it is the whole that is at fault." On the other hand, the living-together in a confined space apart from the society, and an often all too accidental formation of groups may well weaken (if not destroy) that dimension of "the private" which, transcending all bourgeois realizations, remains the indispensable soil of individual freedom. And yet, these communes are not only a refuge (though a most precarious one) from the oppressive and hypocritical order of life in this society, they are (most precarious) islands of a future: the testing ground for human relationships among men. The fact that this entire sphere has also become the refuge of some sick and mad ones (like any other sphere in this society) does not cancel its political potential – to the degree to which the rebels succeed in subjecting the new sensibility (the private, individual liberation) to the rigorous discipline of the mind (*die Anstrengung des Begriffs*). The latter alone can protect the movement from the entertainment industry and the nut house, by channeling its energies into socially relevant manifestations. And the more the insane power of the whole seems to justify any spontaneous counteraction (no matter how self-destructive), the more must despair and defiance be subjected to intellectual and factual *organization*. The revolution is nothing without its own rationality. The liberating laughter of the Yippies, their radical inability to take the bloody fame of "justice," of "law and order" seriously, may serve to counteract the petrification of the movement in another bureaucratic authoritarianism, and may help to tear the ideological veil which protects the purveyors of law and order, but it leaves intact the structure behind the veil. The latter can be brought down only by those who support it, who constitute its human base, who reproduce its profits and its power. They include an ever increasing sector of the middle classes, and the intelligentsia. At present, only a small part of this huge, truly underlying population is moving and is aware. To help extend this movement and this awareness is the constant task of the still isolated avant-gardistic groups. At the same time, they must guard their own consciousness and they must act by themselves.

# VII

†"The Historical Fate of Bourgeois Democracy" (n.d., around 1972–73) is another of the major unpublished texts found in the Marcuse archives in Frankfurt (#522.00). Written under the pressure of Nixon's decisive defeat of liberal anti-war candidate George McGovern in 1972 and Nixon's escalation of the US intervention in Vietnam, it represents Marcuse's most sustained critique of American democracy and growing belief that neo-fascist forces were gaining ascendancy. It anticipates Marcuse's analysis of "the preventive counterrevolution" in his book *Counterrevolution and Revolt* (1972) and stands as one of Marcuse's most passionate engagements with contemporary political reality and as his most sustained polemic against US democracy. It was never published, perhaps because the Watergate affair and eventual downfall of Nixon put in question his analysis of the power of President Nixon and reactionary forces in the current political conjuncture, or perhaps because he was turning to aesthetics and work on what became his last published book *The Aesthetic Dimension* (1979).

# THE HISTORICAL FATE
# OF BOURGEOIS DEMOCRACY†

The elections of 1972 have demonstrated, once again, and clearer than before, the historical fate of bourgeois democracy: its transformation from a dynamic into a static, from a liberal-progressive into a reactionary-conservative society. This democracy has become the most powerful obstacle to change – except change to the worse. On the road from laissez-faire to monopoly and state capitalism, bourgeois democracy in its present form marks the stage where only two alternatives seem possible: neo-fascism on a global scale, or transition to socialism. The former is the more likely one; it would not abolish but only intensify the established system and give it another breathing spell – long enough to cause all but irremediable destruction.

The regressive development of bourgeois democracy, its self-transformation into a police and warfare state must be discussed within the framework of global US policy. Briefly, the policy governed by the myth of an international communist conspiracy (the cold war) came to an end in 1972. Nixon's visits to Peking and Moscow marked the turning point (coinciding with a new turn in the policy of the two communist superpowers? This was suggested by Nixon in *US News and World Report*, June 1972). These visits were followed by a vast economic rearrangement, which opened the USSR (and to a much less conspicuous extent, China) to US finance and corporations. The concurrent political rearrangement is indicated by the amazingly weak verbal communist protests against the genocidal saturation bombing of Vietnam.

At the very same time, [there appeared] the aggressive military and political build-up of the US power-machine, and the fascist organization of the "Free World" progress (Philippines, Puerto Rico). But *against whom* this fantastic world-wide mobilization of power? A global war between the capitalist and communist superpowers (which would be destructive of all of them) is precluded by the sheer self-interest in the survival of the established regimes on both sides and by their "overkill" potential. The profits to be derived from the inflationary continual build-up of the defense industry in the capitalist countries, and the competitive response by the communist countries do not seem sufficient justification in view of the costs of the warfare state to the rest of the national economy.

The answer suggested by the present use of this war machine is: the "national security" of the USA is threatened by the national liberation movements throughout the world. The answer calls for strong qualification:

1 National independence of former colonial countries is *per se* no barrier to imperialism and neo-colonialism is still colonialism; nor is national independence incompatible with dependence on foreign capital (the case of most Latin-American countries, Arab countries, Burma, Thailand, etc.) – it may even be more lucrative than "direct colonialism."
2 The national liberation movements cannot withstand the full use of US military power (incl. "local" nuclear weapons) for any length of time. *Vietnam is no exception*! Nixon was probably right when he declared that "we could finish off North Vietnam within an afternoon." And the trend of communist policy suggests that such fate of Vietnam might *not* provoke a military conflict with the only communist power that might be a match for the USA.

However, the national liberation movements do constitute a threat to the global capitalist systems on two (interrelated) grounds:

a To the degree to which the "domino theory" is correct. Victorious in one strategic country, the revolution would have a snowball effect in subverting satellite regimes in other countries – a spread too much to be taken care of thoroughly! This is the threat to the "living space" of advanced capitalism: not merely control over vital raw materials, cheap labor, etc., but also over space, people, and time. In a strict sense, the economy of monopoly state capitalism is a *political* economy. The acute economic needs are "overlaid" by the long-range need for preventing the growth of the communist potential – not only Soviet or Chinese power, but also the *indigenous*, popular revolution, in Western Europe and in the Third World, a revolution which could make self-determination real and reject all satellite status.
b This world-historical prospect is the spectre that haunts the capitalist metropole, where the insanity of the established system begins to affect the "normal" behavior required for the continued, enlarged functioning of capitalism – the behavior at work as well as at leisure.

The system reacts effectively. Bourgeois democracy is giving itself an enlarged popular base which supports the liquidation of the remnants of the liberal period, the removal of government from popular control, and allows the pursuit of the imperialist policy. The shibboleth of democracy: government of the people and by the people (self-government) now assumes the form of a large-scale *identification* of the people with their rulers – caricature of popular sovereignty. Rousseau is stood on his head; the General Will is incorporated in the government, rather the executive branch of the government. Dissent and opposition are free to the degree to which they are manageable.

This identification, itself an achievement of monopolistic state capitalism at its highest stage (USA), operates in a depth dimension which sustains the power of the system in the individuals: bourgeois democracy has found a kindred instinctual foundation for its regressive and destructive development. The following sections will briefly discuss this dynamic.

Advanced capitalism is characterized by a quantitative *and qualitative* extension of its working class (see *Counterrevolution and Revolt*, Chapter 1). General denominator remains the dependence on capital, the capitalist appropriation of unpaid labor time, the separation from control over the means of production. With the monopolistic concentration of economic power, and the extended extraction of surplus value to intellectual and "unproductive" labor (in the sense of Adam Smith's term) large strata of the middle classes become working class – without being radicalized and "proletarianized." Only in this new historical form is the working class the majority of the population, only in this form culminates the capitalist polarization of society into capital and labor, rulers and ruled. And at the same time, the huge dependent population, the ruled class, provides the popular base of bourgeois democracy – reproducing this democracy in its repressive structure.

*Bonapartism*? Perhaps, but without Bonaparte, without the real or phony charismatic dictator. In any case, the analysis is confronted with structural changes which militate against the freezing of its concepts on previous stages of the development. Bourgeois democracy retains the capitalist class structure; at the same time, the ruled class, the underlying population at large, becomes the subject–object of politics, of democracy: the *people*, "free" in the sense and within the limits of capitalism, and in this freedom, reproducing its servitude.

This dialectic is clearly reflected in the political terminology of the Left. With the exception of some sectarian groups: the emphasis, in theory and practice, shifts from the (traditional) working class to the "people": "power to the people." But *who are* the people? In the official, especially legal lingo, the people are the sum total of the American citizens (including the ruling classes), considered as represented in and by specific institutions and organizations (in this sense: "The People versus X"). This is certainly not the meaning of "power to the people." Nor is, in this slogan, "people" coextant with "working class" in the narrower sense; it includes housewives, racial and national minorities, employees, unemployed, in brief, practically the entire underlying population.

The concept thus contains all these elements: the poor people (*le peuple*), the subjects of a Prince (monarchic or republican government), citizens vested with institutionalized rights and liberties, participating in, or being the government. In fact, the concept seems to have no contrary, because even the members of the ruling class and of the government are taxpayers, voters – subject to the rule of law. And precisely this amorphous Concept reflects the reality: the amorphous masses who today form the human base of American democracy – the harbinger of its conservatives' reactionary, even neo-fascist tendencies.

First, the facts which indicate the popular base of democracy in the USA, the roots of its strength as they appeared in the 1972 elections – only the climax of a long range trend. In free elections with universal suffrage, the people have elected (not for the first time!) a warfare government, engaged for long years in a war which is but a series of unprecedented crimes against humanity – a government of the representatives of the big corporations (and big labor!), a government unable (or unwilling) to halt inflation and eliminate unemployment, a government cutting down welfare and education, a government permeated with corruption, propped up by a Congress which has reduced itself to a yes-machine (after some not very serious criticism). And this government was elected with a considerable labor vote – the people rejecting a candidate who was by no stretch of the imagination a radical, an anti-capitalist[1] who was a member of the Establishment but who offered a reasonable chance to terminate the war crimes and to mitigate some crying inequalities and injustices. In other words: the people were willing (nobody forced them) to "buy" inflation and unemployment, war crimes and corruption, a grossly inadequate health service, the continued rat race of the daily existence – why?

The answer easily presents itself: the GNP is rising, the goodies are still coming in; one makes a living, much better than before, one can travel, have fun. And, after all: if the alternative is socialism, and if socialism is what exists in the USSR and its satellites (and what else is there except the

---

1  Marcuse is referring to 1972 Democratic Party Candidate George McGovern
   [D.K.].

unrealistic notions of some intellectuals), capitalism is vastly preferable. Moreover, the people are manipulated, brainwashed; the media, practically their only source of information, reflect and express government interests and policies – or rather those of the capitalist Establishment, which does not exclude some criticism within limits. And education, if at all, is increasingly functional: oriented on the jobs to be had and to be done: rewarded service to the Establishment.

The answer makes good sense, but it does not tell the whole story. The higher standard of living is bought at the price of enough misery, frustration, and resentment; the insanity of waste, of the inhuman performances on the assembly line, and of the loss of life and limbs in a constant slaughter is too obvious to be effectively repressed. And the submission to the sinister concentration of power in the government demands explanation precisely in view of the fact that it occurred in a democratic way, with civil rights and liberties institutionalized for the majority of the population.

Thus, it is wrong to say that the people are not to blame, that they are powerless to change things even if they wanted to. To be sure, the people have long since introjection continued to determine effectively mind and behavior in the face of its blatant cruelty and obsolescence?

The people *can* do something!

For example, they can vote against the warfare administration; they can come out en masse to protest and demonstrate its will as sovereign. They are free to obtain non-conformist, non-manipulated and non-censored information (the so-called underground press which is not at all underground; even some reports in the better newspapers and on TV; listener supported media, etc.), but it seems that they don't want to, that they do not have the real wish, the *need* to read or see or hear anything that contradicts the accepted truth or falsehood.

Thus people vote freely for their rulers, even where it is not the question of keeping or getting a job – they *identify* with their rulers. And thus they form a thoroughly conservative majority, which perpetuates itself in and through the electoral process, which perpetuates the ruling class and its administration, and which frustrates the opposition.

Here is the vicious circle of bourgeois democracy today: since no revolutionary situation prevails which could generate a revolutionary praxis, the radical Left must combine, and strengthen its *extra*-parliamentary strategy with a parliamentary opposition. But a different government can only be elected by a popular majority, and this is a *conservative* majority. In other words, at best, only a representative of the Establishment (though perhaps one with a more liberal shading) would have a chance to be elected – i.e., a lesser evil (which may even further stabilize the Establishment).

The spectacle of the reelection of Nixon stands as the nightmarish epitome of the period in which the self-transformation of bourgeois democracy into neofascism taken place – the highest stage (so far!) of monopolistic state capitalism. The people's identification with the system finds its most striking expression among the (blue collar) working class. The large labor vote for Nixon, racial discrimination, continued loading of war supplies during a strike, hatred against the "radicals," resulting in brutal beatings of demonstrators, boycott of the ships of countries where organized labor refuses to handle the shipment of American bombs to Vietnam – it would be disastrous for the Left to minimize these actions as non-representative "aberrations," nor to attribute them to the power of the union bureaucracy. They are rather labor's tribute to the social forces which bind the people, beyond the persisting class conflicts, in new ways to the established system.

In new ways: because the interplay between production and destruction, liberty and repression, power and submission (i.e., the unity of opposites which permeates the entire capitalist society today) has, with the help of technological means not previously available, created, among the underlying populations, a mental structure which responds to, and reflects the requirements of the system. In this mental structure are the deep individual, instinctual roots of the identification of the conformist majority with the institutionalized brutality and aggression. An instinctual, nay, libidinal affinity binds, beneath all rational justification, the subjects to the rulers.

The mental structure involved here is the *sadomasochistic character*. Erich Fromm, following Freud, has developed this concept in sociopsychological terms (*Studien über Autorität und Familie*, ed. Max Horkheimer, Paris, Alean, 1936, pp. 77–136. See also, Fromm, *Escape From Freedom*, New York, Rinehart and Co., 1941).

Within the conception of dialectical materialism, we are dealing here with one of the "mediations" between infra- and superstructure, one of the modes by which the social structure is reproduced in the individuals. An affinity prevails between Fascism and the sadomasochistic character (See T. W. Adorno, Else – Frenkel – Brunswik, and others: *The Authoritarian Personality*, New York, Harper and Brothers, 1950, and Wilhelm Reich's writings on the mass psychology of Fascism).

To be sure, instinctual identification is primarily always with persons, not with institutions, policies, a social system. In its emphasis on the sensuous "image," on the "sex appeal" of the political leader, the American system has mastered, in a terribly efficient way, the depth dimension of satisfactory submission beneath the political dimension. The real issues recede before the instinctual affirmation of the image: the people find themselves in their leader. No wonder then that it does not matter much what the leaders do in Vietnam, what unprecedented atrocities are committed under their regime; it does not matter much whether they lie or tell the truth, what they promise and don't keep; corruption and deception at the most august level of government does not cause much trouble . . . All these things are only the enlargement of what is going on daily, what is germane to this society; if the politicians get away with it, they only prove their competitive prowess. The crimes of the administration are indeed crimes only from an "extraneous" *moral* point of view – otherwise they are requirements of national security, free enterprise, self-preservation, etc.

It may be noteworthy that the features of the "image" seem to change in line with the increasing unpleasantness of the system, with the brutality of its accomplishments, with the replacement of hypocrisy by open lies and deceptions. The President, accordingly, as the chief of this giant corporation into which the nation is organized, can now be extremely ugly, without charm and sex appeal, but full of prowess and business morality.

To be sure, capitalism has always been brutal and ugly, criminal, but the presence of a strong and active opposition enforced a certain (ideological) restraint in the advertising of the real capitalist methods and goals. It is this ideological restraint (itself still a form of morality) which has now been abandoned.

In the abandonment of the civilized restraints on destructive power, in the liberation of government from good and evil, in the submissiveness and "understanding" of a free people instinctual drives are at work which threaten to assume explosive force. They constitute a huge syndrome of sadomasochism. Almost unadulterated sadism reigns in the American massacres in Vietnam, in the Saigon dictatorship, but also in the crimes which pervade the metropole, in the police, prisons and mental institutions; in the insane construction of ever more wasteful buildings, in the sports, etc. With a larger masochistic component, sadomasochism is rampant in the rock concerts where the massive audience suffers joyfully and orgastically the gratuitous violence of the noise ("escape from freedom," from politics!). And sadomasochistic is the tolerance of the people – the "free people": tolerance of the crooks and maniacs who govern them.

This sadomasochistic syndrome can be perfectly rationalized in terms of its productivity and power. But just as in the case of the identification mechanism (see above), so here is the overt rationality generated and fortified by the instinctual dynamic. This confluence makes the psychological category into a political one. Sadomasochistic is always an individual and not a society, but where the individual syndrome is displayed by the behavior of the larger part of society, it becomes a social syndrome. This society is delivered over to the *Death Instinct* in one of its most brutal forms. Phrases such as "death of the cities," "dying rivers and lakes," "vanishing forests" must be taken quite *literally*.

For according to Freud, the Death Instinct operates on a long "detour": destroying others before and while destroying oneself. The detour is shortened in the drug culture: what once was an element in the political rebellion, has now become, divorced from political praxis, gradual suicide. American culture is still sometimes described as a "death-denying culture" – nothing could be further from the truth. Or, rather, the neurotic death-denial hides the profound "understanding" of death: its veritable celebration in the daily media reports of violence, of the killing rate in Vietnam, in the advocacy, as *ultima ratio*, of the "final solution" (let's finish them off!).

The terrible option for death does not stop at the next of kin, the husbands and sons. The mother of three students at Kent State, who declared (and released for publication) that her sons should be "mowed down" if they do not obey the guards (see *Counterrevolution and Revolt*, p. 26f.) is probably an extreme case of sadomasochistic madness. The lady who is the former chairman of the National League of Families of Prisoners of War is probably also an extreme case: she approved the resumption of the saturation bombing of Vietnam although this would obviously delay the return of the prisoners, and increase their numbers. But the lady preferred this rather than give in to what she called pressure to sign a peace agreement, which would have returned the prisoners (*Los Angeles Times*, December 20, 1972). She did not believe that her statement represented the feelings of the majority of families concerned. But the extreme cases elucidate the norm: they are publicized, covered by the media – and there is no outrage, no storm of revulsion and hatred; there is no violence to suffocate this violence: for this option for death is an option for the perpetuation of the massacre – an option against peace and against hope. It is a *political* option.

On the road to fascism, advanced capitalism draws largely on primary aggressiveness. Consequently, the reversal of this trend would involve a radical redirection of aggressiveness. The struggle against the sadomasochistic soil of society is also waged on the instinctual level; here it involves, not the suppression but the counter-activation of aggression. Its suppression by the preaching of love and non-violence plays into the hands of the practitioners of hatred and violence. There are instinctual and "political" differences between the manifestations of aggressiveness: the hatred of evil, of oppression and destruction strengthens the Life Instinct, weakens the Death Instinct, the sadomasochistic structure. There is truth in the statement that almost always, the wrong people, i.e., those who stand for liberation, die prematurely: the system of oppression has its physiological roots.

The Marquis de Sade knew it: under this system, cruelty, injustice, vice are invariably rewarded, while virtue, morality, justice are invariably punished. This, and not his administrative organization of sexuality is his message. There may well be conditions under which hatred may be the only authentic mode of loving.

Adorno writes:

> It may well be that our society has developed itself to an extreme where the reality of love can actually be expressed only by the hatred of the existant, whereas any direct evidence of love serves only at confirming the very same conditions which breed hatred.
>
> ("Social Science and Sociological Tendencies In Psychoanalysis," 1946, quoted in Martin Jay, *The Dialectical Imagination* (Boston, Little Brown, 1973), p. 161.)

This liberating hatred is the token of the liberated consciousness, its impression into the instinctual structure. Once the facts have been learned, once it has become apparent why and how they have become facts and what they have done to people, the way is open for the "instinctualization" of reason, for the juncture of rationality and the unconscious. The instinctual need, the desire for freedom, becomes concrete as a *negative*: desire for liberation *from* . . . , for changing the world. The world cannot be changed by love (mankind has not yet learned it in 2000 years) but it can be changed by love that has turned into hatred and will return to love when the struggle has been won. It has never yet been won: not only brute force but also the power of ideology are responsible for the defeat. Ever since the crucified God (Nietzsche has recognized the horror of this symbol), the worship of death, the *Einverständnis mit dem Tode* had held sway over civilization: death as reward, as entrance into life, prerequisite of happiness and salvation. *L'Amour fort comme la mort*: the phrase epitomizes the big lie which has helped to discipline people in patience, obedience, endurance. This ideology has been institutionalized in churches and schools, has been transmitted in education from generation to generation; it permeates bourgeois democracy, it helps, again, and again, to prevent and "contain" revolution.

The subversion of this ideology cannot be achieved through education in materialism, atheism, etc.; it requires much stronger forces. What is at stake is the *conquest of fear*, which is always fear of pain, suffering, loss. Here science could come into its own, by giving mature mankind control over death: making it easy, painless. The rest could be taken care of by a comprehensive and adequate health insurance.

These are some of the extreme issues which confront the radical Left in this period: they operate in zones not yet elucidated and incorporated into theory and praxis. We return to the more acute issues at hand: the strategy of the Left.

The analysis of capitalist integration shifts the emphasis from the *classes* to the "*people*," the dependent population as a whole. In reality, this shift is no more and other than a redefinition of the concept of class in accord with the development of capitalism; thus, the redefinition may well be one of long duration. Thus, the proposition that the collapse will be an internal one, from within the system, holds true (the "within" including the Third World). And the process of transition would involve a radical transformation of bourgeois democracy *prior* to the revolutionary construction of socialism and *within* the framework of monopolistic state capitalism.

This transformation would reduce the conservative–conformist majority but by no means attain a "parliamentary" transition to socialism. This possibility (if it ever was one in the advanced capitalist countries) is all but precluded by the total armed and technical power controlled by the ruling class. The democratic transformation can only lead to the point where the popular support of the system is reduced to such a degree that the radical opposition can mobilize its own popular base – the threshold of civil war.

The following sections will discuss the question of whether the US capitalism generates the conditions for such a development.

One must start from scratch again. The power structure has succeeded in throwing the movement back on the smallest and most discredited means of protest: demonstrations, pickets, even letters to the Editor, to Congress-men, telegrams to the President! Humiliating, ridiculous, depressing – but it counts: the larger the number, the quantity, the more difficult to disregard this kind of protest. Moreover, the issues should be sharpened and not channeled into procedural, legal controversies. For example, if demon-strators against Marine recruiters on campus are being punished, the protest should not be against the use or violation of regulations (academic freedom, academic behavior) but rather against the much more punishable offense on the part of the Administration in allowing Marine recruiters on campus in the first place.

Generally, the *war* must be the primary target: it is the cause of the inflation, the deterioration of education and welfare, the crime culture. Tearing through the whole devilish and deceptive net of procedures and technics, the protest should make it clear that the presence of US forces in Indochina has been an act of aggression from the beginning, and that the nation has been implicated in an uninterrupted series of war crimes ever since. It was a bad blunder on the part of the anti-war movement to play the government's game by working for the release of prisoners of war. The argument: that the enemy was willing to make concessions in recognition of anti-war sentiment in the USA, which in turn would induce the US government to concessions, this argument thoroughly misjudges the strength of the warfare state and the brutality of its Administration.

The Left must realize that never before was the power and the mass base of the ruling class as large as it is in the USA today, and never as ready to use this power with all available means. It is sustained by the sadomasochistic conformism of the people. Liberation depends on a revolutionary struggle in which the prevalent instinctual structure would undergo a decisive transformation. The dominant aggressiveness must not be suppressed but redirected against the real enemies, tangible and visible incorporations of the capitalist system – its lackeys as well as masters: in the government, industry, the army, the universities, churches, etc. Action must be without the anal features, without the cruelty and cynicism which are the prerogative of the Establishment. Such action will go to the very limits of legality wherever transcending these limits would be self-defeating, and it will have to be prepared by a thorough political enlightenment of the respective "community" in order to neutralize its hostility and indifference.

The historically new features of bourgeois democracy in its most advanced form (in the USA) are (a) the strength of its popular base, and (b) its militant reactionary character. The popular base is fortified by an instinctual structure which reproduces the capitalist system in the individuals. The base includes the large majority of the working class. Now *it* is of course not at all a new development that the working class is "bourgeoisified" (*verbürgerlicht*). New is the remoteness of conditions under which this process could be reversed, the absence of a labor party and labor press, the rejection of socialism even as an end. As to the political character of bourgeois democracy today: this democracy does not anymore confront a feudal or post-feudal power; it has conquered, in its entirety, the army, the civil service, the educational institutions. As a result, parliament has been reduced to a minor function. The monopolization of the economy asserts itself in the concentration of power in the executive branch of the government. The self-rule of the bourgeoisie is complete; in the line-up of the population behind this rule, the working class still occupies a class position of its own, against the bourgeoisie, but as a class *in* this society – not transcending it, not its "definite negation." And the class struggle does not interfere with the brutal imperialist policy: international working class solidarity is at a historical low (rather, point zero), and the militant anti-war movement is still concentrated in "marginal" minoritarian groups.

At this stage, capitalism openly displays its own essence: the crime against humanity which it has been from the beginning. The exploitation of man by man, and the perversion of human into commodity relationships, the degrading character and organization of work, the system of domination, the destruction of nature – all these qualities can no longer be concealed or attenuated by their progressive function in the development of the productive forces. The capitalist development and use of these forces, constantly spurred by exploitation and dehumanization, have culminated in the productivity of killing – the killing of the weak and the poor in Indochina: technological, scientific, automatic killing which frees the killers from any sense of personal guilt.

It is as if capitalism now feels safe enough to throw off the brakes on its productive destruction – legal, moral, political brakes (or: as if capitalism can no longer afford to maintain those brakes). The system tears its own veil, its own verification. In its own behavior it demonstrates daily the truth of Marxian theory. Engels' Third Part of *Anti-Dühring*, Lenin's analysis of imperialism are tame and restrained in comparison with reality. The union of big capital and the state is the most immediate and overt: the notion of a conflict between private interest and public government is no longer taken seriously, and, if necessary, abolished by administrative fiat.

With the disappearance of the distinction between business, Mafia, and politics, corruption has become a meaningless term. The higher up it is, the more it is protected – "legitimized" by the very fact that it *is* so high up.

In the American democracy today, the government is by definition (because it was elected by the people, and because it is the government) immune against subversion, and it is (by the same definition) safe from any other than verbal criticism and a congressional opposition which can easily be managed. The separation between person and office, and the recognition of a popular right of resistance (ideas so central in the Protestant and Puritan tradition) are forgotten. The office sanctions the office holder, and this sanction is not affected by his deeds. The President is the President, and he retains the taboo that is due him – whether or not he ordered the dropping of the atom bomb or the massacre of the Vietnamese people. The sadomasochistic mentality of his subjects fortifies the taboo.

And the right to resistance: as exercised by the sovereign *people*, resistance has always been a revolutionary event, a fact rather than a right. The *right* of resistance has never been granted to the people as a whole, acting *en masse*; it has always been vested only in a specific part of the people, some group or council or "estate" considered as *representing* the people them-selves: "magistrates", parliament. But in the American democracy today, even this restricted popular resistance has ceased to operate: with the "balancing" activity of Congress concentrated on the budget and verbal protest, with the ubiquitous controling of power of the Executive, bourgeois democracy no longer presents an effective barrier to fascism.

I have stressed the ambivalent function of civil rights in this democracy: they have to be defended with all available means, though they also serve the protofascist government which controls them ever more openly. I refer to *Repressive Tolerance*: the situation has worsened since. The notion of objectivity, so central to the working of a civilized society, has been invalidated (nay, turned into its opposite) – not by the radicals, the Marxists, etc., but by the very government that indicts them. It drafts tough measures to force the media to have "balanced" programs. In the guise of objectivity: rigid censorship (operating, as everything else, via the money: withdrawal or non-renewal of licenses). But if any redressing of the balance would be needed in order to achieve objectivity, it would be in the opposite direction, namely, equal time and space for opinion and information *critical* of, and refuting those emanating from the government.

The government can afford to allow the airing and printing of critical objectivity as long as the latter remains strictly *quantitative*: ten affirmative letters to the Editor and ten negative on the same page, etc. The equality is deceptive, for the affirmative, conformist opinion is multiplied and fortified by the whole context: the make up of the newspaper, the privileged space allotted to government declarations and spokesmen, vindicative pressure, the sentiment of the community.

Moreover, in this context, objectivity in the allowance of opinion promotes aggressiveness, oppression, and crime to the extent to which it publicizes the most outrageous exhortation to violence – the sadomasochistic violence ingrained in the Establishment. Not a wild Leftist, not a human being, but a Mr Flynn from Anaheim can write to the *Los Angeles Times* that his "only regret is that the United States hasn't seen fit to use nuclear weapons against North Vietnam," and the paper prints this obscenity (December 29, 1972; four days after Christmas) because it also prints, on the same page, the protest. A President sitting safely in the most heavily protected White House in the world is called "courageous" for his order to bomb and bomb and bomb people out of this life and land, and this nonsense is printed, because, on the same page, the same President is blamed for the same reason.

Compared with a *neo-fascist* society, defined in terms of a "suspension" of civil rights and liberties, suppression of all opposition, militarization and totalitarian manipulation of the people, bourgeois democracy, even in its monopolistic form, still provides a chance (the last chance?) for the transition to socialism, for the education (in theory and practice) and organization to prepare this transition. The New Left is therefore faced with the task of defending this democracy – defend it as the *lesser evil*: lesser than suicide and suppression. And it is faced with the task of defending this democracy while attacking its capitalist foundations, that is to say, to separate the political forms of capitalism from its economic structure. Such a separation is made possible by the dialectical relationship between form and content: the bourgeois-democratic form "lags behind" the monopoly and state capitalist structure, and thus preserves liberal institutions germane to a previous historical stage which is rapidly being surpassed. Advanced capitalism is adequately equipped for doing away with these institutions if and when the conflict becomes intolerable, while the Left is still much too weak to transform them into socialist democracy. Overcoming this weakness requires the use of the democratic institutions while combatting the forces which, within this democracy, make the people themselves the harbinger of conservative, reactionary, and even neo-fascist tendencies.

To use bourgeois democracy for reducing its popular base – this is certainly not a new strategy. But today, the task is infinitely more difficult because (a) the impact of material want as revolutionizing force has considerably lessened, and (b) the management of the human being has reached unprecedented depth. Consequently, the raising of consciousness must proceed on a larger base, beyond the working class in the narrow sense, and it must be a job of *education* for a veritable transformation of values and goals which would negate the established system. Under monopolistic capitalism, such political education would indeed be the job of small non-integrated groups, and of individuals!

Élites? Why this notion, which belongs to the propaganda equipment of the Establishment – denunciation of hated radicals in terms appealing to the anti-intellectualism of the people? Why not rather the good revolutionary term "avant-garde". It has always been a small group, and has always included "intellectuals." And its task has always been education.

To be sure, the chance of a socialist revolution emerges in the experience of the revolutionary struggle itself but the point is that today, in the USA at least, in Germany, in Britain (that is, in the most advanced capitalist countries), the revolutionary struggle must first be generated, brought into being, organized. This requires the translation of the objective conditions into political consciousness, socialist consciousness. It cannot be the task of an "élite" (why replace the good Leninist concept of "avant-garde" by that of "élite"? Thus succumbing to Establishment propaganda?) of self-styled leaders, but rather of individuals and groups from *all* classes (*horribile dictu*!) who, in their confrontation with society, have had the liberating experience: on campus, on the streets, in the shops, in the ghettos, and who have become militant socialists in this confrontation. They know that the masses are not socialist, and they work for raising the consciousness of their fellow men and women wherever they may be, and not only among the workers: political education in theory and praxis.

This answers the question: who educates the educators? The answer is simple (once one has freed oneself from the vicious anti-intellectual propaganda in the formulation of the question). The answer is: *the educators educate themselves*. The theory is there, the historical tradition and experience are there, the lessons of the revolutionary struggle are there – they can be learned and communicated. . . .

Today, capitalism imposes on radical political education a new focus and a new "language." Just as, in the advanced capitalist countries, the radical impulse is likely to originate in the existential dimension *beyond* vital material want (privation), so the political education will have to accentuate and articulate this dimension. This means that the need for a fundamental reorganization of manual and intellectual labor is accentuated by a corresponding "ideological" change: education must focus on "cultural," *moral* issues as political weapons.

The minimization of moral issues (as "merely" ideological) has become a major bloc in the development of political consciousness and a major prop for the prevailing capitalist morality. Unless their very concrete political contents are made conscious (after more than a century of repression in which not a few Marxists joined the bourgeoisie), the image of socialism as a qualitatively better society will be a pale and abstract idea, not much worth fighting for. This means, not to regress from scientific to "utopian" or "true" socialism, from dialectical materialism to idealism, but, on the contrary, to recapture the full force of dialectical materialism by recognizing the material content of moral issues, their political substance and potential.

What *is* the political content of moral categories?

If the American workers *en masse* go on strike against the war in Vietnam, they would do so because they could not stand anymore the slaughter of a poor people fighting for liberation, and could not stand anymore the wholesale destruction of its country. This solidarity would be a *moral* category translated into political action. At the same time, such action, quite apart from its effect on the capitalist economy, would break the identification of labor with the ruling class and its interests – a break which is not achieved in the reformist trade union strategy. In short: eruption of socialist morality as political force. Another example: if conditions are established in which such events as the Rose Bowl Parade (attended by over a million people!) simply cannot take place as long as the war against liberation movements continues and the ghettos still stand. This achievement would be morality becoming a political force, and the political cathexis of a target which symbolizes the commercial epiphany of the erotic sphere. At the same time, the suppression of the massive display of beauty in the ugly society would be the radical moral outrage against the celebration of joy in accommodation to the atmosphere of the slaughterhouse.

Conversely, [one sees the] capitalist morality of labor as [a] reactionary force: In 1972, considerable sections of labor in the densely industrial states of the USA voted for the reelection of Nixon because of his stand against school busing. "It appears that the blue-collar worker in Michigan has reached the point where 'the school his kid goes to means more to him than the size of his pay check'" (*New York Times*, October 10, 1972). A "cultural" issue superceding the material economic issues? Is it the *quality* of education which is the concern of these workers, or is it rather the racist morality motivating the political act? The result: a further contribution to the stabilization of capitalism in its most aggressive form. The political force of morality assumes a new historical form under the conditions of monopoly capitalism: it is more deeply rooted and has a much larger radical potential than at previous stages of the social development.

When capitalism has freed itself from its ideological brakes, good and evil must again become political categories. "If "the people don't care" it is because they have long since learned that the Free World and Free Enterprise are above good and evil, truth and falsehood – as long as the system works . . .

Evidently, the liberation from good and evil horribly augments the power of a society which disposes over the means and resources to assert its self-defined interests. They now cover the entire world, inner and outer space. Here is the juncture between the political economy and the existential amorality of the system.

At this stage, continued popular support or sufferance of capitalism depends on "understanding" its monstrous crimes: the material well-being in the metropole rests on the inhuman silence of the conformist majority. The higher standard of living is certainly a goal worth fighting for. In the advanced countries, it must be essentially redefined in terms of human liberation; in very material terms. Can the good life be attained without exploitation and brutalization? On practical as well as theoretical grounds, the answer must be affirmative. But such a development presupposes the revolution which is being suppressed – not only by the government and the ruling class, but also by the people submitting to them.

In accord with the "extension" of the target of political education from the workers to "the people," the New Left in the USA has emphasized the "*community*" as the soil of political education. The concept of "community" is ideological: it suggests a basic identity of interests cutting across class divisions. Nevertheless, there are good reasons for this ideological "deviation." Communities such as the "neighborhood" offer the opportunity to reach people in their daily environment, in the concreteness of their life – after work, but also at work (women!). Moreover, concentration on the community counteracts the bureaucratic-centralized organization of Establishment politics, and of bureaucratic party centralization of the opposition. Community control would be a (tentative) form of self-determination and control "from below"; as such, it could precede and accompany workers' control in the factories and shops, in the ghettos, it would mean an immediate strengthening of the political potential.

The slogan "neighborhood control" (as, for example, propagated by the left-liberal Peace and Freedom or Peoples Party) is not to replace "workers control" nor is it a socialist slogan; it is rather germane to a situation where the large majority of the people (including labor) is decidedly, even militantly, conservative. Thus the question arises: neighborhood control by whom and for what? With the exception of the white and non-white ghettos, the neighborhoods reflect the liberal-conservative structure; the political work in these communities must start from this structure.

This means that the political work would begin with the discussion and collective decision on specific problems facing the community: school, child care, rents, utilities, ecology, etc. They are decidedly "reformist" issues, unpolitical, but as the work proceeds, each of them would reveal its political character within the whole; it would also lend itself to make accessible nonconformist information, and to develop the nuclei of a local organization. Neighborhood organization in the lower middle class communities would also establish a personal link between residence and occupation (shop, office, factory).

Community control for what? In communities still essentially conservative and conformist, self-control would not mean any progress other than, perhaps, progress in efficiency. Just as workers' control in the factories would not mean progress toward radical social and political change unless exercised by radical working men and women, so in the other communities. Here too, political education must be the first step on the long road toward socialist, anti-capitalist control. The aim of control is indeed "rationalization," i.e., an organization of work and leisure less wasteful and destructive of human and natural resources, but precisely this aim can be preserved only by a revolutionary sensibility, imagination, and reason – otherwise, it remains a rationalization of unfreedom, a higher stage in the development of capitalism. Rationalization and progress in autonomous control do not "automatically" assume the features of socialism, of control for freedom. In order to drive beyond the point where they transcend the capitalist framework and toward a radical reorganization of life, in other words, where they assume a different *quality* of work and leisure they must proceed on a qualitatively different human base – expression of a new human potential.

The same structural relation between the quantitative and qualitative elements of the transitional process prevails in the community which plays a decisive role in the radicalization of the integrated society: the *student* community. The counter-culture, the new morality originated largely in these groups – they contained the qualitative difference. What was lacking from the beginning was its adequate political organization. The latter was prevented by the cult of spontaneity and anti-authoritarianism. Admirable efforts at larger-scale organization were made: their highest point (at the Chicago Convention in 1968) was also the beginning of the decline . . .

In this context too, the *Women's Liberation Movement* is of the utmost importance – precisely to the degree to which it becomes a *political* movement. The negation of the values and goals of the male-dominated patriarchal society is also the negation of the values and goals of capitalism – and this on the physiological, instinctual level of the individual. I have been accused of succumbing to the "male chauvinist" image of the woman by attributing to her specific qualities which are actually socially determined (tenderness, softness, etc.). Now it seems to me meaningless to separate in this way socially determined and physiological ("natural") qualities: in the historical development, the former sink into the physiology and become "second nature." In any case, these female qualities have become a *fact*, and as factual, they can be put to political, social use. To suppress them because they are historically determined would be sacrificing to the male Establishment. To be sure, there is the aggressive female, the "devouring mother" (just as there is the soft male, the non-violent man). The goal is to free those qualities (male and female) which pertain to a better society, a society without sexual and other exploitation – regardless of whether these qualities are physiologically or socially determined.

In every revolution, there have been "sur-revolutionary" demands and forces which transcended the economic and political goals of the actual revolutionary praxis. In the absence of a revolutionary mass movement, they appear as historically premature. Today, this is the case in an especially emphatic sense. Conditions and modes of life which are traditionally supposed to be the result and effect of the revolution now precede the revolution, even appear as part of its cause in the advanced capitalist countries. I mean that transformation of values which aims at subverting not only the capitalist economy and politics but also the established consciousness, morality, and aesthetics – and not only of capitalism but also of Soviet model socialism.

Totalization of freedom: the more the capitalist production "overflows" into the market of unproductive goods and services, the less rational becomes the subjection of freedom to necessity. The realm of necessity tends to shrink and to become co-extant with the requirements of the established system and with the laws governing nature (matter).

Thus it is no accident that, at this stage of history, *the transcendent elements of Marxian theory* are being recaptured. The economic categories contain in themselves the imperative of liberation: it is the precondition rather than the result of the analysis. This internal coincidence of imperative and scientific truth is itself grounded in an objective constellation, namely a historical situation where human labor (intellectual and manual) has created the conditions for the abolition of servitude and oppression – goals which are blocked only by the capitalist organization of society. The transcendent content of the economic categories defines the concept of exploitation: the fact of exploitation persists even if the workers' material and cultural needs are more or less satisfied, if he is no longer the impoverished proletarian of the nineteenth century. For the substance of exploitation is the denial of freedom, is to work (and to live) in order to maintain and enlarge a social system the growth and wealth of which depends on the degradation of the human being. The surplus value appropriated by the capitalist is *time* taken away from the workers, time taken out of his life, and this alienation of living time in turn reproduces the human existence as servitude.

The first phase in the subversion of this condition would be the appropriation and use of surplus time for the abolition of servitude: self-determination and self-organization of socially necessary labor. The notion that this would be imaginable only on the highest level of technical progress (automation!) seems no longer tenable. The development of the political economy in China shows a largely decentralized and autonomous modernization within the framework of a general plan. In this respect, the problem is not the construction of socialism "from below" but rather the global political constellation, namely, the capability of the American superpower, and its readiness to suppress such a revolution.

Once again, the complex structure of the Marxian concept of capitalist development must be emphasized. The internal contradictions manifest themselves primarily in the aggravating economic difficulties, but by themselves they will not lead to the collapse of the system. The fascist solution still offers an alternative to revolution. True, no society can be maintained by terror, but a society (and precisely a technically highly advanced society) can be run by terror *plus* satisfaction of needs over and above subsistence needs. American imperialism still has tremendous markets to conquer: the Latin American liberation movements are beaten down by brute force and the business arrangements with the USSR and China promise not only to help further US finance and industry but also to protect the European and Asian flanks of imperialism. There is nothing in Marxian theory that excludes the possibility of such a development, and the force which alone is capable of preventing it is *political* action.

At the stage of monopolistic state capitalism, politics gains precedence over the economy – also in the strategy of the Marxist Left. I tried to show that, in the USA, this means focusing theory and practice on such targets as the war, the military establishment, the power structure's attack on education and welfare, government by conspiracy and undercover agents, the subjection of the legislative and judicial to the executive branch, censorship and intimidation, the rule of the Big Lie. And also the mobilization on the ideological level: coming to grips with the sadomasochistic mentality which supports the political economy of capitalism.

This shift in the strategic emphasis is motivated by the notion of a crisis of capitalism different from the traditional Marxist concept. I suggested it in terms of a structural disintegration while the economy, in its institutions, still operates: a moral disintegration, in the daily practice, at work and outside work. Not revolution but revolt: by individuals and small groups, throughout the society; too spontaneous, too isolated, even too criminal to be an avant-garde; not socialists, and not ready for political organization. As against vicious distortions, it must be reiterated that this is *not* a *Lumpenproletariat*, not "the rabble," the unemployed, etc.: this stratum includes employed workers, blue and white collar, intelligentsia, women, etc. By virtue of their position and their mentality, they can *become* political and nuclei of *organization* through painful and patient education.

If this trend comes to fruition and seizes a good part of the enlarged working class, the conditions have matured in which the taking over of individual factories and shops and the self-organization of work can occur. At this point, too, the open struggle with the (by that time fascist) forces is bound to break out. It is useless to speculate about the outcome but a few general remarks may be appropriate.

1  The chances of the Left depend on the extent of its popular base. This is a truism, but by itself, the popular base is no effective barrier against fascism. In Germany, a majority of the people did not support Nazism prior to 1933. It is precisely an essential feature of fascism to be able to cope with a non-fascist majority: by actual and "preventive" terror, but also by a system of manipulation, and satisfaction, which retains the constitutional paraphernalia. The balance of power depends on the resolution and capability of the political organizations of the Left to fight

with all available means – organizations rooted in the local and regional bases, but coordinated on a larger level.

2 The notion that fascism may be a historical precondition for socialism is a fatal illusion. If anything, it has contributed to weakening and dividing the Left at a time when a strong united front was essential.

3 No foreign power would effectively fight the rise of fascism – nor would any foreign power effectively and actively support a revolutionary movement. Reasons: fear that such intervention might lead to global war and to the overthrow of the power structure in the intervening countries.

4 Fascism can be defined as the totalitarian organization of society for the preservation and expansion of capitalism in a situation where this goal is no longer attainable by the normal development of the market. The principal threat to capitalism is twofold: the existence of a strong socialist-communist opposition within, and the constriction of capital accumulation caused by the lost war, serious depression, etc. In this situation, the capitalist "solution" is sought in a reduction of the wage level, breaking the power of the unions, and embarking on an aggressive imperialist policy. This solution requires the mobilization of the entire population behind the national interest as defined by the ruling class, abolition of the rule of law, the emasculation of parliament as rostrum of the opposition, all-out militarization, and shelving, *de facto*, the democratic ideology.

Now in the development of monopolistic state capitalism, these conditions emerge in the course of growth – with the following modifications:

- the increasing difficulties of capital accumulation and the narrowing of the market do not appear as the result of a lost war or other abnormal conditions, but rather as the result of the tremendous rise in the productivity of labor and constant overproduction even by lowered productive capacity.
- the opposition against repressive economic policy takes the form of union resistance against reduction of the wage level, and workers' resistance against intensified exploitation – not a socialist or communist threat; example: USA.
- German and Italian fascism were defeated in a global war, *not* from within. It is highly unlikely that a similar constellation will arise if fascism is established in the most advanced capitalist country of the present era. The danger of self-destruction is too imminent.

The alternatives? In the optimal case, the Left will be sufficiently united and sufficiently strong and militant to stem the fascist tide – which means: unite and organize *now*, as long as an anti-fascist potential still exists and has some freedom of movement. Or (and this may be concommitant): the communist orbit is reunited and prepared enough to stop and throw back imperialist aggression *without* a global (nuclear) war. Both possibilities are still fairly realistic.

For the Left in the USA, I emphasize again the immediate tasks:

- flooding the politicians, the representatives, the media and their sponsors with letters and telegrams of protest at every instance of political repression and persecution, and at every protraction of the war;
- starting from scratch again by organizing demonstrations, boycotts, picketting;
- providing teams of capable lawyers to defend the prosecuted in the courts (renouncing a "political" trial where the atmosphere for it does not prevail!);
- collecting funds for counter-institutions;
- educational and organizational work on the local bases, in the community, etc.

# VIII

## Watergate: When Law and Morality Stand in the Way

### By Herbert Marcuse

LA JOLLA, Calif.—The treatment of the Watergate scandal has concealed more than it has revealed. With rare exceptions, mainly in the "underground press," the significance of the events has been hidden or minimized by publicizing it as an extraordinary case of corruption in the highest circles of the Government—extraordinary because of its bungling brutality, its violation of elementary constitutional rights. However, this sort of treatment isolates the scandal from the context which makes the extraordinary an ordinary event, not an aberration but the extreme political form of the normal state of affairs.

This context is the present state of American capitalism. It seems that it cannot function, cannot grow any more without the use of illegal, illegitimate means, without the practice of violence in the various branches of the material and intellectual culture. The rule of law, and the political morality stipulated by it, were appropriate to the period of liberal capitalism: the age of free competition and free enterprise. On the open market, certain legal safeguards, generally observed, sufficed to protect private enterprise from undesirable interference; their observance did not unduly

a series of conspiratorial agreements, and its political counterpart operates through latent or manifest interven-

holder, one of the most liberating achievements of Western civilization, has collapsed. Now, not the office of

the sanity of the people. Reading the documents on the planning and organization of the super-intelligence agency, one must assume that in 1970, students, Panthers, Arabs, etc., were about to take over the country.

No, the vast, secret, illegal intelligence apparatus would not and could not suppress any real threat to national security, but well it could (and indeed did) suppress a threat against the established policy, domestic and foreign. While Congress was surrendering ever more of its balancing and controlling powers to the executive, while intimidation and self-censorship of the media became ever more noticeable, while inflation and unemployment continued unabated, while the power to wage war anywhere in the world was handed over to the President, the militant opposition was concentrated in the New Left.

Even without the full-scale implementation of the "game plan" to hunt down suspects and enemies all over the place, the operation was at least temporarily successful. The student movement has been broken up; the opposition has retreated. Temporarily, because the spirit of 1968-70 lives on, all over the nation, and not only among the young and the intelligentsia. And here, the all but irresistible

as a whole—of its "normal" behavior. But what remains "operative" and unscathed by revelations and ex-

Donald Evans

†"Watergate: When Law and Morality Stand in the Way" (1973) was published in *The New York Times* on June 27, 1973 when serious allegations were being made about the crimes of the Nixon White House that led to his resignation. In a June 14, 1973 letter to *New York Times* editor Harrison Salisbury, Marcuse wrote: "Enclosed is my piece on Watergate. I hope you are not too angry with it." It was published a couple of weeks later with a passage cut on the Gestapo-like tactics of the Nixon administration and with the conclusion taken out which suggests the presence of "an authoritarian regime resolved to do away with the still exiting liberal-democratic safeguards." We restore the text, otherwise unedited by the *Times*, to its original version by putting the excluded passages in notes.

# WATERGATE: WHEN LAW
# AND MORALITY STAND
# IN THE WAY †

The treatment of the Watergate scandal has concealed more than it has revealed. With rare exceptions, mainly in the "underground press," the significance of the events has been hidden or minimized by publicizing it as an extraordinary case of corruption in the highest circles of the government – extraordinary because of its bungling brutality, its violation of elementary constitutional rights. However, this sort of treatment isolates the scandal from the context which makes the extraordinary an ordinary event, not an aberration but the extreme political form of the normal state of affairs.

This context is the present state of American capitalism. It seems that it cannot function, cannot grow anymore without the use of illegal, illegitimate means, without the practice of violence in the various branches of the material and intellectual culture. The Rule of Law, and the political morality stipulated by it were appropriate to the period of liberal capitalism: the age of free competition and free enterprise. On the open market, certain legal safeguards, generally observed, sufficed to protect private enterprise from undesirable interference; their observance did not unduly hamper good business, nor was free competition under the rule of law altogether detrimental to progress: the competing powers developed the productive forces, and provided the goods and services to satisfy the basic needs of an increasing part of the population.

But the picture begins to change with the period of the World Wars. Competition generates oligopolies and monopolies; gradual saturation of the capital market at home leads to an aggressive imperialist policy, and the rapid rise of giant corporate interests transforms ever more independent enterprises into direct or indirect dependencies. At the same time, the growing power of organized labor threatens the corporate dominion, and the sharpening conflicts now demand the intervention of the state which the liberal phase restricted to a minimum: politics becomes part of business, and vice versa. The Rule of Law, the morals of legitimacy, based on the relative equality of competitors and on their general and common interests, becomes, under the changed conditions, an obstacle to business and power on the one hand, and an inadequate safeguard for the weak on the other. Monopolistic competition and imperialist expansion become the vehicles of growth on the national as well as international levels: the economy functions through a series of conspiratorial agreements, and its political counterpart operates through latent or manifest intervention in foreign countries: surreptitious or overt entry.

These tendencies change the composition, function, and behavior of the ruling class. To the degree to which it no longer develops but rather distorts and destroys the productive forces, it turns into a vast network (or chain) of rackets, cliques and gangs, powerful enough to bend the law or to break it where existing legislation is not already made or interpreted in their favor. In terms of liberal economics, today's conglomerates and multinational corporations would, by their very structure, exercise conspiratorial and illegitimate power. The difference between the Mafia and legitimate business becomes blurred. The purveyors of violence, as entertainment or as part of the job to be done, find sympathetic response among the underlying population whose character they have shaped.

There is no reason why the political sphere should remain immune from these developments. A wave of political assassinations and assassination attempts has swept the country. The previously progressive institutions of the Republic have been made into barriers against social change, stabilizers of the status quo. The electoral process has long since been dominated by the power of big money, the separation of powers turned into a Presidential dictatorship. The distinction between the office and the office holder, one of the most liberating achievements of Western civilization, has collapsed. Now, not the office of the President, the President himself is taboo: he defines and implements national security. Above right and wrong, his definition and implementation override dissent. He is also above logic: his statements are neither true nor false, they are "operative" or "inoperative" (according to his Press Secretary, R. Ziegler, April 17, 1973).

"Operative" means: having force, being in effect; it is neutral to moral values and legal norms. Watergate would have been operative if it would have worked; since it has been bungled, it has become inoperative. And this means that it disrupts the cohesion of the political system: as (and only as) a bungled undertaking, it becomes dangerous, compromising: it comes under the jurisdiction of moral and legal norms; it becomes a series of crimes, offenses . . . They must be publicized, televised, punished, because at stake are not only the prestige and the efficiency of the government but also of the society as a whole – of its "normal" behavior.

But what remains "operative" and unscathed by revelations and exposures of abuse is the notion of national security. The White House insists, understandably, on rigid secrecy to protect sensitive government documents – insists understandably, for it is precisely this secrecy which protects not only such documents of the government but also its policy from being revealed in its paranoic aggressiveness. The national security of this country is not now, nor in a foreseeable future threatened by anyone anywhere in the world – neither at home nor abroad. What may indeed be threatened is the further expansion of the American world empire, and secrecy serves to prevent the people from finding out what is being done to them under a false flag.

Popular awareness of these facts is combatted by the vast intelligence network which makes spying a normal activity. Its extent, its means, and its targets stand in no relation to national security: they are an insult to the sanity of the people. Reading the documents on the planning and organization of the super-intelligence agency, one must assume that in 1970, students, Panthers, Arabs, etc. were about to take over the country. No, the vast, secret, illegal intelligence apparatus would not and could not suppress any real threat to national security, but well it could (and indeed did) suppress a threat against *the established policy*, domestic and foreign. While Congress was surrendering ever more of its balancing and controlling powers to the Executive, while intimidation and self-censorship of the media became ever more noticeable, while inflation and unemployment continued unabated, while the power to wage war anywhere in the world was handed over to the President, the militant opposition was concentrated in the New Left.[1]

Even without the full-scale implementation of the "game plan" to hunt down suspects and enemies all over the place, the operation was at least temporarily successful. The student movement has been broken up; the opposition has retreated. Temporarily, because the spirit of 1968–1970 lives on, all over the nation, and not only among the young and the intelligentsia. And here, the all but irresistible protest against the Watergaters and the

---

1  The chairman of the Senate Investigation Committee spoke of the "Gestapo mentality" in the planning and execution of the illegal police apparatus (Gestapo mentality also in its language: "plumbers," "game plan," etc.): breaking the law and disturbing the order were to insure the law and the order imposed on the American people by the Leader. (Our leader and comrade: thus was Nixon addressed on a plaque handed to him by some of the POWs who owed their release so much to the anti-war efforts of the New Left.)

Gestapo mentality on the most august levels of government may well indicate the possibility of changing the course.

*This* opposition does not come from the Left: it comes from those conservative and liberal forces which are still committed to the progressive ideas of the Republic.

It is too early to write the obituary on Watergate, too early to say which side will win. The powers responsible for Watergate may survive: basic tendencies in the capitalist society support them, especially the increasing concentration of power, the amalgamation of big business and politics, the repression of radical dissent fostered by the aggravating economic difficulties.[2]

---

2  These tendencies may well make for an authoritarian regime resolved to do away
   with the still existing liberal-democratic safeguards. It might be worth noting that
   in Europe between the two World Wars, big scandals prepared the soil for
   extreme rightist and fascist governments: such scandals gave rise to the cry for the
   strong man, willing to clean up the stable of Augias – to do away with the whole
   "system." But the triumph of these forces is not inevitable. Those who insisted on
   tearing the veil of secrecy which protected the disastrous policy (no matter what
   their motives may have been) have done a great service: the chance of a change in
   the aggressive political climate in which the people, and their representatives, have
   surrendered to the powers that be.

# IX

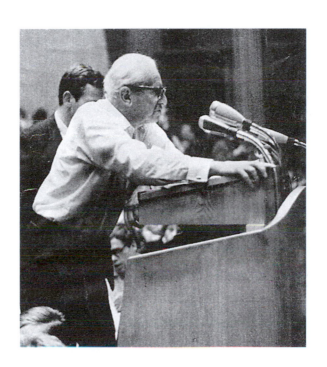

†A Revolution in Values" (1973) was first published in *Political Ideologies*, James A. Gould and Willis Truitt, eds (New York: Macmillan, 1973, pp. 331–6). A lecture delivered at a conference on Science, Technology, and Values, February 1972, at the University of South Florida, in Tampa, Marcuse continues his reflections on cultural revolution and provides one of the most focused presentations of his call for a "revolution in values."

# A  REVOLUTION  IN  VALUES[†]

At the beginning, I have to say briefly what I mean by values in this context. I mean norms and aspirations which motivate the behavior of social groups in the process of satisfying their needs, material as well as cultural, and in defining their needs. In this sense, values are not a matter of personal preference: they express the exigencies of the established production relations and the established pattern of consumption. However, and this is decisive, at the same time, values express the possibilities inherent in but repressed by the productivity of the established society. Let me give you a few very familiar examples of this two-fold character of values: on the one hand, to be bound and confined to the existing social system, on the other hand, to transcend it by aiming at possibilities still denied by the system. For example, the value of honor in feudal society expresses, first of all a basic exigency of feudalism; namely, the requirements of a hierarchy of domination and dependence founded on direct personal relationships assured not only by force but also by the sanctity of contracts. The value of loyalty, proclaimed in a society of oppression and inequality, was idealized, sublimated, in the great court epics, the romances, the court ceremonial of the time, but it would be nonsense to say that heroes like Tristan, Percival, and others are nothing but feudal knights and vassals, that their ideals, adventures, and conflicts do not transcend the feudal society; they certainly do. In and above the feudal framework, we find universal human possibilities, promises, sufferings and happiness.

Similarly, the values of liberty and equality express first of all the exigencies of the capitalist mode of production, namely, free competition among relative equals, free wage labor, exchange of equivalents regardless of race, status, and so on. But, at the same time the same values project better forms of human association, still unrealized possibilities. The same ambivalence we have in another of the decisive values characteristic of the modern period, namely, the concept of work as calling and vocation. Work is a necessity for the entire adult life, and in most cases an unpleasant necessity; still, or precisely because of it, work is said to be the vocation of man sanctioned by religion. Now, for the vast majority of the population work has always been dehumanizing, painful, alienated labor, that is, an activity in which a human being cannot develop and satisfy his or her own individual faculties and capabilities. At the same time, this concept of work as calling and vocation projects a very different attitude and position of work in life; namely, the self-realization of a human being in creative work.

After these preliminary and very sketchy definitions, I would like to discuss two main aspects of my theme, namely, the role of values in social change and the contemporary revolution of values as an unprecedented transformation. Let me start by taking the Marxian theory of how a transformation of values takes place. Socially effective new values replace the established ones if and when they express the interest of an advancing, ascending class in the struggle against the existing ruling class. But, the new values articulate the particular class interests in a general form, claiming that the class interest is at the same time the universal interest and in this way, class-determined values assume the form of a universal truth. This is the ideological character of values. Values are ideological inasmuch as they abstract from their restriction or denial in reality. In capitalist society, liberty and equality remain abstract, partial liberty and equality – a privilege. But the very same ideology becomes a material force in the process of change as soon as it begins to impel political action on a mass scale aiming at the full realization of the distorted and denied values.

Now, it is important to notice that the Marxian conception does not mean a simple chronological sequence, namely, first basic change in the class relations, then a revolution in values. To say that the new values of socialism can only be the products of new social and economic institutions is vulgar, not dialectical materialism. Rather the articulation of new social values almost invariably *precedes* the institutionalization of new class relations and of a new mode of production. Examples abound in history; I shall mention only two: the Enlightenment prior to the French Revolution, and socialist theory itself. This situation illuminates the role of the intelligentsia in the process of social change, which I shall discuss subsequently. The transformation of values is not merely the ideological reflex of the social structure. A radical transformation rather articulates radically new historical possibilities, forces not yet incorporated into the process of social change.

An intellectual, "cultural" revolution precedes social revolution, projects the latter, is the catalyst of the latter.

The transition from an established value system or an established value hierarchy to another one is a dialectical process. Thus, the bourgeois ideology cancels the feudal contract relations by generalizing this relation in the idea of the social contract which binds all members of society while submitting all of them, in very different ways, to the overriding laws of the exchange economy. Similarly, socialism is to cancel the abstract and exploitative structure behind the bourgeois ideology of liberty and equality, and to make work truly a vocation, namely, the self-realization of the individual in an association with free human beings. The translation of the ideology into reality is to take place in the revolutionary action of the proletariat. How does this conception apply to the situation in the advanced capitalist countries today?

Today's cultural revolution (and I speak only of the cultural revolution in the West) involves a transformation of values which strikes at the entirety of the established culture, material as well as intellectual. This attack on the entire traditional system of values finds its peak in the rejection of the Performance Principle. According to this principle, everyone has to earn his living in alienating but socially necessary performances, and one's reward, one's status in society will be determined by this performance (the work–income relation). The rejection of the Performance Principle also rejects the notion of progress which has up to now characterized the development of Western civilization, namely, progress as increasingly productive exploitation and mastery of nature, external and human, a progress which has turned out to be self-propelling destruction and domination. Note that this rejection of the Performance Principle does not only strike at the principle governing the existing capitalist society, but at any society which maintains the subjection of man to the instruments of his labor. Now as against this Performance Principle, the cultural revolution calls for an end to this domination, for freedom and solidarity as a quality of the human existence, for the abolition of a society which condemns the vast majority of its members to live their lives as a means for earning a living rather than as end in itself.

At this point, a warning against any false romanticism. There can be no such thing as a total abolition of alienation. Dialectical materialism recognizes the inexorable objectivity of nature, of matter, the inexorable struggle of man with nature confronting the human subject and limiting its freedom no matter in what form of society. It is not the question of abolishing alienation altogether but abolishing what I might call surplus alienation, namely the alienation exacted by the existing society in the interest of

maintaining and enlarging the status quo. This surplus alienation has been
the soil on which quantitative progress has taken place: it has sustained the
separation of intellectual from manual labor, the need and the growing need
for dehumanizing, parasitarian and destructive work, the need for repression; it has wasted and polluted the available resources – technical, natural
and human. Quantitative progress now could, and should, turn into quality:
a new mode of life which would free the potentialities of man and nature
by negating the established system of exploitation and its values. This
transformation of values would not only invalidate the existing political and
economic institutions, it would also make for a new morality, for new
relations between the sexes and generations, for a new relation between man
and nature.

The scope of these tendencies and their radical character assume a
new force at the present stage of capitalist development. In all preceding
revolutions of values these demands remained largely abstract, marginal;
they kept "above" an order of social as well as instinctual repression which
was in itself rational and legitimate as long as it really developed the
productive forces. To date, however, this organization of society is becoming
incompatible not only with further progress but also with the very survival
of mankind as a human race. And accordingly, today's revolution of
values no longer proceeds within the established continuum of quantitative
progress, but it tends to break this continuum. It is a *qualitative leap* into
the possibility of an essentially different way of life.

Let me try merely to enumerate the main aspects of this break with, and
transcendence beyond the established continuum. The foundation and the
aim would still be the shift from self-propelling productivity to collectively
controlled production for freely developing individual needs: socialism.
It implies the shift from utility values to aesthetic values, the emergence of
a new sensibility, new modes of perception, or experience. Aesthetic values
are inherently non-exploitative, non-repressive; their articulation in radical
political movements suggest the striving for a change also in the instinctual
foundations of civilization. In the last analysis, this tendency would
counteract the male aggressiveness of patriarchal civilization and thereby
subject more effectively aggressive to erotic energy, to the life instincts. One
sees today a widespread rebellion against the domineering values of virility,
heroism and force, invoking the images of society which may bring about
the end of violence.

This is the historical and psychological depth dimension of the
Women's Liberation Movement. It does not yet seem conscious of its truly
subversive radical potential, which could propel a decisive transformation
of the entire material and intellectual culture, could reduce repression,

and provide the psychological, instinctual foundation for a less aggressive Reality Principle.

The ascendence of new radical values is more than a merely ideological revolution; rather it tends to become a material force generated by the very dynamics of advanced capitalist society and foreshadowing the internal weakening, perhaps even disintegration of this society. This ideological revolution, which is all but a reversal of values, reflects a new historical stage of social development, namely, the stage where society has achieved the satisfaction of basic needs for the great majority of its members while sustaining oppression and misery at home and abroad. This society must, under the pressure for enlarged capital accumulation, incessantly create and stimulate needs over and above the needs of subsistence, in other words cultural and luxury needs. Thereby, this society is invalidating the legitimacy of perpetuating profitable repression. The attained level of the productivity of labor would allow the reduction of working time required for the reproduction of society to a minimum and thus eliminate the necessity of full-time alienated labor – but full-time alienated labor is the foundation of the system. It is undermined by the constant production of goods and services which are superfluous in terms of subsistence. Spending one's life in "earning a living," life as a means rather then as an end-in-itself: this mode of existence becomes evermore blatantly unproductive, obsolete, irrational – rational only for the maintenance of the status quo. Under these conditions, demands are generated for a radically different social division and organization of labor, for the abolition of the work–income relation: "transcendent" needs of freedom which cannot be satisfied within the framework of institutions based on the rule of Performance Principle.

Corresponding to this stage of development, a new pattern of social change is gradually emerging, namely, the possibility of a revolution on the grounds of satisfied basic needs and unsatisfied transcendent needs. It would be a revolution under the pressure of the vital need for self-determination, the need for joy, for no longer being an instrument of the ever-present apparatus. This is not simply the well-known pattern of rising expectations, better offerings from the available "cake", but rather the awareness of goals subverting the established hierarchy and priority of values and aiming at a new rationality, new sensibility, new morality.

Now how does this revolution of values manifest today as a material force, as radical social ferment? Here, I can only indicate the most conspicuous features of this process. First, we have in this country some sort of "Keynesianism with a vengeance". Max Weber characterized the spirit of capitalism as "inner-worldly asceticism", the drive to save and save and save, to invest and to invest in order to produce more and more profit, work, and to accept even the lowest and most inhuman work as "calling", as the vocation of man. Today, we see the negation of this principle: the urge to spend, and the revolt against prevalues of production; work discipline and responsibility are weakening; people question effectively the necessity for life-long alienation.

Secondly, and related to the trend just discussed, there is a pervasive deterioration of the commodity world itself, of the quality of goods and services and a recurring disruption of the process of production in a more than "normal" way: wildcat strikes, strikes against the entire organization of work and not only for higher wages and better working conditions. A high rate of absenteeism prevails, and individual and group sabotage are frequent. And in this general climate, the ecology drive articulates the need for a new relation between man and nature as his life environment – a drive which, if sustained and extended, can become a political force, striking at the very institutions which create and perpetuate pollution.

Behind all this is the awareness, the feeling that one can live as a human being without running in the rat race, without performing dehumanizing jobs, the awareness of the repressive and destructive impact of the "consumer society". Given the structure and organization of advanced capitalism, it is no wonder that the new values are not carried by one ascending class in its struggle against the ruling class. These values do not express the immediate interests of any specific class. They are, at the present stage, still carried by non-integrated groups among the youth, the women, the black and brown population, the young workers, the intelligentsia.

They are minorities; they are by themselves no revolutionary groups, nor can they in any sense replace the working class as the basis of radical social change. But they are indispensable today, the sole catalysts of change, and they articulate needs which are in reality the needs of the entire underlying population. And, if and when the working class becomes the carrier of revolution, it will be a very different class, in which the blue collar labor will only be a minority, a class which will include large strata of middle classes, and in which intellectual work will play an increasing role.

This trend accentuates the importance of the colleges and universities in the process of change. The students, far from being merely a privileged élite without a material base, are in fact the potential *cadres* of the existing as well as the future society. The construction of a free society, the abolition of poverty the world over, the reduction of necessary but inhuman work to a minimum of time, the rebuilding of towns, the restoration of the countryside, the control of disease, of the birth rate – these tasks require a high degree of scientific progress, also in the humanities and social sciences!

The progressive elimination of violence, the emancipation of the senses, far from implying a rejection of reason and rationality, demand a new and more rational rationality, a new and more rational reason, capable of organizing and developing also non-instrumentalist, non-utilitarian, non-repressive goals. The question arises whether there is not some surplus aggressiveness and violence in the established science and technology, in their very structure, perhaps the reflex and at the same time the stimulus of the service of science and technology to destructive social powers. Can we, in any sense, rationally speculate on a change, not only in the application of science but also in its direction and method? A change perhaps generated by an entirely new experience of nature, a new relation to nature and to man? The ascent of aesthetic values as non-violent, non-aggressive values suggest at least the possibility of a different formation of scientific concepts, a different direction of scientific abstraction; a more concrete, more sensuous, more qualitative science and technology, including a science of the imagination, as a creative faculty of human beings.

A few words in conclusion. The tendencies which I have tried to sketch here draw into the process of change the instinctual structure itself, the senses, minds and bodies of men and women: they enlarge the scope of the potential revolution. It seems that the established society is fully aware of the scope and depth of the challenge. The power structure answers with intensified, legal and extra-legal repression, with the organization of the preventive counter-revolution, preventive because no successful revolution has preceded it in the advanced industrial countries. Under these circumstances, the prospects are not very exhilarating. The initiative today is with the forces of repression. There is no historical law according to which capitalism will inevitably be followed by socialism. The socialist tradition itself has always recognized and retained the alternative: either a free and human society, socialism, or a long period of civilized barbarism, a society entirely in the hands of an omnipresent and all-powerful administration and management – some kind of neofascism. I believe that it is not too late. I think that barbarism, neofascist barbarism, can still be fought. If it is not fought today, it may be too late because we know of no case where a fascist regime, once established, has been defeated from within. So it is not yet too late, but if this generation doesn't fight it, it may very well be too late.

# X


BRANDEIS UNIVERSITY

WALTHAM 54, MASSACHUSETTS
February 16, 1961.

Dear Leo:

I am disturbed. I am disturbed. I am disturbed. From a
catalogue of the so-called Free Press, I see that you and
Lipset are editing a book on Riesman. It is none of my
business to judge whether your mental and other energy
is productively spent on such an undertaking. But since
you are dear to my heart I must tell you that I am
grieved to see you tied up with your colleague, Lipsit whose
book POLITICAL MAN is, in my view, one of the most repulsive pieces of closetdeckel sociology I have ever seen.
I think you know what I mean. Do you think you will get
over it?

I may have told you that I am going to have my sabbatical
next year and that we intend to spend most of the time in
Paris. What about seeing you - either there or in this
country before we leave?

Give my love to Marjorie.

Do not resent my frank opinion. It is motivated entirely
by loyalty.

*Herbert*

*Marcuse*

# LETTERS

Herbert Marcuse carried out an extensive correspondence with Leo Löwenthal, who became one of his closest friends. The Löwenthal archives, not yet open to the public, contain a rich collection of correspondence with various members of the Institute for Social Research and a large collection of letters to and from Marcuse, as well as some manuscripts, not found in the Marcuse archives. Accordingly, our letter section opens with correspondence between Marcuse and Löwenthal where Marcuse indicates his desire to help Löwenthal obtain a suitable teaching position and in which Marcuse expresses his views of current social theory and mentions work on *Eros and Civilization*. The Marcuse–Löwenthal section concludes with a letter written by Löwenthal to Richard Popkin, then Chair of the philosophy department at the University of California, La Jolla, where Marcuse would teach from 1965 until his enforced retirement in 1970. Thanks to Peter-Erwin Jansen and the Löwenthal archives for permission to publish letters from the Löwenthal–Marcuse correspondence.

Marcuse continued to maintain a regular correspondence with Max Horkheimer, T. W. Adorno, and Frederick Pollock after they returned to Germany. This rich correspondence contains comments on their respective works, intellectual and political tendencies of the day, their academic pursuits, and personal vicissitudes. The exchange selected opens with a letter from Marcuse to Adorno where he makes provocative comments concerning phrases of Adorno's and allusions to friends who were claiming that Adorno was promoting cold-war ideology; Marcuse notes that he found no such evidence in Adorno's writings, but was disturbed by some comments in a recent introduction to Paul Massing's book on anti-Semitism by Horkheimer and Adorno. Horkheimer and Adorno together respond, aggressively defending themselves, but prompting Marcuse to write a sharper response that was never sent, but which we include in the letter selection. A subsequent letter to Adorno notes that Horkheimer met with Marcuse in the US, "clarified" some of the points under contention, claiming that he had wanted to modify some of the statements, but that the letter was sent before this was possible. This letter to Adorno is conciliatory and does not take up the polemic that would later emerge in the 1960s under the pressure of the student movement – a dramatic development that will be a topic of the next collection of Marcuse's works that will appear in the Routledge *Collected Papers* series that will engage Marcuse's contributions to *Foundations of the New Left*.

In addition to his extensive correspondence with original members of the Frankfurt School, Marcuse frequently corresponded with Raya Dunayevskaya, who founded a Marxist-Humanist group in Detroit, was a prolific writer, and engaged activist. While they differed significantly on their appraisals of the revolutionary potential of the proletariat, they shared a passionate interest in Hegel and Marx and had an extensive and often illuminating exchange of letters. I have chosen a selection of letters on the topic of automation that appeared in 1960 when Marcuse was working on *One-Dimensional Man*. Dunayevskaya presents a detailed overview of literature on automation and her own views. While Marcuse sharply differs on some major points, some of the literature Dunayevskaya recommended and some of her arguments appear in *One-Dimensional Man*.

Marcuse carried out a sporadic correspondence with Frederick Pollock on automation and Marxian theory, as well as the affairs of the Institute of Social Research. Pollock published a book on *Automation* in 1956 and Marcuse occasionally wrote him about the topic and other issues in economics and Marxian theory. We publish here a memorandum of a discussion between Marcuse and Pollock in 1960 and a letter on the conversation by Pollock. It is interesting to see that the form of the memorandum presents Marcuse as the questing student and Pollock as the omniscient professor; it would be interesting to know Marcuse's response to Pollock's positions, but his archives do not contain letters in which he responds.

Thanks to John Abroweit for translating the letters and the concluding reflection on Marcuse by Jürgen Habermas, as well as providing notes to the letters he translated.

## HERBERT MARCUSE TO LEO LÖWENTHAL, MARCH 26, 1955

*Brandeis University*
*Waltham, Massachusetts*

*Leochen:*

This Brandeis thing is dragging on at a snail's pace.[1] I think I have so far blocked the consideration of people like Robin Williams of Cornell and Charles Page, but I have not yet succeeded in presenting you as the only candidate. Max Lerner is constantly en route in and outside the hemisphere – I now made a definite appointment with him for the Easter week. Nothing is going to happen until after the spring recess, that is, April 20.

Why don't you write how you like it there, and how you put up with teaching these healthy suntan-smelling artefacts of California students?[2] I have heard nothing definite from Frankfurt, except that the *Festschrift* still isn't out. My book is with the publisher for routine copy-editing – I still don't know how to handle the German edition; the Institute seems to have other zores. Any idea? I talked with Koehne, but he apparently has no time for translating the book.[3]

I must disappoint you (*es fällt mir schwer*): we have no two copies of de Maistre, and this is the one work which I had in mind for myself – as "fee" for my work as executor. You wouldn't want me to sacrifice it? Wouldn't you do with the Burke? The library is in all probability going to be sold to the University of West Berlin, which would pay in Dollars. But the house is not yet sold, although we bought a very nice place in Newton, a suburb of Boston halfway between Cambridge and Waltham. We expect to move around June 1.

An "appreciation meeting" will be held for Franz at Columbia on April 11: Schuyler Wallace, Kirchheimer, and I will speak.[4] You should be here. I miss you anyway – strange as it may seem. And I still regret your sojourn to the Unterwelt of the Misbehavioral sciences next year – I shall do my best to get you out of it.[5]

Inge sends you her best wishes and greetings – as do I.

*Yours Herbert*

---

*Editor's notes*

1  Marcuse had recently received a tenured position at Brandeis and was working to get Löwenthal a position there, while blocking potential conservative appointments.
2  Löwenthal was teaching at the University of California at Berkeley; ironically,

Marcuse himself would be teaching "suntan-smelling artefacts of California students with his appointment to the University of California at San Diego in 1965.

3  Marcuse refers, first, to the *Festschrift* for Max Horkheimer published later in the year in the Institute publication series; he then refers to his own *Eros and Civilization* published in 1955 by Beacon Press which he had submitted to the Institute for a German translation, but, as I discuss in the Introduction, was not included in their publication series.

4  Marcuse's good friend Franz Neumann had just been killed in an automobile accident and Marcuse participated in a memorial session for Neumann at Columbia. His reflections were published as a Preface to a collected volume, Franz Neumann, *The Authoritarian and Democratic State*, ed. Herbert Marcuse (New York: Free Press, 1957), pp. vii–x. On Marcuse and Neumann, see *Technology, War, and Fascism*, pp. 7ff. and 93ff.

5  Löwenthal was appointed for the following year as a fellow at the Stanford Institute of Behavioral Sciences which Marcuse ironically refers to as "the Unterwelt [Underworld] of the Misbehavioral sciences."

---

## HERBERT MARCUSE TO LEO LÖWENTHAL, SEPTEMBER 9, 1955

*Brandeis University*
*Waltham, Massachusetts*

*Dear Leochen:*

Your letter reached us after our return from our short but more than beautiful vacation in Maine. I am happy that you took to Kluckhohn – he is indeed an exceptional being.[1] I have not yet gotten in touch with him but shall do so soon. My book is supposed to be out by the end of October. The Institute does not seem to be eager to publish the German edition – understandably if the "Frankfurter Beiträge" really set the model for publication. Lazarsfeld will have his joy (and, I guess, his Hohn) about the "Gruppenexperiment." I don't remember whether I wrote you that Fromm is going to reply to my critique, which appeared separately in "Dissent". *Reason and Revolution* will come to you directly from the publisher – I shall personally inscribe it when we see each other – when?[2] I envy you for the opportunity to do nothing but thinking and writing – but what about the company in which you find yourself? Which reminds me: at the psychologists' conference at San Francisco, a certain Untermensch from Yale named Robert E. Lane (*NY Times* Sept. 3) gave a paper which beats everything in Untermenschentum: it is on the "personality traits affecting political interest" and I would be extremely grateful to you if you could secure a copy for me.[3]

I have not been at Brandeis for a long time, but I have seen the president and some of my colleagues: there is no new development re sociology, and I doubt that Coser will get the chair. But who knows? I shall keep after it.

Is the Horkheimer *Festschrift* out? How could it happen that they allowed the terrible mixture of Latin and German in the title *Soziologica*?[4]

The very best to you andMarjorie (no space between the "and" and her name)

*also from Inge*
*your very old*
*Herbert*

---

*Editor's notes*

1   Marcuse is referring to the American anthropologist Clyde Kluckhohn whom he obviously respected.
2   Marcuse's book *Reason and Revolution* had been republished by Columbia University Press in a new edition in 1954.
3   Robert Lane, a political scientist at Yale, was author of a book *Political Ideology* (New Haven: Yale University Press, 1963) and obviously not respected by Marcuse.
4   See Note 3 to the previous letter.

---

## HERBERT MARCUSE TO LEO LÖWENTHAL, FEBRUARY 16, 1961

*Brandeis University*
*Waltham 54, Massachusetts*

*Dear Leo:*

I am disturbed. I am disturbed. I am disturbed. From a catalogue of the so-called Free Press, I see that you and Lipset are editing a book on Riesman. It is none of my business to judge whether your mental and other energy is productively spent on such an undertaking. But since you are dear to my heart I must tell you that I am grieved to see you tied up with your colleague, Lipset whose book POLITICAL MAN is, in my view, one of the most repulsive pieces of closetdeckel sociology I have ever seen. I think you know what I mean. Do you think you will get over it.[1]

I may have told you that I am going to have my sabbatical next year and that we intend to spend most of the time in Paris. What about seeing you – either there or in this country before we leave?

Give my love to Marjorie.

Do not resent my frank opinion. It is motivated entirely by loyalty.

*Herbert Marcuse*

---

*Editor's note*

1   See Seymour Martin Lipset, *Political Man*, New York: Anchor Books, 1963.

## LEO LÖWENTHAL TO RICHARD POPKIN,
### MARCH 31, 1964

*Professor Richard H. Popkin*
*Chairman*
*Department of Philosophy*
*University of California*
*San Diego, California*

*Dear Dick:*

This is in answer to your letter of March 25th, 1964 in which you request my opinion of Professor Herbert Marcuse of Brandeis University and his suitability to join the faculty of the San Diego campus.

I have known Mr Marcuse for 34 years. He joined the Institute of Social Research at the University of Frankfurt of which I was a senior research associate in 1930 and in 1931 he became attached to the branch office of the Institute at Geneva, Switzerland, where the other members joined him in 1933 after Hitler came to power. From then on we worked very closely together, first in Switzerland and from 1934 on in the United States where the Institute established its headquarters in affiliation with Columbia University. We closely collaborated on our publications and lectures, and have ever since remained in very close professional and personal contact.

I consider Mr Marcuse one of the outstanding scholars and intellectuals of our time and definitely one of the leading figures among his generation. His scholarly background is of the highest caliber. This is particularly true with regard to his superior knowledge of the history and problems of philosophy, but it is no less applicable to his unusual familiarity with the fields of political science, cultural history, sociology, and depth psychology. I am speaking advisedly about thorough familiarity because the scope of intellectual and scholarly materials which is at his beck and call is of unimpeachable solidity and reliability.

To remind you of one example of his gift for acquiring new knowledge I may just cite his well-known studies of Soviet Marxism for which he, already in his fifties at that time, prepared himself thoroughly by learning Russian in order to be able to read the material in its original text. He is, by the way, completely tri-lingual in English, French, and German.

I don't think it will be necessary to say much about his publications. The academic community is well aware of this outstanding record. I would like, however, to mention his first book on Hegel, published about 35 years ago in Germany which already showed the enormous productivity and intellectual imagination of this man. He was fortunate enough during his younger years to be taught by the greatest scholars in philosophy and cultural history at German universities of whom I will only mention the name of Edmund Husserl, who wanted him to join the teaching staff of the University in Freiburg but was not able to do so because of the anti-Semitic inclinations of Heidegger who occupied a second chair of philosophy at that university.

Every book he has published since has set a new landmark. His *Reason and Revolution* is the definitive work on the development of political philosophy from Hegel to the threshold of the contemporary situation. His work on *Soviet Marxism* enjoys the highest reputation among the experts in the field. His *Eros and Civilization* has triggered significant discussions on the philosophical implications of Freud for the last ten years and his latest book, *One-Dimensional Man*, as may be seen already from the few reviews which have appeared, will again get the closest attention of the intellectual community.

My first-hand knowledge about his teaching is, of course, limited. From all I hear, he is one of the most idolized and successful instructors at Brandeis. I have seen him lecturing several times at Columbia University, and I had also the pleasure of attending some of his classes at Brandeis while there on a research visit. From my own point of view, it was an intellectual as well as aesthetic pleasure to see him lecture to the students and his style of presentation and discussion was delightful and of the highest quality. I should not forget to mention that he not only has been twice invited for lecture courses by the Sorbonne, but that this venerable institution has also tempted him a year or two ago with an offer of permanent tenure.

It will hardly be necessary to speak of the personal qualities of this man. Everybody who has worked with him, including myself, has only gained from this experience. He is a thoroughly decent person, of complete integrity and his conduct in his relations to follow scholars, administrators, and students is one of great tact, a remarkable sense of humor, and humility. I could not wish for a better associate or friend in daily contact. It may be appropriate to mention that Mrs Marcuse is a charming lady of great intellectual qualities and scholarly knowledge of her own and I would not hesitate to say that an addition of this family to a faculty community would be an asset highly to be cherished.

I should be more than happy to give you any further information if so desired.

*Cordially yours,*

*Leo Löwenthal*

## HERBERT MARCUSE TO T. W. ADORNO,
## JANUARY 24, 1960

*26 Magnolia Ave.*
*Newton 58, Mass.*

*Dear Teddie,*

You will recall the conversation that we had in Sils Maria. I told you about some people who had claimed that some of the things that you say or write seem to promote the ideology of the Cold War. I read your *"Theorie der Halbbildung"*[1] and could not find there anything at all that would justify such a claim. You agreed with me that our critique of the East has to remain linked to a critique of the West – for reasons that are for both of us as serious as they are self-evident. But now I read in the preface that you and Max wrote to Massing's book about a certain "Jahn,[2] who stands in high regard today with the *Fronvögte*[3] in the Eastern zone." I don't see anything about the *Fronvögte* in the Western zone, who may not hold Jahn in high regard, but others instead who have done just as much to promote anti-Semitism. That you should have devoted at least as much attention to them here is not a mechanical but a substantial demand. Otherwise it really does look like you believe that there are *Fronvögte* only in the East. No doubt, those in the West are different: their bosses have more money and thus can afford more freedom. But I believe that it is still really an open question which *Fronvögte* are doing more damage to the cause of humanity. It seems to me that the old *Fronvögte* in the West are every bit as dependent upon the power of the occupying forces as their counterparts in the East (at least until he has his own atomic weapons), and that they are the ones who are working most decisively and with obstinate rage against pacification. And what happened in the past few weeks in the West makes the association of anti-Semitism with the East ring very hollow. Does it have to be so? You write hardly anything that doesn't have to be – why on this topic? Or does it have to be this way for tactical reasons? That does not speak well for the West. Finally: the Eastern *Fronvögte* are dependent upon those in the West to maintain their power and vice versa – this sinister symbiosis permits no abstraction.

I don't have the least right to assume the role of a moral judge. But I identify myself with you so much that I view everything you write if not as written, then at least as signed by me. I would like to maintain this identification. Write me what you are thinking and doing. I'm working hard on my new book.

*Warmest regards,*

*Herbert*

*Translator's notes*

1  Theodor Adorno, Gesammelte Schriften, Vol. 8 (Frankfurt, 1972), p. 93.
   Translated by Deborah Cook in *Telos #95* (Spring, 1993) as "Theory of Pseudo-
   Culture."
2  Friedrich Ludwig Jahn (1778–1852), founder of the German gymnastics movement.
   He was a nationalist agitator during the wars of liberation and continued to
   propagate a romantic vision of nationalism (that was not free of Anti-Semitism)
   throughout the *Vormärz* period. His pedagogy stressed the importance of physical
   education.
3  *Frönvogte* are overseers of compulsory labor; historically, in the Russian context,
   they were the ones who directly oversaw the labor of serfs.

## MAX HORKHEIMER AND T. W. ADORNO TO HERBERT MARCUSE, FEBRUARY 12, 1960

*Frankfurt am Main*

*Dear Herbert,*

Since your letter of the 24th of January concerns both of us, we wanted
to respond together.

Your criticism, that we are promoting cold war ideology, is in fact based
on mere semblance. We assume that your choice of the word "seems"
[*scheinen*] in the context of your criticism was well considered. But let
us turn to the matter in question. That one must remain critical of the West,
and not just the East is a theoretical consequence which needs no justification. The publication of the Massing book speaks clearly enough; it does,
after all, examine the historical origins of anti-Semitism in Germany and
destroys the sorry excuse that it broke through from the outside, like a
natural catastrophe. The sentence from our preface that you or whoever else
finds incriminating belongs to a publication about the West, not the East.
So in this respect the balance you demand has been maintained.

But the desideratum would itself be all too mechanical if one were to insist
that every time something was said against the Russians, something else
should immediately be added against the West, just to avoid offending the
well-known sensibilities of tender Mr Khrushchev, who recently made
anti-Semitic remarks in public. Even though his more recent policies have
done much to address the criticisms at the 20th party convention of the
so-called cult of personality, he still stands for a government that not
only exterminated millions of people, but also liquidated, painfully and
disgracefully, the theoretical and practical inaugurators of the Russian
revolution. That he wants to avoid a nuclear war with America doesn't mean

that he's willing to relinquish his totalitarian claim to power, which even now he is using in several satellite states to terrorize poor Jews. Our theory can't be subordinated to keeping score [*Auszählverfahren*]. This way of viewing things calls to mind censorship and precisely that spirit of heteronomy which our common thinking refuses.

If we are not mistaken, the conviction that "Diamat"[1] still has something to do with our philosophy stands behind the demand for some sort of balance in the criticism of East and West. But loyalty can turn into disloyalty, if it refuses to see the transformation of the content of its supposed object. We cannot overlook the fact that it is possible for us in the West to write and even to accomplish real, if modest change, whereas in the East we would without question have been killed long ago; nor do we fail to see that for the time being a freedom of thought exists in the West that can only be called paradisiacal when compared to the other side. That this freedom has a material foundation is nothing new for us. This is the basis of all types of freedom, as is well-known.

On the other hand, we can hardly believe that you would accept the argument that one should view the horror in the East merely as a preliminary step on the correct path. Precisely this preponderance of the means over the ends in theory leads to the triumph of the means over the ends in practice and to the justification, in the name of the eventual creation of something better, all that's bad *hic et nunc* [here and now]. That sometime in the future the Chinese can expect wonderful times is not enough for us to justify the fate of a single taxi driver who is unable to visit his pitiful *Schrebergärtchen*[2] in the eastern section of Berlin because he lives in the West. You, of all people, who are so close to the Aristippian[3] spirit in philosophy, should be skeptical of this type of deferment, which is tantamount to denial. If this argument resonates with something like a critique of the so-called philosophy of history itself, it is not contrary to our intentions.

In short, we are not willing to accept any limitations on our freedom to criticize, least of all in the name of a notion of justice, which we cannot presume nor believe is substantial. That one must, when writing, take possible misunderstandings into consideration, is part and parcel of that mechanical way of thinking which, in its insistence upon the unity of theory and practice, ends up undermining its own purpose. The reference to the *Fronvögte*[4] does indeed strike at the heart of the matter. The illusion currently spreading and being carefully maintained in both the East and the West consists above all in the prevention of reflection upon internal relations through an overemphasis on foreign policy. But the solemn words of the flighty statesmen in the West express the social reality of those they represent just as poorly as the jovial laughter of the boyars, when they pat the bellies of farmers in the Midwest. The key to the administered stupification and regression in the East is simply that they are terrorizing people into adopting a work ethic in just a few decades which was established in the West over the course of centuries of misery and crises. This is what the *Fronvögte* are doing there. This situation is to blame for the fact that every thought that ventures beyond the established guidelines is interpreted as "sabotage," namely as a potential reduction of the volume of production; allegiance has become as fetishized as only the commodity once was. It's no coincidence that Schostakovitsch recently claimed in an interview the main problem with decadent music is that it doesn't sufficiently encourage people to find joy in their work. And Turnvater Jahn[5] certainly led the way when it comes to cheerfulness. By the way, the fact that you object to this passage in particular, which refers to the synthesis of communism with this full-bearded anti-Semite, has an irony that you should be the first to recognize; not least of all because the same ones here in the West whom, according to you, we should have included in our criticism and which we in fact did, also consider themselves to be his descendents. Despite their conflicting interests, the irreconcilable opponents are one.[6]

*Warm regards, to Inge as well,*
*Max*
*Dein Teddy*

---

*Translator's notes*

1 "Diamat" refers to the philosophy of "dialectical materialism" being developed and according to Marcuse in the Soviet Union. In his book, *Soviet Marxism,* Marcuse criticizes "Diamat" as a reified and bureaucratic form of Marxist discourse constructed to serve the interests of the Soviet state.
2 A "*Schrebergärten*" is a parcel of land, normally located on the outskirts of a city, used as a garden by people who have no room for one in their urban dwellings.
3 Aristippos (435–355 BC) was the founder of the Greek philosophical school of hedonism. He recommended orienting one's life to the present, not the future or the past.
4 See footnote in the letter from Marcuse to Adorno of January 24, 1960.
5 Friedrich Ludwig Jahn (1778–1852), founder of the German gymnastics movement. He was a nationalist agitator and stressed the importance of physical education.
6 "*Trotz der Interessengegensätze sind die Unentwegte eins.*"

## HERBERT MARCUSE TO T. W. ADORNO

*Dear Teddie,*

A detailed reply to your letter had already been written when Max arrived here. The conversation turned to your letter and before I had a chance to say anything about the content of my reply, Max explained that your letter contained a real mistake: the example of the taxi driver. It was left in only due to an oversight: the secretary sent the letter without incorporating the corrections that Max wanted to make. But my response was for the most part directed at this example (I remembered your claim that examples are not incidental!). Thus is it not necessary to send my reply – but I have included a few excerpts that still seem relevant.

In the meantime I have read your "*Erfahrungsgehalte der hegelschen Philosophie*"[1] and I have to tell you that I was really thrilled. That is really the best that one can and must still say about Hegel today. I wish you would have these essays along with the "*Aspekten*" published in English.

I liked "*Aufarbeitung der Vergangenheit*"[2] as well – it fulfills the desideratum that I insisted upon in my response. With the exception of the sentence on German democracy, in which social life is reproducing itself more happily than it has for as long as humankind can remember.

How nice it would be if we could discuss all of this in person! But I do at least have everything that you publish sent to me – I need it for my the good of my soul [*Seelenheil*].

*All the best to you and Gretel, also from Inge,*

---

*Translator's notes*

1  "The experiential contents of Hegel's Philosophy"; probably an earlier version of Adorno's *Drei Studien zum Hegel*, Gesammelte Schriften, Vol. 5 (Frankfurt, 1970), p. 247. Theodor Adorno, *Hegel: Three Studies*, trans. Shierry Weber Nicholsen (Cambridge, Mass., 1993).
2  Certainly a version of Adorno's "Was bedeutet: Aufarbeitung der Vergangenheit?" *Gesammelte Schriften*, Vol. 10 (2), p. 555. For the English version see, *Critical Models: Interventions and Catchwords*, trans. Henry Pickford (New York, 1998).

---

## HERBERT MARCUSE TO MAX HORKHEIMER AND T. W. ADORNO (UNSENT LETTER)

*Dear Max and Teddie,*

Your letter confirms too much of what I suspected. Only a discussion in person can help. But I would like to respond to at least a few of your points.

First: you misinterpreted my position. Nowhere in my letter did I defend the Soviet regime – so it wasn't necessary to correct me. Everything you wrote – on the relationship of means and ends, "Diamat" and "*Arbeits-freude*,"[1] and the ideology of the "*Zwischenstufe*"[2] – I treated myself in *Soviet Marxism*[3] and I emphasize all the time in my lectures. But I did pose the certainly not very apologetic question of which *Fronvögte*[4] do more damage to the cause of humanity, and I claimed that the link between Western and Eastern *Fronvögte* is by no means mechanical . . .

You talk about the spirit of heteronomy, which our common thinking refuses, and that our theory can't be subordinated to keeping score. I couldn't have put it better. This is precisely what I wanted to say in my letter, namely that there is heteronomy in the West and the East. I wanted to defend the autonomy of thought against its subordination to the more pleasant type of heteronomy. I find it horrible – so horrible that your example of the taxi driver living in West Berlin who can't visit his pitiful *Schrebergärtchen*[5] in East Berlin, seems like a pitiful travesty to me (Teddie, didn't you say that examples are not merely incidental but illuminating?). It seems inhumane and hopelessly heteronomous to me, to play off, with the indifference of an American businessman, this inaccessible *Schrebergärtchen* against efforts to ameliorate the real misery of millions – even if they succeeded only in providing access to decent hospitals and doctors. "That sometime in the future the Chinese can expect wonderful times" (a saying borrowed from the Western *Fronvögte*!) might not be able to reconcile you with the inaccessible *Schrebergärtchen* (it would me, without any pangs of conscience – I admit it!) – but this is not at all the issue. The issue is that the Chinese are *already* doing better *today* than they were before and that the Western *Fronvögte* are doing a lot which causes the amelioration of their suffering to proceed painfully slowly. Once again I have to quote. The taxi driver with–without the *Schrebergärtchen* is concrete and singular; the Chinese are abstract, far away and many. Millions of victims that one does not see and hear count less than one up close and personal. But the dialectic is no fiacre that one can stop at will. And the others are there.

But it is completely unfair to claim that I want to link the critique of the East with the critique of the West "just to avoid offending the well-known sensibilities of tender Mr Khrushchev, who recently made Anti-Semitic remarks in public." (By the way: where and when??) Whether his sensibilities are finer that those of Mr Adenauer, which can't be offended in the West, because they are doing so much for the atomic bombs, I don't know. The sensibilities of statesmen are not exactly in the back of my mind – and certainly not *in* my mind. But you write that Khrushchev stands "for a government that not only exterminated millions of people, but also liquidated, painfully and disgracefully, the theoretical and practical inaugurators of the Russian revolution." So he stands not for his own government, but for its predecessor, whose crimes he is attempting to atone for – much more so than Adenauer. He stands no more and no less for the extermination than the *Fronvögte* of the West zone stand for the (not yet sublated) past. The break between the past and present (and future!) seems to me to be smaller in the Western zones than in the USSR. In the West they are negotiating with Franco right now about missile bases and training grounds; "punishing" Sepp Dietrich with a fine of 8000 German Marks (how many pennies is that per Jew?); giving pensions to Hitler's officers; rehabilitating and strengthening the very same capital that played such an important role in the wonderful times hardly past. Who is subordinating his theory to keeping score: he who insists on a "mechanical" linkage, or he who refuses it?

No doubt, in the West there is "freedom of thought," that "can only be called paradisiacal when compared to the other side." Which thought? Does it also get printed and published? I wouldn't deny it. But I have found neither in your writings nor elsewhere an autonomous critique of what is happening in the West – nothing that matches the concreteness of your critique of the East. Once again "keeping score." When and where does one begin to count and assign the bodies that the respective governments have on their consciences? Why begin in 1928? Should I not include the others? The others that were exterminated in the West? Did you not rightfully say and write that the Hitler regime was no accident, rather that it was rooted in the system that still exists in the West? No doubt, this concerns the future. But since when is our theory allowed to limit thought to that which is present, and to ignore determinate and determinable tendencies?

And all this because of Turnvater Jahn.[6] *Mea culpa*![7] But I really believe that old Turnvater Jahn was completely harmless compared to the atomic fathers in new uniforms, who are walking around today in the West.

It may be that "despite their conflicting interests . . . the irreconcilable opponents are one." But those interested in reconciliation shouldn't make this alliance so easy for them.

------------

*Translator's notes*

1  "Joy in work," literally translated. Horkheimer and Adorno used the term in their letter to refer to the ideology accompanying the Soviet regime's compulsory labor plans.
2  The idea that the repressive aspects of Soviet domestic policies are an unpleasant but necessary "intermediary stage" on the way toward realising a fully liberated socialist society.
3  Herbert Marcuse, *Soviet Marxism: A Critical Analysis* (New York, 1958).
4  See footnote in letter from Marcuse to Adorno of January 24, 1960.
5  See footnote in Horkheimer and Adorno's letter to Marcuse of February 12, 1960.
6  Ibid.
7  I am to blame.

## HERBERT MARCUSE TO RAYA DUNAYEVSKAYA, AUGUST 8, 1960

*Dear R. D.:*

I feel pretty bad for not having answered your various notes and letters, the main reason being that I am neurotically busy with my new book and equally neurotic about the slightest interruption. Please accept my apology. I am sure you will understand. I should even feel worse about it because I am writing you now to ask a favor. I may have told you that my new book with the tentative title *Studies in the Ideology of Advanced Industrial Society*, is some sort of western counterpart of *Soviet Marxism* – that is to say it will deal, not only with the ideology but also with the corresponding reality.[1] One of my problems will be the transformation of the laboring class under the impact of rationalization, automation and particularly, the higher standard of living. I am sure you will know what I mean if I refer to the discussion among the French sociologists in *Arguments* and especially Serge Mallet's articles. It is a question of a changing – that is to say – a more affirmative attitude of the laborer not only towards the system as a whole but even to the organization of work in the more highly modernized plants. Mallet's field study of French workers in the Caltex establishment in France points up sharply the rise of a highly co-operative attitude and of a vested interest in the establishment.

Now, what I should like to ask you is first, your own considered evaluation as far as the situation in this country is concerned, and secondly, if it isn't asking too much – reference to American literature on this problem pro and contra. I know that your own evaluation runs counter to the thesis of reconciliatory integration of the worker with the factory but I would also like to know whether there is any sensible argument for the other side.

I hope that I do not intrude too much upon your time. How is your own work coming along?

With best wishes and greetings,

*Sincerely,*

———————

*Editor's note*

1  Marcuse's "Studies in the Ideology of Advanced Industrial Society" was eventually published as *One-Dimensional Man* (Boston: Beacon Press, 1964). For a comprehensive contextualization of the Marcuse–Dunayevskaya correspondence, see Kevin Anderson, "The Marcuse–Dunayevskaya Dialogue, 1954–1979," *Studies in Soviet Thought* 38 (1990): 89–109. Thanks to Anderson for making fresh copies of the letters available and for permission to publish the Dunayevskaya letters.

## RAYA DUNAYEVSKAYA TO HERBERT MARCUSE, AUGUST 16, 1960

*Dear HM:*

It was good to hear from you. (Your letter was delayed because you sent it to the old address; please note new one: 4482 – 28th St.)

Your letter of the 8th came at a suspicious time since the special issue of *News and Letters*, which will be issued as a special pamphlet, *Workers Battle Automation*, has just come off the press and should be of value to you both because you will see the workers speaking for themselves on the conditions of labor and the alleged high standard of living. I know, from the time I last spoke to you, that you consider these views as being the result of my influence. While it is true that Charles Denby and some (by no means all) of the writers of this pamphlet are Marxist Humanists, you would make a serious mistake if you considered their views so exceptional that they did not represent the American proletariat.[1] They represent a very important segment of the American workers and in all basic industries – auto, steel, coal – and the conditions they describe are what they experience on the line, not what some sociologists see in a "field study." I would like to call your attention also or especially to p. 6, "Which Way Out" because, contrary to the monolith not only of Communists but radicals who think they must have a "united voice" when they face the public, workers here disagree openly. Angela Terrano, whom you may recall I quote in *Marxism and Freedom* because she has raised the question of what kind of labor in the true Marxist sense, and who then used the expression that work would have to be totally different, "something completely new, not just work to get money to buy food and things. It will have to be completely tied up with life" (p. 275) here rejects Automation altogether whereas the editor insists that if the workers managed the factory it would not be a House of Terror and works along the more additional channels of workers' control of production, shorter workday, etc.[2]

Secondly, I happen to know a Caltex engineer who says some very different things than Serge Mallet. I had him add a special paragraph on the question you raised, but this study of "Oil and Labor" published in the FI in 1948 was quite a comprehensive one and as I doubt you have it I enclose that too. (But when you have finished please return at your convenience.) At the same time I am not sure that you have my article in *Arguments* on "State Capitalism and Bureaucracy" which deals with some of the sociologists you no doubt have in mind as, C. Wright Mills, who speak on somewhat a higher level than the epiphenomenal "Organization Man", and contrasts that to a state capitalist analysis of the times we live in. Since it was simultaneously published also in English I am enclosing the *Socialist Leader* of January 2, 1960 which does so. I will also try to locate the "Two Worlds" article at the beginning of the year which dealt with the American economy in the postwar years as it goes from recession to recession.

Now then the American literature on the subject: I have long since stopped paying attention to sociologists who have rather degenerated into the school of "social psychology" which the workers in the factory rightly call "head shrinking" so my list cannot be exhaustive but I can give you the major references. Since the class struggle was never accepted in American sociology as the framework of analysis, your reference to those who speak of alleged cooperative attitude of worker to management and even "organization of work"(!), must have in mind ex-radicals and near radicals whose recent toutings of the virtues of capitalism are sort of summed up in the person of Daniel Bell and his strung-out articles called a book, *The End of Ideology* by which they mean, of course, the end of the class struggle. Certainly they are struggling no longer now that their philistenism cannot even assume the veneer of the West European enders of the class struggle (Not only the French but even the British "New Left") but the crassest apology for State Department "culture." (Now, isn't that a better euphemism than "the line"?)

Perhaps the most solid of these is Seymour Martin Lipset. His *Political Man: The Social Bases of Politics* is dominated by his attempt to "document" the attenuation of the class struggle: The modification of late capitalism by welfare legislation, redistribution by taxation, powerful unions and "Full Employment" legislation. Lipset's thesis is that "the fundamental political problems of the industrial revolution have been solved; the workers have achieved industrial and political citizenship; the conservatives have accepted the welfare state; and the democratic left has recognized that an increase in over-all state power carries with it more dangers to freedom than solutions to economic problems." (Even here the American is very different from the French who when they espouse the attenuation of the class struggle go for the Plan with a capital P while the American remains "the free enterpriser" although the State Department itself when it is a question of export of ideology goes for "people's capitalism.")

A book that has recently gotten a lot of attention both because it is new and sort of summarizes in bright journalistic language some half century of sociology is *The Eclipse of Community* by the Princeton University sociologist, Maurice R. Stein. There are all sorts of shouting on "the End of Industrial Man" (Peter Drucker), "the end of political man" [*The Politics of Mass Society* by William Kornhauser]. Now none claim that the end of this economic, industrial, political man, even as his thinking too has been taken over by the electronic brain, is happy or content with his work. In that respect the ambivalence is seen clearest in Daniel Bell's "Work and Its Discontents" whose claim is that the attenuation of the class struggle has nevertheless occurred, if not in the factory, then by "the new hunger [for] the candied carrot." How much have we heard of those TV sets and "occupational mobility" and David Riesman's flip side record from *The Lonely Man* to *Individualism Reconsidered* of the need "to increase automatization in work – but for the sake of pleasure and consumption and not for the sake of work itself." At least Bell has one good catch phrase that the descriptions that issue from the so-called "human relations" projects are "not of human, but of cow, sociology."

If you take the economists, you also have a choice of the flip side so that Louis M. Hacker now touts "The Triumph of Capitalism" and while everyone is ashamed of such past as "The Decline of American Capitalism" which, like all so-called Marxist books from Corey to that Stalinist apologist who passes for "the" Marxist authority (even Joseph Schumpeter's monumental but quite lopsided or, as we say more appropriate in Jewish "tsidreit", work, *History of Economic Analysis* refers to him as such) Paul Sweezey are one and all underconsumptionist so that, whether you take the period of the 1930s when "all" were Marxists to one degree or another and some serious works were done, or you take now when nearly the only works against capitalism are issued by the Stalinists, there really is no genuine Marxist analysis of the American economy either historically, sociologically or as economic works. But, at least, from the economists one does get figures and they do show that in *The Affluent Society* some are very much more affluent than others. Otherwise the sociological works, even before McCarthyism for whom they prostrate, were specialized studies of one or another aspect, like occupational mobility by sociologists Reinhard Bendix and S. M. Lipset, or the Lynds' *Middletown* or Lloyd Warner's *Yankee City* or Louis Wirth's *The Ghetto* or Florian Znaniecki on the Polish peasant in America. Even the more broad dislocations as *Class and Caste in a Southern Town* by Dollard had no comprehensive view of American society as a whole. When both the muckrakers before World War I (Lincoln Steffens' *Autobiography* if you happen not to have read it will do for that) and the specialized studies of the 1930s and some in World War II stopped flowing, we then went into the most famous Elton Mayo's Hawthorne studies on "The Human Problems of an Industrial Civilization", which were to replace, I suppose, the statistical studies of sharecroppers, breadlines, etc.

Now everything has moved to Automation. In addition to those I list in *M & F* [*Marxism and Freedom*], there is now *Automation and*

*Technological Change*, Hearings before Joint Comm. on the Eco. Report, 84th Congress, Wash, D.C./. H. B. Jacobson and J. S. Roucek *Automation and Society* (Phil. Library), C. Walker's *Toward the Automatic Factory* and *Automation and the Worker* by Floyd C. Mann and L. Richard Hoffman, which, despite its title, is not what the worker feels but a specialized study in power plants by the U. of Mich. There is a good bibliography, issued in 1959, called *Economic and Social Implications of Automation: a Bibliographic Review*, Michigan State U., East Lansing, Mich. I doubt any of these are really what you wish to waste your time on, but it is a fact that the new (since 1958) "The Society for the History of Technology" with its journal *Technology and Culture* (Vol. I, #1, Winter 1959) at least doesn't write with the guilt complex that the sociologists do and therefore can both be somewhat more objective as well as free from the attempt to identify the end of its ideology with that of the "masses." Not being concerned much with the masses (their outpost away from the publishing center here at Wayne State U. and its editor Melvin Kranzberg of Case Institute of Technology, Cleveland, is really Chicago and the *Christian Humanism* of the sociologist-technologist U. Nef.) it can pay attention to the technological base as it impinges on other fields. For example, it would definitely be worthwhile if your book is not going to press right this minute to get its next issue which it promises to devote entirely to that monumental 5 volume study *A History of Technology*, which is edited by Charles Singer and which series of articles on it, critical and otherwise, will be prefaced by him.

Now then, as you see, I could not give you the listing of the American literature on the subject without giving you my views as well. I wish now to summarize my considered evaluation not merely of books on the American society as I see [it], which differs very radically from your views. If I may, I would like to say that I hope at least that you have not, in your pre-occupation with "the transformation of the laboring class," fallen into the trap of viewing Marxian socialism as if it were a distributive philosophy. I do not mean to insult you and put you in the underconsumptionist category but such great revolutionaries as Rosa Luxemburg were in it, despite the fact that her *Reform or Revolution* was based precisely on removing the question of the class struggle from its reduction to a question of "personal fortunes" to one of production relations. Engels certainly wrote many works on production relations and never was even conscious of any deviations, and yet by not being the dialectician and humanist Marx was, wrote tracts that were far afield. Hilferding had undertaken his *Finance Capital* as a bringing up to date of *Capital* yet the "organized capitalism" with its "stability" inclinations reduced socialism to a matter of "taking over" not reorganized from the ground up, least of all by the spontaneous actions of the workers. Of course, you may say that is exactly where Marx was "wrong" and you of course are not only entitled to your view but writing probingly for many years, and I may be doing you great injustice since I do not have your MSS at hand (I do hope you will send it to me so that view can be concrete instead of based on assumptions) but I just have a feeling that this preoccupation with the alleged high standard of living shifts the weight from what you yourself state in the Preface to my book as "the integral unity of Marxian theory at its very foundation: in the humanistic philosophy."

Therefore, allow me to recapitulate some fundamentals although all are familiar to you. First you no doubt recall that on p. 125 of *M & F* where I quote from *Capital vol. I*, pp. 708–9 on law of accumulation I argue against the popular concept that now that the worker is "better off" etc., pointing to Marx's statement that "in proportion as capital is accumulated, the lot of the laborer, be his payment high or low, *must grow worse*." (Emphasis added.) That his lot has grown worse is evidenced in the conditions of labor under Automation and in the unemployment it has produced. The "pockets of depression" may sound very incidental to those who do not have to live in them but when, in 1960, even a Jack Kennedy (now that electioneering is in the air) must stand appalled at conditions in West Virginia where actual cases of mothers selling themselves into prostitution to try to keep from starvation, isn't it time for the exponents of higher standard of living to take a breather and look into the lot of the 5 million unemployed who with their families make up 13 million. And it isn't only the unemployed, nor even the snail pace of the rate if growth of the American postwar economy which has produced 3 recessions, but the so-called normal conditions under Automation. I have seen miners' shacks who had an outhouse instead of a toilet but had a TV on the installment plan but that did not signify either contentment or that they "chose" thus the "candied carrot," but only that TV could be installed whereas before plumbing could be it would need a great deal more that a $5 down payment – you'd have to root out altogether those hovels, including the miserable excuses for roads leading to them in this most road-conscious industrially advanced free land.

The answer of those who seem to take the opposite view is that, (1) they have never even bothered to build a LP [i.e. Labor Party], (2) the labor leadership they have they "deserve" since they voted for the Reuthers, Meanys, Hoffas, and (3) that they are not "active" i.e., rechanging society this very movement. Striking, wildcats, and organization of their own thinking seem not to count for very much. For the moment I'll accept this non-acceptable view and ask whether that is any more than the "bourgeoisification of the British proletariat" Marx and Engels so bemoan or "the aristocracy of labor" that Lenin saw as the root cause of the collapse of the Second International.

This brings me to the second basic Marxian view, on the question of going to ever deeper and lower strata of the proletariat for its revolutionary essence. You may recall that on p. 187 of *M & F* I bring Marx's speech of Sept. 20, 1871, after the collapse of the Paris Commune and the cowardly running even before then of the British trades union leaders. (I have seen that Speech only in Russian, but it may be available in German I don't know.) I there also show that Lenin hadn't "discovered" this which he now called "the quintessence of Marxism" until he himself was confronted not only with the betrayal of the Second but with the ultra leftism of Bukharin who was thereupon ready to castigate not only the Second's leadership but the proletariat itself. It is the last par. on that p. 187 where I deal with Lenin's approach on two levels, the real and the ideal, that I would now like to call to your attention, if I may.

It is true that Automation and state capitalism are not only "quantitative" but qualitative changes in our contemporary society and that that predominant fact would also affect a part of the proletariat. But a part is not the whole. Indeed, the fact that gives the appearance of an affluent society not only in the bourgeois sector but in the masses – the millions of employed so that the 5 millions unemployed look "little" – does not show that those unemployed are predominantly in the production workers. No suburbia here. It is all concentrated in the industrial centers, among an organized but wildcatting proletariat and aggravated by the Negro Question which is by no means quiescent and among a youth that has shown that they are not rebels without a cause but with one. I know you do not accept my view that they are in search of a total philosophy and are not getting themselves ready for the dustbin of history. But it is a fact that not only among the proletariat and the million that were striking just when Khrushchev was visiting and Eisenhower wanted to show him American superiority in industry, not industry at a standstill, it is a fact that in just the few months that Negro college youth began sitting in the whole question of freedom and youth "coming up to the level of the West European" has been moved from the stage of the future to that of the present.

That will do until I actually see your book in manuscript and get the development of your thought. I should be very happy to write again then. Meanwhile, my work – and I still labor with the Absolute Idea despite the activist pressures you are free from – moves slowly, but I do hope after Labor Day to get more time to concentrate on the book. Perhaps I'll get to Boston in winter – I did get there last March but I was there for only two days and two lectures and had no chance to try to contact you. If the invitation to speak will be repeated this fall, I will try to see and talk with you.

———————

*Editor's notes*

1   Charles Denby's pamplet *Workers Battle Automation* was discussed by Marcuse in *One-Dimensional Man.*
2   Marcuse published an Introduction to Dunayevskaya's *Marxism and Freedom* (New York: Bookman, 1958), pp. 7–12.

═══════════

## HERBERT MARCUSE TO RAYA DUNAYEVSKAYA, AUGUST 24, 1960

*Dear R. D.*

It was wonderful to get from you such quick and good help. I read at once the issue of *News and Letters.* Don't misunderstand me: I agree with practically everything that is said there, and yet, somehow, there is something essentially wrong here. (1) What is attacked, is NOT automation, but pre-automation, semi-automation, non-automation. Automation as the explosive achievement of advanced industrial society is the practically complete elimination of precisely that mode of labor which is depicted in these articles. And this genuine automation is held back by the capitalists as well as by the workers – with very good reasons (on the part of the capitalists: decline in the rate of profit; need for sweeping government controls, etc.; on the part of the workers: technological unemployment). (2) It follows that arrested, restricted automation saves the capitalist system, while consummated automation would inevitably explode it: Marx, *Grundrisse der Kritik der politischen Oekonomie.* p. 592–593. (3) re Angela T.: you should really tell her about all that humanization of labor, its connection with life, etc. – that this is possible only through complete automation, because such humanization is correctly relegated by Marx to the realm of freedom beyond the realm of necessity, i.e., beyond the entire realm of socially necessary labor in the material production. Total dehumanization of the latter is the prerequisite.

But all this has to be discussed orally. I hope we can do so in the winter. And again, my great gratitude!

I am sending $10 – to help *News and Letters.*

═══════════

## FREDERICK POLLOCK TO HERBERT MARCUSE, DECEMBER 8, 1960

*Montagnola/TI*

*Dear Marcuse,*

For some time now I've been intending to write down some notes from our memorable conversation in New Haven, insofar as it addressed theoretical problems. But not until now did I get around to writing the enclosed memo. (No, my memory is not so impressive, but as a reminder I jotted down a few key terms on the return trip.)

I kept thinking about your claim, that the quality of cars is getting worse and worse, while driving hundreds of miles in a rented 1959 Chevrolet during our week in California. The car already had many miles on it and it ran splendidly. Many cars were no doubt better ten years ago than the products that bear their names today. But the comparison is not so simple. To make a judgment one would have to convert the current price into dollars from 1940 or 1950 and compare the quality of today's cars with similar models from 10 or 20 years ago. I suspect this would demonstrate that the later model is an improvement.

This doesn't mean that it wouldn't be possible to produce better cars for the same price, if one didn't spend so much on unecessary chrome und plating.

I've heard of Vance Packard's *Wastemakers* only in a few conversations, since the book is still on the way. But I suspect that he generalizes from what are really outrageous exceptions. Considering the overcapacity in most branches of industry (national and international), the producers of consumer goods etc. cannot exploit the consumers as long as they would like.

Although I haven't forgotten your biting final remark – that according to me everything is in order in the current economic system – I still don't want to reopen the debate. Measured by standard of what could be, it is in horrible disarray. But if theoretical attempts to understand this system are to be meaningful, they can't be satisfied with showing the monstrous *faux frais* it produces; they also have to see how capable it still is of avoiding crises. You remember the tragi-comic condemnation of the latter-day Galileo, Eugen Varga, because he gave the capitalist system some [. . .].[1]

Mr Kennedy and his advisors seem quite familiar with the weak points in the current system. Whether they will succeed in Congress with drastic reforms combined with equally drastic tax increases, is another question.

I also wanted to draw your attention to two publications: Günther Wagenlehner, *Das Sowjetische Wirtschaftssystem und Karl Marx* (Cologne, 1960); reactionary, but contains much interesting material.

Furthermore: *Comparisons of the United States and Soviet Economies* (Hearings before the Joint Committee, Nov. 13–20, 1959, Washington, 1960, invoice number 48448.) 292 pages packed full with material.

The three lines that I wanted to write have turned into a long letter. From this you can see how much I would like to talk to you more about these questions.

*Sincere Season's Greetings from my house to yours.*
*Your*
*Frederick Pollock*

———————

*Translator's notes*

1   Illegible word in the original letter.

———————

## MEMORANDUM: HERBERT MARCUSE AND FREDERICK POLLOCK, NOVEMBER 10, 1960

*Theoretical Problems, discussed with Herbert Marcuse in New Haven*

1   M:   Are colonial products vital for capitalistic countries?
    P:   No, except some war materials.
2   M:   Are expanding armaments vital for them?
    P:   No. See #8.
3   M:   In view of automation etc. can value theory be maintained?
    P:   No, if one interprets it in the sense of orthodox [Marxist] theory.
4   M:   If one views all labor time paid by the market as socially necessary doesn't one abandon critical theory?
    P:   No, because the critique is brought back in with the reinterpretation of what is "socially necessary." One only needs to consider how trash is "necessary" in this society and how many goods, services and institutions, that would be absolutely necessary in a good society, are "too expensive" today. The concept "socially necessary" is used just as ironically as Galbraith's "Affluent Society."
5   M:   Are all qualities getting worse in late capitalism?
    P:   No, the opposite is true, unless the life of certain commodities is

artificially shortened (light bulbs etc.). But this is the exception. In general, the industrial products of today are higher in quality than fifty years ago. Compare the rubbish that was originally sold with the label "Made in Germany" or "Made in Japan" with the quality of today.

6   M:   Would not technical progress in the economic sphere, particularly automation, be much further advanced in an ideal society?

      P:   The question does not make much sense. Does it mean, perhaps, that if the arms budget were used instead for automation, that it would be much further advanced? Then it is a tautology. Clearly the question cannot be posed in such general terms. Does this "ideal society" exist in only one country or across the entire globe, and therefore does not need an arms budget? Is the labor process increasingly mechanized or are the workers in this society part of a team that has responsibility and a positive relationship to the labor process? (à la Georges Friedmann)

7   M:   Is not automation being artificially impeded today?

      P:   What do you mean artificially? That everything technically possible is not implemented, rather only what is profitable, or what does not harm industrial relations too much? But neither are "artificial" in the current phase of capitalism – on the contrary, both are "natural."

8   M:   Is a serious crisis unavoidable if the arms budget is not constantly raised?

      P:   It is not "unavoidable," because in principle the expansion can be maintained today with other public expenditures, and by economic policy in general, as suggested by Kennedy. That would be another step in the direction of state capitalism and it is doubtful that a Congressional majority would support this as long as the crisis is not apparent to everyone.

9   M:   What does it mean that foreign investment of American capital has increased to 30 billion dollars? Is this not a new form of imperialism?

      P:   One could respond positively, insofar as greater profits are made abroad due to lower labor costs and taxes. But even so one should not lose one's sense of proportion. The seemingly gigantic sum of 30 billion is 20% less than that which American private business invested in America in the year 1959, namely 37 billion dollars.

# XI

Jürgen Habermas' "The Different Rhythms of Philosophy and Politics. For Herbert Marcuse on his 100th Birthday" was published in German in *Die postnationale Konstellation. Politische Essays* (Frankfurt: Suhrkamp, 1998, pp. 232–9) and has been translated here by John Abroweit. Habermas was a long-time and close friend of Marcuse and first published these reflections on Marcuse's work in *Neue Zuricher Zeitung*, July 18–19, 1998. We would like to thank Jürgen Habermas for providing permission to translate and publish his reflections on Herbert Marcuse.

# AFTERWORD

## The Different Rhythms of Philosophy and Politics For Herbert Marcuse on his 100th Birthday

### *Jürgen Habermas*

After the death of his first wife Sophie, Herbert Marcuse wrote to Max Horkheimer and Friedrich Pollock on March 3rd, 1951: "The idea that death belongs to life is false, and we should take much more seriously Horkheimer's thought that humanity can become truly free and happy only with the abolition [*Abschaffung*] of death." The possibility of eternal life in this world – Marcuse adopted this unprotestant thought, which can be traced back to Condorcet, and lent it a vitalist inflection of his own. Despite progress in gene technology, it has not been realized in the meantime. If it had, Herbert Marcuse would have been able to observe the peculiar association of the hundredth anniversary of his birthday with another memorial: "1898 – 1968 – 1998" was the motto guiding commemorations of Marcuse – at the conference in Genoa in June, 1998, for example. Although scholarly friends of the philosopher were also present at the conference, passionate interest arose only when looking back at the student revolts and at Marcuse's ambivalent role as a mentor. It seems it was the coincidental concurrence of his birthday with the anniversary of 1968 more than the resonance of his philosophical work that prevented him from being forgotten.

When the philosophical reception of writings once published in numerous editions comes to a halt, it is often just a passing symptom of exhaustion following a period of intense interest. This is what happened to Adorno. His work has, however, for good reasons, remained a challenge to the present. Interest remains even in Horkheimer's work within the context of the tradition he inspired. But in the case of Herbert Marcuse, the profile of the scholarly [*wissenschaftlich*] author has been obscured by his historical role as political teacher and inspirer. We are familiar with the peculiar ebb and tide in the reception of significant or less significant philosophers. The after-effects of political interventions, which are bound much more closely to their historical context than philosophical works, are subject to different, short-lived rhythms. In the case of Marcuse, it seems that the conjunction of the historical rhythms of the reception of his work, on the one hand, and his political person, on the other, has caused a certain short-circuit. The weight of his philosophical arguments has been drawn into the maelstrom of criticism of his political *engagement*. It is tempting to make oneself the spokesman of the one at the expense of the other. But, if my argument contains a kernel of truth, there is a danger of optical distortion in both directions – in respect to his political activities no less than his philosophy.

Compared to the other members of the inner circle around Horkheimer, Marcuse certainly had the most political temperament. In 1918, he joined a Berlin soldiers' council, and sixty years later he still talked about the disappointment "that the failure of the German revolution my friends and I experienced . . . with the murder of Karl and Rosa." During the Second World War, Marcuse worked in the political division of the Office of Strategic Services and participated in his own way in the fight against the regime that had forced him to flee from Germany by carrying out "analyses of the enemy." In the early sixties, the Civil Rights Movement politicized him once again, before he joined the opposition to the Vietnam War and eventually influenced the student protest movements on both sides of the Atlantic. This occasional activism cannot, of course, allow one to forget that Marcuse, even in comparison to Horkheimer and Adorno, was an academic figure in the more limited sense of the word – that is, someone who observes the rules of the profession and writes scholarly books.

With Heidegger he familiarized himself with the themes and standards of contemporary philosophy. The first "Heideggerian Marxist" wrote his *Habilitationsschrift*[1] in a conventional style and published at the time, around 1930, works in leading academic journals. Not Adorno, but Marcuse

---

1  In Germany one is required to write a second dissertation, or *Habilitationsschrift* in order to qualify for a professorship at the university.

assumed the role of the philosopher in the division of labor Horkheimer established at the New York Institute. He was the one who wrote the commentary to the programmatic essay "Traditional and Critical Theory." In 1941 Marcuse earned recognition within his discipline as well with a historical-systematic investigation of the development of social theory out of Hegel's philosophy. *Reason and Revolution* compares favorably in all respects with Karl Löwith's famous *From Hegel to Nietzsche*. Even *Eros and Civilization*, his most radical and in a certain sense "most characteristic" book, Marcuse understood as a contribution to a disciplinary debate. *One-Dimensional Man* is his best known, though not his best book. It appeared in 1964 and concluded, deeply pessimistic to the end, with Walter Benjamin's words, "It is only for the sake of those without hope that hope is given to us" – that is, without the link to praxis that the students soon created on their own.

In the preface to *Reason and Revolution* Marcuse justifies his study of Hegel with the following words: "the rise of fascism calls for a reinterpretation of Hegel's philosophy."[2] Now, if it is true that Marcuse's work has drifted into the shadows of a past political relevance, we must draw a different conclusion from the changes in the historical situation that have occurred since then. We do not need "to see his philosophy in a new light," but rather to re-examine our own preconceptions concerning the political role of the author.

The thorough documentation that Wolfgang Kraushaar recently presented in *Die Frankfurter Schule und die Studentenbewegung*[3] makes it possible, using the example of the Federal Republic of Germany, to re-examine the direct influence of Marcuse's arguments on the '68 movement. Some of the most important ideas were already present in the speech Marcuse gave on May 22, 1966 at a conference on Vietnam organized by the SDS at the University of Frankfurt. Marcuse's point of departure is the "contrast between social wealth, technological progress and the domination of nature on the one hand, and the implementation of all these forces to perpetuate the struggle for existence at the national and global level . . . in view of poverty and misery, on the other."[4] Today, after the end of the arms race between the super powers, the "destructive implementation of accumulated wealth" is certainly less obvious than it was during the Vietnam War. But in the context of a globalizing capitalism, which causes

---

2  *Reason and Revolution*, (Boston, 1960), p. xv.
3  *Die Frankfurter Schule und Studentenbewegung: von der Flaschenpost zum Molotowcocktail 1946–1995*, 3 volumes, ed. Wolfgang Kraushaar, (Frankfurt, 1998).
4  Ibid., Vol. 2, p. 205.

unemployment and the price of stocks [*Aktienkurse*] to rise more or less in unison, Marcuse's central diagnosis of a "fatal unity between productivity and destructivity" has been confirmed in another, no less drastic way.

Marcuse saw that the forces of production are unbound rather than bound by the existing relations of production, and consequently called the productivist model of social emancipation into question. Long before the Club of Rome, Marcuse fought against "the hideous concept of progressive productivity according to which nature is there gratis in order to be exploited." The environmental movement has since made everyone aware of this idea. Marcuse saw the difference between socialism and capitalism "not so much in the development of the forces of production as in its opposite. This is the prerequisite for the abolition of labor, the autonomy of needs and the pacification of the struggle for existence." This argument as well makes sense in light of the thesis of the "end of the laboring society." According to a widespread estimate, in the OECD[5] countries, the gross national product could be produced by 20 per cent of the population able to work. But if a constantly increasing part of the working population becomes "superfluous" for the reproduction of society, the close connection between occupational success and social recognition can hardly be maintained.

Marcuse's estimation of the potential for protest was not unrealistic either. He certainly did not see the Soviet Union as an alternative to the capitalist West. Nor did he share the view that the general interests of society are expressed solely in the suffering and resistance of the exploited masses. A different relationship between majority and minority was already becoming apparent at that time in the US, where an integrated majority stood opposed to marginalized minorities, which had no effective means of redress. This is why Marcuse placed his hopes in the moral sensibility of youth, intellectuals, women, religious groups, etc. These normatively motivated groups must ally themselves with the material interests of the weary and oppressed: "One of the things that I have learned is that morality and ethics are not mere superstructure and not mere ideology." Like a good idealist, Marcuse spoke of the "solidarity of reason and sentiment." Since sociologists have observed a certain shift from material to so-called post-material value orientations, even this claim has become more plausible.

The strong resonance Marcuse found then among the student population cannot, of course, be explained primarily in terms of the arguments themselves. It was the suggestiveness of a Freudian tinged vitalism which ensured Marcuse's place among the generation of his grandchildren. Marcuse, who was himself influenced by the youth movement at the turn of the century,

---

5   Organization for Economic Cooperation and Development

had a sense for the culturally revolutionary character of the new youth
movement – for the motivations of revolt and for the self-understanding of
those rebelling: "This is sexual, moral, intellectual and political opposition
all in one. In this sense it is total, directed against the system as a whole."

But this formulation also reveals why such an existentialist description
makes it so easy to link the youth revolts to a concept of transforming
the totality taken from the philosophy of history, namely the concept of
"revolution." Although Marcuse himself did not mistake the revolts for a
revolution, he did believe that they might serve as the initial spark and he
suggested to his listeners that they could understand themselves as being part
of a future revolutionary movement. His ambivalent statements on the
question of violence demonstrate this as well. He distanced himself from the
liberal faction of the SDS already in July, 1967 in Berlin with a comment
directed against Knut Nevermann: "I by no means equate humanity with
non-violence. On the contrary, I have spoken of situations in which it is in
the best interest of humanity to use violence." This tendency is supported
by an understanding of philosophy and enlightenment based on an uncritical
concept of reason and an elitist notion of education which was imparted to
Marcuse and others in his generation by the politically questionable
curriculum of the German *Gymnasium*.[6] Hannah Arendt, for example, was
also not so far from this conception.

The fanciful equation of rebelling youth with a forerunner of the
revolution may partially explain why the reception of the philosopher
Herbert Marcuse has more or less come to a standstill. The all-too-topical
reception then makes it difficult today retrospectively to dissociate the
accomplishments of the academic scholar from the unrealized *Kairos*,[7]
that is, the historical context that Marcuse himself inflated to a distorting
standard of judgment. But it is not the first time that a philosophy has
perished in the historical context it itself made the criterion of *veri* and
*falsi*. This judgment has of course a suspiciously smug air about it, because
it does not do justice to the truth content of Marcuse's analyses. Marcuse
conceptualized the peculiar entwinement of the productivity of economic
growth with the destructivity of its social consequences in imploring
[*bewschwoerend*]-totalizing terms, that is, with concepts that have become
foreign to us. With his diagnosis Marcuse confronted us with an image of a
totalitarian closed society because he believed it was necessary to introduce
a vocabulary that would open clouded eyes to things that were no longer
perceived at all, by casting a harsh light on seemingly familiar phenomena.

---

6  German élite high schools.
7  The decisive or perfect moment for something.

The situation has changed. No one who reads the newspaper today can deceive himself about the entwinement of productivity and destructivity. Driven by a highly efficient "*Standortkonkurrenz*",[8] our governments have let themselves become entrapped in a deregulatory race to lower costs leading in the past decade to obscene profits and drastic disparities of income, deterioration of cultural infrastructures, increasing unemployment and marginalization of an increasingly large, impoverished population. We do not need a new language to recognize this because we no longer imagine we are living in an "*Überflussgesellschaft.*"[9]

The intellectual situation has changed as well. Postmodernism has disarmed the self-understanding of modernity. One no longer really knows if the democratic conception of society that realizes itself politically through the will and consciousness of its unified citizens has assumed the characteristics of a utopia that is endearingly old-fashioned or rather simply dangerous. Hand-in-hand with a pessimistic anthropology, neo-liberalism reconciles us more each day to a new global situation in which social inequality and exclusion are considered facts of nature. Existing constitutions point to a completely different view of things. Perhaps we need a renovated language after all, so that the pressure to conform to functional imperatives does not lead us to forget this normative viewpoint.

----

8  Geopolitical competition.
9  Affluent society.

# INDEX